|| JUSTICE AT WORK ||

Justice at Work

THE RISE OF ECONOMIC AND
RACIAL JUSTICE COALITIONS IN CITIES

Marc Doussard and Greg Schrock

University of Minnesota Press
Minneapolis
London

Copyright 2022 by the Regents of the University of Minnesota

All rights reserved. No part of this publication may be reproduced, stored in a retrieval system, or transmitted, in any form or by any means, electronic, mechanical, photocopying, recording, or otherwise, without the prior written permission of the publisher.

Published by the University of Minnesota Press
111 Third Avenue South, Suite 290
Minneapolis, MN 55401-2520
http://www.upress.umn.edu

ISBN 978-1-5179-1304-5 (hc)
ISBN 978-1-5179-1305-2 (pb)

Library of Congress record available at https://lccn.loc.gov/2021061686.

Printed in the United States of America on acid-free paper

The University of Minnesota is an equal-opportunity educator and employer.

"Justice?—You get justice in the next world, in this world you have the law."
—William Gaddis, *A Frolic of His Own*

Contents

	Introduction	1
1	The Upside of Globalization: City Power in the Urban Age	15
2	Economic and Racial Justice Coalitions: Diverse Social Movements Challenge Inequality	35
3	Urban Policy Entrepreneurs: Networked Policy Change from the Grassroots	63
4	Organizing for Better Jobs: The Fight for $15 Transforms Urban Politics	87
5	Good Jobs for All: Targeted Hiring Fights Racism at Work	115
6	Justice beyond Work: Sick Days, Fair Schedules, and the Politics of Social Reproduction	137
7	"Wall Street Is a Racist Conspiracy": Racial Justice and the Fight against Austerity	161
	Conclusion: The Promising Work of Justice	187
	Acknowledgments	203
	Notes	205
	Bibliography	209
	Index	233

Introduction

The news about American cities provides ample opportunity for both hope and despair. In terms of economies, population, and stature, cities are undoubtedly thriving. Most major U.S. cities gained population in the 2010s (Frey 2020), and they are propelled by technology, finance, and advanced services—twenty-first-century boom industries that need urban density and diversity to flourish. This economic importance translates into social and cultural prestige. If you are a student reading this book, you most likely plan to move to a city upon graduation. The television shows Americans obsessively watch are overwhelmingly set in cities. Conservative media and intellectuals, who previously and unsubtly championed suburbs as white alternatives to racially diverse urban centers, now celebrate the so-called triumph of the city. Cities dominate both economy and cultural imagination in a way that would have been difficult to imagine even at the turn of this century.

On the other hand, Charles Dickens remains dismayingly relevant 230 years after the French Revolution. The urban boom has led to great times for some, but evidence that too many of us live in the worst of times dominates the news. Separating the urban boom from rampant economic and racial inequalities requires mental contortions that few of us can muster. Evidence of polarization, of just about everything, comes from all corners. Work pays too little, provides too few opportunities for advancement, and offers few promises of stability. The quality, and even the availability, of basic public services depends on a person's neighborhood: the right income and right skin color entitle residents to private schools, magnet schools, or (a true rarity) well-financed urban public schools, while residents in communities of color face forty-year-old textbooks, armed security guards, and overstuffed classrooms. The police terrorize those same communities, while caring for the white, propertied class. Gentrification, the diminished availability of shelter for working people, and the specter of low-income people of color losing their homes when elites "discover" a neighborhood, are everywhere.

The Great Recession, the reactionary political responses it fed, and the 2010s made these inequalities too stark and obvious to ignore. The crises of 2020—Covid-19, police violence, and the worst job losses in ninety years—revealed our underlying inequities to be not just deeper and more pervasive than imagined but also more interconnected. Until recently activists, scholars, and policy makers divided urban problems into small and self-contained pieces, such as housing affordability gaps, mismatches between jobs and job skills, and "performance gaps" in public schools. The response to Covid-19 revealed a significant adaptation in reformers' thinking. The Covid crisis, critics insisted, constituted a simultaneous work crisis, housing crisis, austerity crisis, and above all a crisis of systemic racism. Reversing long-term trends, the intellectual and advocacy response to Covid began to relink problems that critics had previously separated. The emboldened reformers seized public attention with surprising ease. The summer of 2020 provided the strange, shocking sight of outlets such as *Forbes* indicting structural racism (Weller 2020), and former U.S. *secretary of defense* John Podesta writing an op-ed entitled "Covid-19 Relief and Economic Recovery Must Dismantle Environmental Racism" (Podesta and Martinez 2020).

These crises are monstrous, yet seeing our problems so clearly offers hope. Our brief in what follows is to ground these increasingly precise and exacting demands for justice in the realities of cities and social movements today. Intellectually, organizationally, and in the realm of policy, movements for social and economic justice are on the offensive, together. Combining resources and objectives, and doing so effectively, marks a significant change for community, labor, and racial organizing movements that long struggled to collaborate. Rather than accepting the few material scraps the remains of the New Deal settlement provide, they articulate and enact visions for justice writ large. They aim to realize these visions through a modified, multiracial approach to economic justice—one that argues for and wins better jobs and more public resources for the poor and marginalized by directly addressing the foundational racism on which economic inequality rests. The prospect of obtaining that justice originates in the city itself, and in decades of intellectual and practical work to reshape justice movements in order to take advantage of the opportunities of economic globalization and the urban renaissance.

OPPORTUNITY IN THE URBAN AGE

The current urban age heightens the inequalities central to capitalist urbanization from the beginning. The rise of cities as "command and control centers" (Harvey 1989b), the dynamic sites from which businesses coordinate global supply chains and economic empires, also provides new opportunities to contest those inequalities. Density is the key for capital: it allows specialized professionals and businesses to find one another, it pushes scientists and engineers to innovate more radically, it multiplies the number and speed of financial transactions, and it makes housing more reliable as a sink to absorb the staggering surplus of capital that cities generate. That same density provides opportunities for activists, who can now work through thick and diverse networks whose structure can at least in part level the playing field with mobile, multinational capital.

Rather than ask how the economies of cities are changing, we ask how communities and peoples' organizations respond to those changes, and what their organized responses mean for how we think about action against inequality. Because capital needs cities, cities provide key bargaining sites for community struggles against inequality (Lefebvre 1991; Castells 1983). Significantly, municipal public policy appears to play a driving role in realizing those struggles and—crucially—in shaping justice movements and political claims. Citizens are increasingly effective at winning what lay observers would call "progressive" economic policy, as a flourishing and increasingly vibrant body of scholarship shows (Pastor, Benner, and Matsuoka 2009; Milkman and Ott 2014). The study of urban government likewise notes that economic globalization brings both inequality and chances for cities to engage in forms of economic redistribution that were previously infeasible (Savitch and Kantor 2002; Schragger 2016).

We bring these perspectives together, both to enrich them and to answer pressing questions about how, why, whether, and how much movements for economic justice succeed in cities. For decades, scholars have rightly noted that the study of the changes sweeping cities has more or less been the study of capital (Herod 1997). Just as major newspapers have multiple business reporters and no labor reporters, research on urban government, policy, and elections centers capital's elites: corporations, financiers, and the political institutions (e.g., the Chamber of Commerce, the American Legislative Exchange Council) of the well-financed and reactionary right. Scholarship descended from the regime and growth machine traditions of urban politics does something functionally similar by steering attention toward mayors, political machines, and growth coalitions (Stone 1989). In the late twentieth century, cities needed capital investment in order to compensate for federal disinvestment, state disinvestment, and population flight. The resulting scholarship was usually the study of how influential elites gain and hold power, occasionally the story of how homeowners and elite citizens' groups challenge that power, and almost never the story of how working people, communities of color, and everyday citizens work to center the agenda on issues that matter to them (Weaver 2021; Imbroscio 2006).

When the poor and the marginal *do* show up in these political accounts, they do so in a one-off, anecdotal way that is very much the point. Capital operates at the scale of the globe and real estate investors have portfolios that span dozens of cities. Mayors coordinate elegantly structured political operations that assemble power by the block, neighborhood, and ward. Citizens' challenges to this power are by contrast treated as individual and parochial. They appear to develop epiphenomenally and in isolation, and by implication do not possess the scale to adequately challenge the forces creating the innumerable inequalities cities face. These frameworks take off the table the possibility that resistance to economic and racial inequality—resistance strengthened by the insight that economic globalization deepens capital's reliance on cities—is itself well-organized, varied, networked, and worth deeper study.

The neglect of the role peoples' movements play in urban politics grows harder to justify by the day, because evidence that they are large, well organized, and effective seems to be everywhere. In the 2010s, city minimum wages transformed from an idea without a name into a policy commonplace. Austerity and endless budget cuts to basic public services felt as inevitable as death, taxes, and rush-hour traffic—until striking teachers in Chicago initiated a national wave of activism that won the unthinkable (unthinkable in America, that is) goal of securing more resources for basic education. Seen this way, focusing on businesses, technology, and mayors doesn't just tell an incomplete story—it *misses* developments as fundamental to city economies and politics as the next disruptive innovation or fiscal crisis.

We also ask what the constraints and opportunities of local government mean for a blooming scholarship on urban social movements (Almeida 2019; Pastor, Benner, and Matsuoka 2009). Here, understanding systematically the factors that make local governments entertain equity reforms draws attention to the important question of how those movements use their power. Looking at justice movements in U.S. cities more closely provides new and provocative information about how they build networks, combine visions of racial and economic inequality without subordinating one to the other, and expand the range of issues citizens can contest.

Linking these developments to a more structured understanding of urban politics, and specifically of the bargaining conditions and legislative powers available to justice movements, allows us to answer more systematically the question of how social movements *use* the power they build. Neglecting that question has consequences. The influence urban social movements exert on a wide range of urban policies (for example, employment standards, affordable housing, basic income programs, universal childcare, police reform) is significant in itself. We argue that the networks urban social movements use to exert that influence constitute an equally important development. Making sense of these networks is both important in its own right and useful diagnostically, as a way to understand and link the related transformations of the globalization of urban economies and the (parallel, adaptive) networking of movements for social and economic inequality. Doing so also offers hope—grounded hope—that peoples' movements have adapted to counter social and economic inequality more effectively.

Accordingly, we aim not just to add peoples' movements to the conventional story of urban politics, but to do so in a way that fully integrates them into the picture as a recognizable and revealing subject of systematic social-scientific study. Who organizes? When, where, why, and how do citizens' movements shape policy and politics? What is their potential to address additional symptoms of urban inequality, and its root causes? How will this form of power develop, and what threatens it?

OUR INNOVATIONS: ECONOMIC AND RACIAL JUSTICE COALITIONS, URBAN POLICY ENTREPRENEURS

We use two developments in the structure of community, labor and political organizing to place peoples' movements on the agenda. First, we focus on the ongoing project of building what we term *economic and racial justice (ERJ) coalitions*. ERJ coalitions have roots in the community and labor organizing of the post–World War II era, but build their work around the goal of overcoming that era's limitations. The potential of unions to create durable economic justice and build power on a scale to rival that of major corporations was historically limited in the United States by the severe racism of many local unions and the labor movement's neglect of organizing. The two problems are of course related: focusing on the narrow needs of their predominantly white and predominantly male membership meant a focus on manufacturing and deserved mistrust from communities of color. A movement that represented a shrinking slice of the population, in a shrinking slice of the economy, had few prospects for increasing power over the long term (Katznelson 1982).

Community organizations had similar problems. Community organizers in the United States worked off the pragmatic, deal-making models developed by Saul Alinsky and his peers in the immediate postwar era. Alinsky's basic approach worked well at the time. He counseled organizers to avoid ideology, to identify incremental and winnable goals, and to focus on building their organization rather than broader movements. These concessions allowed communities to bargain for the surplus of a growing economy and expanding public services. The model faltered, however, as elites undermined the political-economic settlement in which Alinsky developed his methods. Deindustrialization, disinvestment, and austerity left communities bargaining for scraps, a problem of structure that incremental, deal-oriented organizing could not address. Alinsky's greatest concession to pragmatism aged even more poorly. In *Rules for Radicals,* Alinsky counselled community organizers to avoid the issue of race, which he observed had the power to destroy coalitions, undermine consensus for a deal, and lose allies (Lesniewski and Doussard 2017). Foregrounding race, he argued, injected volatility into a delicate process. Alinsky rejected this position toward the end of his life. More important, organizers themselves began to rebel against this teaching in the 2000s. ERJ coalitions emerge from unions and community organizations embracing what they previously shunned: ideological critique, antiracist messages, and demands for transformation rather than negotiation.

The spark to unite community and labor organizing in cities came from the living-wage movement of the 1990s. Organizing for pay increases to service-sector jobs put in place several long-term transformations. For unions, these campaigns focused resources on low-wage service jobs that employers couldn't relocate, that could not be organized effectively without support from public policy, and that were held by people of color and commonly by women of color. For community organizations, mobilizing to win city-level policy changes meant working with unions their members had long viewed as racist; building citywide coalitions with the size and scope to win policy battles in the city council; and joining a *national* network of urban coalitions that developed policies, expert testimony, campaign messages, and organizing techniques. Living-wage campaigns initiated these changes by spurring hierarchical labor unions and grassroots community organizations to work together, and putting both to work on campaigns that dealt directly with racial inequality, which they treated as an important end in itself.

Today, ERJ coalitions sit behind the proliferating body of campaigns and messages that tie together economic, social, racial, environmental, and (the list continues to grow) other justices. The events of 2020 provide a harsh reminder that justice movements must grow in order to stand still: injustice itself is dynamic, hungry, and developing in ways that today's organizers and scholars cannot yet see. Rooting our work in the long-term development of activism provides a fuller picture of the challenge justice movements face—a functionally longitudinal analysis, rather than a snapshot of the current balance of power within a longer struggle. Acute challenges, such as Covid, mounting pressure on state and local budgets, and the threat of the Justice Department deploying the last U.S. Attorney General's personal police force to cities, understandably drive headlines. These threats add to the chronic challenges of fiscal austerity, asset poverty for communities of color, segregation, environmental racism, and work that simply doesn't pay. Our optimism about ERJ coalitions originates in the work they have done to contest those chronic conditions, and from the structure of their membership and claims on power. The maturation of these coalitions suggests that urban social movements are overcoming the schisms that historically divided them, including the separation of work and home in both life and politics, and the frequent separation of economic justice campaigns from racial justice campaigns (Katznelson 1982).

FROM MOVEMENTS TO POLICY

Focusing on ERJ coalitions ties our work to a long-standing tradition of scholarship on neighborhood politics, affordable housing development, community development corporations, and other basic components of community and neighborhood development. We draw attention, however, to the way that the members of this roster conceive, develop, and execute their work through networks to achieve urban policy change. These are large, diverse, and complex networks: networks within neighborhoods and across neighborhoods; across the boundaries of race, ethnic identity, and individual policy issues; networks joining cities to suburbs and urban regions to states; networks across U.S. cities; and an emergent, de facto national network of city-based justice alliances. The members of these networks use them, instrumentally and efficiently, to make public policy—a development that conventional studies of urban politics miss because they focus on politics in a single city. We conceptualize participants in these networks as *urban policy entrepreneurs,* strategic actors on whose work conventional political science sheds significant light.

The figure of the policy entrepreneur plays an important part in the study of federal politics, where her significant but constrained powers reveal important characteristics about lawmaking in Washington. In the classic formulation, the policy entrepreneur develops a policy—then waits. She waits for public attention, with its limited bandwidth, to lurch toward a problem her policy addresses. Then she waits for politics—usually via elections—to make elected officials scramble to address the problem. When these conditions align, she presents her policy as the solution and major legislative change happens. Urban policy entrepreneurs take up this same work, but they do so as a network that strategically shops for policy venues. The progressive policy proposals of this network enter the agenda in cities, counties, and states where conditions are ripe: where electorates are supportive, where elected officials can be made to answer, where ballot initiatives can circumvent hostile legislators.

We argue that urban policy entrepreneurship differs from its federal-level counterpart in one crucial respect. Urban policy entrepreneurs benefit from the resources of the city itself, which allow them to set the agenda with an ease that interest groups in Washington cannot. A protest in a civic plaza, a speech from an ally on the city council, a few appearances on Spanish-language media, education sessions with rank-and-file members: policy entrepreneurs across the United States have set the legislative agenda in their cities with these simple, cheap, and comparatively democratic tools. Similarly, they can push the point with ballot initiatives, or rival candidates for elected office. And because cities are more politically homogenous and left-leaning than the country as a whole, the policies that result are, well, bigger: more than a dozen jurisdictions have now doubled the federal minimum wage of $7.25.

Understanding this process as the work of a national network of policy entrepreneurs has several advantages. First, it draws attention to the ways that the resources of the city itself can sustain and fuel politically progressive movements—a development that reverses the prior conclusion that city policy is a dead end for community organizing and the social movements organizers fuel (Lesniewski and Doussard 2017). Second, our approach provides a way to operationalize the study of multicity politics. Scholars have drawn attention to the need to expand politics on urban scholarship beyond the study of individual cities for nearly thirty years (Cox 1993); many social movements scholars take up this challenge by focusing on networks that link multiple cities and countries (Pastor, Benner, and Matsuoka 2009; Almeida 2019). Following the work of those multisited networks provides both methods and objects of study that can realize not just the goal of understanding multisited movements, but the related goal of understanding the bargaining possibilities different cities and political institutions offer. Ideas about social movements' skill in diffusing and shifting the scale of activism provide a mechanical structure for investigating these capabilities (McAdam, Tarrow, and Tilly 2003).

Third, the mechanical components of the policy entrepreneurship approach provide a rigorous way to understand why activists win on some issues (but not others) and why progressive policies win in some places (but not others). Some problems, such as low pay, resonate with the public, and easily lend themselves to attention-drawing campaigns (McAdam, Tarrow, and Tilly 2003). Similarly, some coalitions have better resources with which to apply pressure to elected officials, and heterogeneous local political institutions can either magnify or dissipate that pressure (Almeida 2019). Finally, problems like low pay have simple policy responses, while others, such as fiscal austerity, do not. Because it is based in these component parts, the concept of policy entrepreneurship provides a framework for making comparisons about how, why, and where a given policy is enacted.

It also helps to clarify questions about the current and future frontiers of activism. Finding a way to peer into the future is important because ERJ coalitions remain a work in progress, and the political-economic realities in which they operate currently change by the day. We make sense of the future by diving deep into policy entrepreneurship on behalf of four policies that respond to different portions of the demand for equity: the $15 minimum wage (job quality), targeted hire laws (access to good jobs), earned sick time and fair workweek laws (social reproduction), and fiscal austerity (collective consumption).

PLAN OF THE BOOK

In order to evaluate ERJ coalitions, and to make sense of the work of urban policy entrepreneurs, we must understand the sources of their bargaining power. In addition to becoming command-and-control centers for a planetary economy, cities have changed in ways that allow communities to exert power without causing businesses or investors to flee. Accordingly, we start with the question of how the very economic changes that create so much inequality also provide peoples' movements with leverage they previously lacked. Chapter 1 reassesses the now-conventional story of the supposed triumph of the city with an eye toward that leverage. We focus both on reversals to the rampant conditions of population loss, job loss, and disinvestment in late twentieth-century U.S. cities, and the unexamined impact of those reversals on scholarship. Arguments that city power cannot support distributive fairness originated in an era of widespread economic contraction and population decline in central cities. Triumphal narratives about the resurgence of cities have mostly failed to trigger a reexamination of these foundational theories—a significant oversight (Schragger 2016).

The flip side of current inequalities, we show, is increasingly opportunity and leverage, especially for cities with strong unions and central labor councils, robust networks of community organizations, and state legislatures that support experiments in municipal policy (Pastor, Benner, and Matsuoka 2009; Doussard and Gamal 2016). Manufacturing job loss means that the remaining employers cannot easily relocate as a protest to policies that distribute wealth and power downward (MacDonald 2017). Similarly, the demise of large, vertically integrated firms means that businesses need cities' policy assistance in ways they previously didn't, and the growing importance of finance to all businesses as a source of profit makes them reliant on city policies that securitize investments in the built environment. The urban era, in short, provides communities with leverage—and some communities and places with more of it than others. Recognizing these changes makes the question of how, where, and when cities gain leverage increasingly important to the study of urban politics.

Chapter 2 introduces ERJ coalitions, and shifts focus from cities to social movements. To understand how we arrived at a period when the mayors of most large cities label themselves as progressives and even reactionaries sign off on high minimum wages, we trace the evolution of economically left urban movements. We begin with the neighborhoods movement of the 1970s and 1980s, which was followed by the 1990s living-wage movement, a brief and failed 2000s movement for community benefits agreements and, finally, the current period of ERJ coalitions. Contemporary ERJ coalitions differ from even the movements of a decade ago in significant ways: They are organized as multineighborhood, multicity, and multiscale networks; they embrace racial justice and anticapitalist ideology (both stances that their predecessors strategically downplayed); and they seek to tie justice *at* work to justice *beyond* work.

Chapter 3 introduces the idea of urban policy entrepreneurship, which solves a number of persistent problems in the study of urban politics. Scholars have for decades pointed to general flaws in the status quo approach to urban politics, which focuses on single cities rather than networks of cities, fusses too much over capital mobility, and treats the growth of finance as an afterthought or grace note to familiar ideas about an economy based on physical production. We agree with these critiques, but take as our point of departure the challenge of converting them into an alternative research program. The idea of urban policy entrepreneurs does that. Studying these networks provides a way to shift focus from city hall to peoples' movements, from single-site studies to multisite politics and from elite policy circles (the subject of policy mobilities research) to policies developed and championed by activists. We contrast urban policy entrepreneurs, who can shape the agenda in cities with protests and their own organizations, to conventional policy entrepreneurs in Washington, who must wait for exogenous events to steer attention to their pet issues. This comparison helps us to bring the study of policy and legislation to urban politics, which rarely considers what people in power do with their legislative powers. That in turn sets the stage for four policies we study in depth.

In Chapter 4, we apply the urban policy entrepreneurship framework to the $15 minimum wage. We show that the minimum wage evolved through strategic experimentation within a national network of linked city-level movements. We focus on three cities where campaigns for the $15 minimum wage matured: SeaTac, Washington, where organizers conducted an old-fashioned, resource-intensive door-knocking campaign that won a $15 minimum wage but did not generate a reproducible model; Seattle, where organizers used a single city council candidate and the city's vigorous social movements to focus an entire election around the minimum wage; and Chicago, where organizers adapted Seattle's methods to their less favorable political circumstances. Our empirical work shows the maturation and circulation of ideas for running these campaigns, and explains the subsequent diffusion of the $15 minimum wage as a commonplace and noncontroversial policy in cities and states with Democratic electorates.

The minimum wage sets a floor on job quality and deals with the problem of work that pays too little. Chapter 5 examines targeted hire policies, which address the social dimension of job quality: who, socially and demographically, gets access to the limited supply of jobs that pay for life's basic necessities? Matching jobs to people entails complexity and challenges beyond those involved with the comparatively simple mechanisms for expanding the minimum wage. The strength and weakness of targeted hiring programs are their roots in specific communities. Advocates for these programs create an audience by drawing attention to intense and prolonged inequalities in access to work. Improving that access, however, requires winning the acquiescence of historically racist trade unions and building relationships with regulators to ensure they enforce the law. We compare targeted hiring initiatives in Chicago, New Orleans, and Seattle, finding that the programs are shaped as much by the structure of a place's social inequalities as by capable policy maneuvering. Targeted hiring programs are thus unlikely to win by themselves the goal of diversifying access to good jobs. However, they develop intersectional organizing and convene new advocacy coalitions who go on to address inequality in other forums.

Minimum wage and targeted hiring laws together enact a limited but meaningful program for winning justice *at* work: they improve the quality of jobs and enhance access to good jobs for communities of color historically shut out of those opportunities. Winning and maintaining justice at work, however, also requires a vision for winning justice *beyond* work, in the realm of social reproduction. These policy areas amount to a proving ground for community-labor coalitions that strive to unite work and home, economic production and social reproduction (Castells 1983). Chapter 6 explores policies that attempt to win this broader vision of justice through further adjustments to the employer-employee relationship. A growing number of jurisdictions are passing laws that provide paid sick time and fair—predictable, stable, remuneratively sufficient—work schedules. However, the policy entrepreneurship underlying these laws is fragile. Activists have not convincingly defined sick time and scheduling as problems that capture public attention, in substantial part because the work of social reproduction remains invisible and unvalued. The current success of these policies reflects not the underlying power of the ideas, but rather the current political power of ERJ coalitions, who for the moment extract commitments from politicians with ease.

Policies that tie working conditions to problems in social reproduction have limited scope to address the full range of problems—housing, health care, transportation, food, education—facing low-income communities and communities of color. Accordingly, chapter 7 examines the current frontier for ERJ coalitions, action against fiscal austerity. We examine advocacy for social goods (childcare, elder care, education) and against the *fiscal racism* of inequitable tax burdens and public expenditures. Both of these problems are place specific in ways that make it difficult for activists to adapt policy solutions with the tools of policy entrepreneurship. Yet surprisingly, we find substantial recent success in advocacy against each set of problems, thanks to the racial justice component of economic and racial justice coalitions. Foregrounding critiques of racism and the language of antiracism allows organizers to simplify complicated fiscal policies into resonant messages about fairness, and expands the territorial and scalar reach of the coalitions available to win policy change. This work remains incomplete, but offers a grounded, realistic path to imagining a more equitable future obtainable in the short and medium term.

The text of the book ends with the reality of justice being incomplete; that same reality focuses the bigger intellectual project we wish to begin. Justice is never full and progress never comes easily, but it does come, and there is no reason to consign the study of equality to normative texts that focus on the ideal-typical goals of justice over the work of actually making it happen. Cities, states, and their political and economic systems develop unevenly, but their citizens increasingly share experiences, ideas, strategies, and collaborators for making their world better. No magic formula for a fairer world exists, but multisited movements are in a way their own formula. They need to be at the center of the discussion when we talk about cities. And centering these movements provides a way to imagine a future in which justice movements do not just respond to crises like those they currently face, but head off other potential crises and move the terrain of contestation from mitigating the inequalities of state and market to creating institutions, norms, and life worlds that deliver just and fair economic growth and fully flourishing humans.

1
The Upside of Globalization
CITY POWER IN THE URBAN AGE

The chorus of voices against social and economic inequality has moved from the margins to the center of political conversations in the United States. For decades, activists, scholars, and elected officials who sounded the alarm about the mounting social and economic gaps in American life shouted into the figurative wind. Today, warnings about inequality come from Chicago economists, Federal Reserve chairs, business leaders, and even conservative public intellectuals, who warn that "free markets alone won't solve our problems" (Brooks 2020).

America's new gilded age has dismayingly predictable winners (white people, men, the highly educated, asset owners) and losers (people of color, women, high school graduates, renters), with the notable exception of central cities, the new darlings of the global economy. The urban rebound is both real and selective. It includes New York, Chicago, and Los Angeles, smaller cities on each coast (Seattle, Portland, and San Francisco; Boston, Philadelphia, and Washington), as well as the Twin Cities, Denver, Pittsburgh, Austin, and many points in between (Frey 2020). These cities share some common traits. They rely comparatively little on manufacturing, their citizens have higher levels of educational attainment, and they grow not as islands but as the centers of economically expanding urban regions (Benner and Pastor 2015). For the most part, the exclusions from this list are its mirror image: manufacturing-dependent cities in the Midwest and Northeast with shrinking populations and few mechanisms for sharing prosperity between central cities and the regions they anchor (Hackworth 2015). White working-class resentment of the new economy thrives in these regions, where it complicates efforts to address both racial and class inequalities (Metzl 2019).

The size and diversity of America's urban system resists effective simplification. We will discuss it through the paired examples of Detroit, a clear loser in postindustrial economies, and Chicago, a consensus winner. Detroit's dependence on auto manufacturing, its high levels of segregation (supported by racist institutions), and the political barriers separating black Detroit and Wayne County from white suburban areas have mostly exempted Detroit from the urban rebound (Thomas 1990; Reese, Sands, and Skidmore 2014). We add the qualifier *mostly* because even Detroit contains pockets of gentrification and growing investment (Mah 2020), and dynamic and skilled community organizations (Kinder 2016). Its community organizers necessarily respond to extreme segregation by building a regional agenda to share resources between Detroit and suburbs (Pastor, Benner, and Matsuoka 2009, 87–93). Even under these extreme circumstances, citizens have found a way to use municipal public policy to redistribute power and resources to the poor: in 2018, Detroit became one of the first U.S. municipalities to institute a citywide community benefits agreement covering all development (Berglund 2020). Thus, the urban rebound we take as the subject of this book is both uneven and not restricted to the largest and most obviously thriving cities.

At the other end of the Great Lakes, Chicago dramatizes with clarity the pathway from twentieth-century manufacturing city to inequitable present-day boomtown. At the dawn of the Reagan era, Chicago faced continued, seemingly ceaseless, decline. The city had lost nearly 400,000 residents and tens of thousands of manufacturing jobs during the 1970s. One of the consolations for families who remained in the city was housing, which was cheap if not good: land and property values stood at a fraction of present levels, prodding mayors and city council members to direct public resources toward stabilizing land values, particularly around the Loop. All the while, a police force that had openly assassinated Black Panther leaders continued to kill black citizens with impunity (and without the documentary evidence of social media).

The problems today's Chicagoans face are equally daunting, but they do not concern disinvestment. Politics in Chicago now revolves around the central problems of investment and gentrification. Property values near the "El" rapid transit lines, the lakefront, the Loop, and previously gentrified neighborhoods continue to grow, with more than two-thirds of the city's community areas facing some form of gentrification. Black flight has supplanted white flight, with residents of color responding to school closures, public transit cuts, and disinvestment in outer neighborhoods by moving away (Zotti 2019). Austerity and debt-financed spending in the city center chip away at funding for public services, to the point that the City has closed many libraries, schools, and bus routes, nearly all of them in low-income neighborhoods of color (Farmer and Noonan 2019). The city's politics are similarly transformed. After the 2019 elections, the self-designated "progressive" bloc on the city council totaled more than one-third of its members. Five of them are self-declared socialists, and the mayor, Lori Lightfoot, constitutes the exact opposite of the classic machine pol: black, queer and a self-declared outsider.

This transformation challenges the foundational ideas about urban politics in the United States, which were developed during a now-distant period of systemic disinvestment. They were correspondingly circumspect: cities, generations of scholars warned, could not act on inequality without scaring off investors. Yet the once omnipresent politics of growth is being pushed aside by a politics of fairness. Understanding the shift from disinvestment to investment—why and how it happened, who it impacts, how it changes institutions, power, bargaining, and leverage—constitutes an essential first step in understanding when, where, why, and for how long justice movements can win their goals.

The urgency to act on these goals responds to both the stark challenges of contemporary inequality and the realization that the current urban boom, like past booms, will only exist in its current form for so long. Technology and investment do not respond to price signals from low-cost regions as quickly or thoroughly as economists supposed, but they do diffuse. New firms and industries can relocate to cheaper locales within predictable windows of opportunity (Storper and Walker 1989). While the economic benefits to agglomeration often outweigh the costs, the advantage is not absolute. Firms, people, and investment eventually diffuse from larger cities—a phenomenon the Covid-19 pandemic's large-scale experiment with remote work will likely accelerate. These pressures add to the imperative for justice coalitions to act now, yet diffusion may have the effect of creating leverage for smaller cities that have gained little in the current boom. In the analysis that follows, we attempt to walk a middle ground between triumphalism and despair: current opportunities are real but limited, and they will shift in ways that will more likely transform than eliminate the capacity for social movements to influence public policy.

We argue that this shift has taken three specific, related forms: the emergence of "post-Fordism" as a basis for capitalist urbanization; the growing importance of the service sector to the urban economy; and the primacy of financialization and real estate in shaping the urban context. Each of these shifts has exacerbated economic and racial inequality within cities—but each also provides leverage and opportunities for organizers to intervene to shape the urban political economy.

FROM DISINVESTMENT TO REINVESTMENT: NEW URBAN FORTUNES

For decades, urban activists and progressives in the United States have begun their formal education with the disappointing admonition that they need to go outside of cities to fix problems *within* cities. Central cities, scholars agreed, lacked the bargaining power to make demands of the wealthy, influential, or well-resourced. Every year, they lost residents, businesses, and investors. Worse, the immediate problem of disinvestment was rooted in the structure of the U.S. government itself. U.S. mayors have limited formal power and need cooperation from private interests to govern effectively (Stone 1989). Cities also lack money: in distinction to most of the industrialized world, U.S. cities possess few financial resources with which to build infrastructure or public programs (Kantor 1995; Mooney 2001). For good measure, cities themselves exist at the leisure of states, who can change the rules of the game as they wish. The 2011 Detroit bankruptcy, for example, was initiated in part by the Michigan state legislature deciding to keep more of Detroit's tax revenue for itself (Peck and Whiteside 2016).

Against this backdrop, urban political economy's mandate was less to make sense of power than to explain cities' powerlessness over economic distribution. Three key challenges drove the agenda. First, the development of "post-Fordism" replaced mass production, mass markets, and collective consumption with niche industries, fragmented markets, and public policy that emphasized flexibility over equitable distributions of income (Amin 1994; Harvey 1989a). This gradual transformation during the final third of the twentieth century forced cities to negotiate new economic roles for themselves. The large company towns of the Midwest, from Dayton (National Cash Register Corporation) to Detroit (autos) could no longer count on growing sales, wages, or production from their signature employers. Cities in the South and West often benefited from new investment in small-scale manufacturing and technology, but those industries delivered uneven pay, tenuous security, and few long-term promises (Glasmeier and Leichenko 1996; Markusen et al. 1991). City economies and political regimes that had flourished when the U.S. economy delivered continuous growth now had to adapt to instability.

Second, the related transformation of deindustrialization shifted the employment base from manufacturing to services, making downtown offices rather than manufacturing plants the center of cities' economic activity (Scott 2014; MacDonald 2017). The contours of this, the best-known part of the story of cities' economic transformation, should be familiar to most readers. Manufacturing jobs in the postwar era delivered stability in multiple forms: high and growing pay, insulation from layoffs, and health care, vacation, retirement (Harrison and Bluestone 1990). The service-sector jobs that replaced them offer fewer certainties. They are split between highly paid jobs in design, advertising, marketing, finance, law, and so forth, and low-wage, unstable, short-term jobs in entry-level services such as food service and retail (Wright and Dwyer 2003; Doussard, Peck, and Theodore 2009; National Employment Law Project 2011). Where economic growth previously drove gains for the middle of the employment distribution, growth now produces multiple inequalities.

Third, the rise of the finance industry and financial activities intensified these inequalities, both directly and through housing markets. Finance employment, whether in the finance sector or in the investment departments of other businesses, compensates its winners extremely generously. The typical urban resident, however, is far more likely to experience the impact of finance in soaring rents and home sale prices, for the simple reason that the profits extracted by financiers need to be invested somewhere (Krippner 2005; Ashton, Doussard, and Weber 2016; Peck and Whiteside 2016; Fields 2017). The entrepreneurial strategies cities used to rebuild their downtowns also turned land into a portable security for investors (Weber 2002), paving the way for systematic, omnipresent, and functionally global gentrification (Smith 2002; Lees, Shin, and López-Morales 2016).

The major theoretical perspectives in urban politics provided something close to unified analyses of these problems. They saw "growth machines" of landed interests use their power to intensify investment in the built environment, pressure local government to remain lean and entrepreneurial, and secure the central business districts vital to coordinating postindustrial economic production (Logan and Molotch

1987; Jonas and Wilson 1999). The related perspective of regime theory focused on an "urban regime" in which mayors compensate for their de facto and de jure lack of power by partnering with private interests (Stone 1989). The mechanisms differed, but the problems were the same: disappearing manufacturing jobs, booming downtowns, and increasing reliance on local government to secure investments in the built environment (Reese, Sands, and Skidmore 2014). Both approaches agree that the needs of capital shape urban politics in the United States. This position approached the rare status of scholarly consensus, and it explained the problems of its time extremely well. At the same time, this perspective was limited by its focus on formal city powers, such as land use and economic regulation (Schragger 2016).

The immediate problems with which studies in the growth machine and regime politics traditions contended have long since transformed the basis of urban politics and economies. Seemingly countless scholarly works excavate these changes in minute and impressive detail. Rather than recount the particulars, we focus on the simple transition from disinvestment, the de facto context in which the classic theories developed, to contemporary reinvestment. Central cities today may only house fractions of the manufacturing production jobs they once held, but their downtowns provide indispensable staging sites for professionals engaged in the work of coordinating multinational manufacturing production, sales, and distribution (Sassen 2001; Glaeser 2011). Crucially for urban social movements, and for the hope that cities might use their powers to mitigate these inequalities, this economy requires cities to work, in the sense that Chicago's politicians once referred to their hometown as "The City That Works." In order to coordinate international production and multinational markets, businesses of all descriptions began to need the dense urban centers they had long shunned. Thus, work again lies at the center of the urban boom, but in a new way. Once businesses made job security a relic of the past, they needed the density and diversity of central cities to provide the workers they used to train themselves: as Greenberg and Lewis (2017) memorably put it, the city itself is the "factory" of contemporary capitalism. This arrangement makes central business districts the intellectual assembly sites of the new economy, strategic centers where highly specialized engineers and designers could combine and recombine to consistently generate new ideas, products, and services (Scott 2014). Post-Fordism, deindustrialization, and financialization create both the problems these cities negotiate and the potential for greater economic rewards.

Businesses also need the downtown as a show piece: a bustling beehive of professional activity where the skilled winners of the new economy convene to work, play, and live. In the growth machine era, scholars could take their pick of bungled downtown projects from which to fashion cautionary tales—the Renaissance Center on the Detroit riverfront was a particular favorite. Today, the amount of public investment, governance, and effort that goes into central business districts often defies measurement. In Chicago, for example, the city has authorized hundreds of millions of investment through tax increment financing and sunk billions of dollars into lakefront parks and facilities (Spirou and Judd 2016; Weber 2015). Those investments also spill over to the people who labor in downtowns. Federally funded, locally staffed and orchestrated workforce development programs, for example, devise job-training and retraining programs to mitigate persistent employment crises in small, unstable, and highly specialized manufacturing firms (Lowe 2007; Schrock 2013). Community college systems, labor unions, manufacturing standards organizations, and incubators all work, often quietly, to ensure that the production networks replacing large factories function smoothly (Clark 2013).

The reversal of disinvestment now leads business-friendly economists to declare the "triumph of the city" (Glaeser 2011), and place cities at the center of a supposed "new geography of jobs" (Moretti 2012). The major problems on city agendas—gentrification, schools, sorely needed infrastructure investments—are problems of growth, rather than decline. And for good measure, violent crime rates have fallen by half or more since the turn of the last century. The old insight that cities have little choice but to support businesses' quest for growth still stands. But the way businesses grow has changed. And that creates opportunities.

NEW OPPORTUNITIES AND EVER-PRESENT PROBLEMS: THE CONTINUING MARCH OF SOCIAL AND ECONOMIC INEQUALITY

The problems those opportunities must solve, however, appear to grow worse by the day. The public policy changes authored by the Trump administration and its appointees read like lazy jokes about what the corporate class would do with unfettered power. To wit: the Tax Cuts and Jobs Act of 2017 made the federal tax code significantly more regressive (Gale, Khitatrakun, and Krupkin 2017). The border wall, unchecked authority for ICE, and pervasive extreme racism directly threaten immigrants, their descendants, and urbanized populations of color (Paik 2020; Castañeda 2019). The *Janus* Supreme Court decision used the First Amendment to read union-busting right-to-work legislation into the Constitution (Milkman 2019). The reader can insert her own list of new problems here.

Reaching further back, the U.S. middle class (or at least the proxy measure of midwage employment opportunities) has been shrinking since 1973 (Harrison and Bluestone 1990). Unions have been in decline for even longer (Freeman and Medoff 1984; Rosenfeld 2014). Democratic control of the federal government has at a minimum failed to slow the spread of inequality. Scholars now understand urban machine politics, urban renewal, and the policies enacted by the powerful midcentury New Deal coalition as instruments for intensifying the wealth, assets, and power of white people, men, and the wealthy (Rothstein 2017; Bledsoe, McCreary, and Wright 2019). Freedom itself, in the most literal and physical sense, constitutes yet another form of inequality for the extraordinary number of people, and specifically people of color, that the United States incarcerates (Gilmore 2007).

Cities do not just concentrate these inequalities, but actively produce them. In the largest U.S. metropolitan areas, the "80–20" income ratio, or the multiple of income earned by households at the eightieth percentile compared to those at the twentieth, increased by nearly one-quarter in the past twenty years (Figure 1). This measure presents a bottom-line account of the cumulative impacts of post-Fordism, deindustrialization, and financialization on economic opportunity. The earnings of the top 10 percent and top 1 percent have consistently expanded faster than those of everybody else (Mishel et al. 2012; Piketty 2014), and at the other end of the spectrum, concentrated poverty grows continually more concentrated. In 2012, we found that one-third of the Chicago-area households with a low-wage earner received *all* their income from low-wage earners (Doussard 2012). To the extent that the increasing impoverishment of low-wage workers has leveled off, it has done so because they have organized themselves to raise the minimum wage (Reich, Allegretto, and Godoey 2017; Congressional Budget Office 2014).

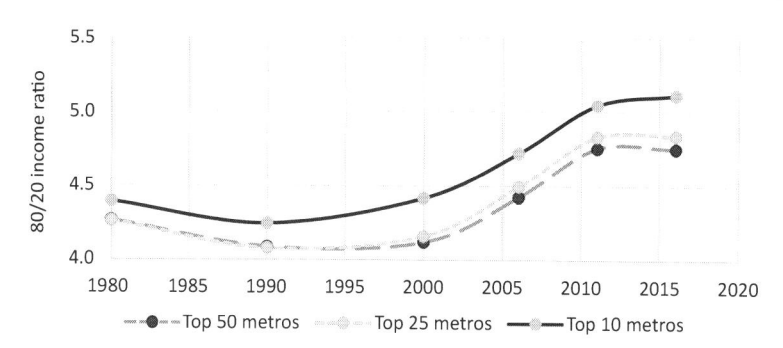

FIGURE 1. 80/20 Household income ratio, largest U.S. metros, 1980–2016

These material disparities grow even wider when viewed through the lens of race. The ratio of the black poverty rate to the white poverty rate has fallen to "just" 2:1 in recent years. That alarming, but diminishing, multiple represents the good news. Overall, average household income for black households in U.S. cities remains around half that of their white counterparts (Figure 2).

These glaring inequalities drive, rather than elude, the study of urban politics, which for decades has focused on the growth of "dual" cities, economic winners and losers, and the ongoing inequalities wrought by economic globalization (Karjanen 2016; Sites 2003; Mollenkopf and

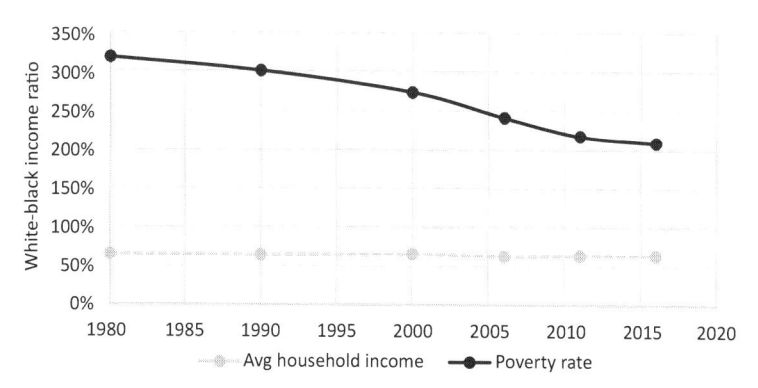

FIGURE 2. White-black income and poverty ratio, large U.S. cities, 1980–2016

Castells 1991). The problem to date is that recitations of the chapter and verse of inequality contain considerably greater clarity and detail than answers to the question of what to do about this central problem. The challenge of prescribing a path toward fairer cities typically founders on the belief, inherited from generations of political economists, that cities and urban social movements lack the leverage needed to drive a better bargain with capital.

CITIES SUPPOSEDLY CANNOT ACT ON INEQUALITY

Justice activists today put to use lessons they learned from decades of fighting against the growth machine. Historically, those struggles were more likely to oppose the use of city power—opposing segregation or defending black and Latino communities against environmentally destructive uses of land—than to redirect that power toward the needs of the poor and communities of color (Morello-Frosch, Pastor, and Sadd 2001; Pastor, Benner, and Matsuoka 2009). Today, the improved bargaining position of cities vis-à-vis organized capital presents those same activists the opportunity to use city agencies and legislation to advance their visions of fairness.

Now-commonplace financial interventions, such as tax increment financing, were first developed in this era (Weber 2014; Frieden and Sagalyn 1991). In the industrial Midwest and Northeast in particular, manufacturers also sought assistance—literally, direct financial assistance—from local government, nominally in response to falling profit rates and out of a desire to keep jobs, but primarily as a payoff for declining to relocate (Bluestone and Harrison 1982). These conditions inspired, or perhaps compelled, generations of activists and residents to demand that city government invest in neighborhoods and people, rather than firms (Clavel 1986; Jonas 1998). The achievements these movements won were victories either *against* the state, or against nonstate entities such as landlords and large corporations. The change in urban fortunes provides an opportunity for these movements to refocus attention toward using the power of local government on their own behalf.

The shift in investment tracks a broader change in the role of cities within the economy (Scott 2014). We now live in an urban age, an era in which the economy revolves around dense agglomerations of firms, knowledge, professionals, and consumers (Beauregard 2018).

Businesses and investors (both private and institutional) as well as households now need cities to maximize the return on their many personal, educational, and financial investments. A rapidly expanding body of academic work celebrates the ascent of cities as centers of economic and cultural life. We do not join this celebration, for the current triumph of cities comes with an immense human toll, entails ever-deeper inequalities, and rests on unseen labor violations, environmental degradation, and creeping political authoritarianism. We seek to evaluate, rather than celebrate, the current moment of leverage for movements that seek a fairer economy: Why and where do they succeed? What are the sources of (and threats to) their power? And where can they expand advocacy focused on work to better address the complex inequalities workers face beyond the workplace?

PUBLIC POLICY SHIFTS TO INEQUALITY

City minimum wage laws dramatize the changing opportunity structure within cities with unique clarity. Growth machine theory, regime theory, and other ideas based on the balance of public and private power at the end of the twentieth century argue, quite simply, that municipal minimum wages should not happen. From a Marxian political economy perspective, the naked distributive consequences of establishing a $15 wage floor position cities as capital's antagonists, and invite reprisals in the form of capital flight, population flight, and a negative reputation in the global competition for footloose capital. Rational-choice theorists suggest a different path to a similar outcome, pointing to the propensity of mobile firms and high-income residents to veto distributive legislation by "voting with their feet" (Peterson 1981). Regime analysis takes yet another path to the same conclusion, finding that elected officials cannot endorse economic redistribution without losing the business support they need to govern effectively (Morel 2018; Reese, Sands, and Skidmore 2014; Stone 1989). On this case of potential redistribution, ideological opposites who agree on little find consensus: using city government to address inequality will backfire.

These classic arguments cannot explain the past decade of urban policy. More than fifty U.S. cities and counties now have minimum wage laws on the books. The wage floors they enact are often twice as high as those activists proposed a decade ago: $15 in Los Angeles, San Francisco, Seattle, Chicago, Minneapolis, and St. Paul; $13 in the

District of Columbia, and $10 or more in dozens of other jurisdictions. Moreover, the movements that win these gains often win pay raises of equal or larger size in state houses: California, Illinois, New York, Massachusetts, Connecticut, Maryland, and New Jersey will all move to a $15 minimum wage in the next five years. Florida will reach that level via a ballot initiative. Arguments that cities cannot pass distributive legislation predict, at a minimum, that these laws would generate enormous controversy as they work their way through city councils. To the contrary, they are extremely popular. Major candidates in Seattle's 2014 mayoral election publicly fought for the mantle of being the $15 minimum wage's most enthusiastic champion. Chicago mayor Rahm Emanuel moved from opposition to the minimum wage to rallying support for the Chicago law and a series of related measures on pay and working conditions. His successor, Lori Lightfoot, signed off on a follow-up series of workplace laws that mandates paid time off and regular work schedules. Those measures passed the City Council 50–0 and induced little protest from business leaders.

Chambers of commerce, retailers, and restaurant trade groups still oppose minimum wage increases and other employment standards. Mayors and city councils either ignore or co-opt them, because retail business interests now pose a smaller threat to a mayor's capacity to rule than do the well-organized activists who demand change. When Chicago's Emanuel entered office in 2011, he was a business-friendly candidate who began his tenure by picking fights with public employees and public employee unions, especially the Chicago Teachers Union. Yet in 2013, he signed an extremely strict, labor-backed wage theft bill, and he loudly claimed to want a minimum wage higher than the $13 he signed a year later. It takes only passing familiarity with Emanuel to trace his motivations to public pressure rather than a conversion to the cause of economic justice. He responded to both acute political pressure to act and changing economic ground conditions that made distributive economic policy palatable to Chicago's organized business interests. Emanuel and his peers continued to serve the interests of economic growth—and found the means to reconcile growth with distributive fairness.

Chicago and other large cities today remain committed to old-fashioned types of support for growth as well. Financial support to developers, once controversial, now stands as a commonplace (Weber 2015). Thirty years after scholars first spotted the key role cities would play as the "command and control centers" of a globalized economy (Harvey 1989b; Friedmann and Wolff 1982) they continue to make themselves indispensable to capital accumulation in obvious, subtle, and insidious ways (Scott 2019). In simple terms, the growth imperative has not disappeared. Instead, it has changed in ways that provide social movements leverage to make the local state do their bidding.

GOVERNANCE AND PLACE: WHERE SOCIAL MOVEMENTS FIND LEVERAGE

Evangelists and critics of the new urban age agree that the economic changes driving the current city boom also intensify inequalities. Scholars from the Left and Right see an inevitable trade-off between growth and equity: Cities can maintain their older institutional protections for the less fortunate (such as unions, public housing, robust public employment) and stagnate, or they can grow unequally (Glaeser 2011). This perspective ignores abundant evidence that the central role of cities in capital accumulation produces new forms of leverage—potential, actual, and increasingly incorporated into advocacy strategy—for urban justice movements. Businesses do not just need cities, they need certain things from cities in order to increase their rate of return: central business districts, a skilled workforce, consumption amenities, and development assistance. America's remaining union members are disproportionately concentrated in the industries that produce, transport, and deliver those goods and services (MacDonald 2017, 4). This central position gives them bargaining power, which they increasingly use in the service of "social unionism" (Frege, Kelly, and Kelly 2004)—activism for the public goods, collective consumption, and defense of identity that defines urban social movements (Castells 1983). The urban boom provides these activists with leverage or, if you will, levers: Specific points where justice activists can steer the process in their favor (Figure 3).

Post-Fordist economic growth ushered in the modern era of inequality by eliminating manufacturing jobs, demanding concessions from workers who kept their jobs, and replacing manufacturing production with the complex and skilled work of coordinating manufacturing production somewhere else. Related but separate, the growing class of urban professionals created skyrocketing demand for personal services, residential construction, restaurants, dry cleaners, spas:

GROWTH PROCESS	RESULTING INEQUALITIES	LEVERAGE FOR JUSTICE ACTIVISTS
Post-Fordist expansion *Firms close manufacturing plants, invest in downtown "command and control" centers*	Deindustrialization eliminates midwage jobs and places downward wage pressure on remaining manufacturing jobs	Mergers, acquisitions, and new fortunes destabilize local business elites and weaken ability to act as a class
	Firms in all sectors demand flexibility in hiring, firing, paying, and scheduling workers	Political values of the growing class of urban professionals move toward equity and sustainability
	Firms disinvest in basic and advanced job training	Businesses turn to public sector to train workers and coordinate complex multifirm networks
Deindustrialization and service sector growth *Personal services and entertainment expand to support the expanding professional workforce*	Low-wage work grows in the aggregate and as a share of all employment	Low-wage industries require location for profit. They cannot easily relocate
	Low-wage work deteriorates: wages fall at the bottom of the pay distribution, employers routinely violate basic labor laws, and workers lose control of their schedules	Restaurants, hotels, and other prominent low-wage employers are "consumer facing": visible mistreatment of workers threatens sales volumes and brand loyalty
	Routine subcontracting pares regulatory oversight to a minimum	Place-based strategies of businesses facilitate place-based organizing
	Growth centers in previously nonunion industries that resist unionization	Deconcentrated industries oppose employment legislation less effectively than larger, more concentrated employers
	Growth centers in deconcentrated industries with small and spatially diffuse workplaces	
Financialization and real estate–led growth *Firms and households invest their growing profits in financial instruments and property*	Steady increases in real estate investment capital produce mass gentrification and rolling housing affordability crises	Widespread public assistance to developers creates pressure points (permits, zoning changes, hearings) for organizers
	Public sector relies increasingly on financial markets and the proausterity "discipline" of ratings agencies	Investment growth creates opportunities for distribution (jobs, housing, public goods)
	Public spending on support for developers and real estate–adjacent amenities crowds out budget room for social investment	Growing importance of finance as a profit source to all industries shrinks the relative cost to employers of improving wages and working conditions
	Gentrification and austerity intensify disparities in school funding and capacities	Organizing for school funding unites and expands previously disparate advocacy constituencies

FIGURE 3. Major economic changes and resulting policy leverage

place-based service jobs in which cost-based competition is the norm, unions represent few workers and small, spread-out employers evade the enforcement of labor laws. These same changes grew through and fed the growth of finance industries. Institutional investors and individuals park increasing amounts of their swelling assets in the built environment and in cities in particular. For the typical urban resident, the results were disastrous: unaffordable housing, frequent moves that uprooted stable social networks, and diminished public spending on schools, transportation, and the other public goods that could mitigate shrinking economic opportunity.

The structural economic changes that rain these inequalities on cities, however, also provide leverage for justice activists, particularly in the housing process. The shift in cities' economic base from manufacturing to services steadily diminishes the formerly all-powerful threat of capital mobility. Most footloose manufacturers are gone from cities, and the goods producers who remain need something from the city itself: access to key customers, a priority position in labor markets for uniquely skilled designers and engineers, access to consumers, or spillovers from others' innovation activities (Sassen 2001). Hotels, restaurants, dry cleaners, and cleaning services, furthermore, use business models that value location, often to the block. They continue to pour into cities, not because cities are cheap, but because urban density and urban incomes offer the highest return on a dollar of capital spent.

More subtly, these changes in the structure of business change who businesspeople are, sociologically and interpersonally. Members of the new professional class habitually patronize low-wage employers, but they are also more likely to vote for self-proclaimed progressive politicians who oppose the conditions of low-wage work (Fraser 2019). The transition to a post-Fordist economy has also decimated the formerly tight hold of old growth machine members on power. If you present Logan and Molotch's canonical list of growth machine members— newspapers, utilities, large manufacturers—to students today, they will scratch their heads. Technology firms, developers, and financiers dominate the list of institutional representatives of organized business today, and while their motives are not benevolent, they are different. Labor costs rarely play an important role in their profits and losses, and their employees voice concern about climate change and even the threat of inequality itself. Readers will protest that those professionals have themselves worked hard to create our current inequalities, and they will be right. But their potential receptiveness to the problem nevertheless matters.

More substantively, businesses and investors need things from cities, beginning with social reproduction writ large (Castells 1983). They also need investments in transit to deliver their workers, financing for public amenities that lock in their property values, public agencies to broker trade deals and support technology development, training for workers, planning approvals for massive retail development and high-rises (Castells 1996). Savitch and Kantor's multinational comparative study of city bargaining power found that cities possess the greatest leverage to bargain with capital when they provide services needed by globalizing firms (Savitch and Kantor 2002). Those services, and the bargaining opportunities they provide, are growing in number and scope. Routine public assistance for expensive real estate development in particular supplies justice activists with expansive opportunities. The search for leverage against mobile capital led cities to attach demands and conditions to redevelopment assistance as long as forty years ago (Clavel 1986). Boston successfully introduced a growth fees program requiring developers to contribute to affordable housing and community development funds in the 1980s; however, the momentum for this approach to development stalled (Goetz 1990; Dreier and Ehrlich 1991). Rising real estate valuations in the 1990s and 2010s, however, rejuvenated these efforts, at least on a case-by-case basis. Today, community benefits agreements, project labor agreements, and developer support for community funding and organizations—support often provided outside the framework of a formal negotiation—is common (Marantz 2015). Large housing developments, such as the former Gates Rubber factory in Denver, commercial developments including Los Angeles's Staples Center, and a rebuilt Yankee Stadium in the Bronx, all came with binding promises to hire union workers, pay above-market wages, and provide financial support for housing and social services (Wolf-Powers 2010).

The community benefits agreement approach keys on the legal mechanisms central to such deals, essentially tying regulatory approval to investor support for public services. Increasingly, however, these negotiations or transactions occur without such minute legal wrangling. In especially high-value locations in cities such as San Francisco and New York, for example, developers have *preemptively* offered to invest in park space, community centers, and affordable housing

(Stabrowski 2015; Hong 2016). We will dissect the mechanics of these negotiations, and the ways in which organizers and activists understand, create, and use leverage, in later chapters. For the time being, simply note that this leverage exists, that it exists in many places, and that it takes on multiple forms.

A related, less obvious type of leverage comes from the day-to-day, technical involvement of local government agencies and community organizations in the operation of business. Workforce development organizations, manufacturing standards organizations, and infrastructure development alliances all work behind the scenes to train workers, link them to employers, and make government agencies at multiple scales attentive to the needs of a region's distinctive businesses (Schrock 2013).

These individual mechanisms of leverage also add up to something greater than the sum of their parts. Valuing cities writ large creates entry points for justice activists. This reality is visible in the recent return of protests (for teachers, for Black Lives Matter) to central business districts, in the diversity of activist organizations that assemble to demand change, in the reality that citizens respond differently to appeals to economic justice for "their" baristas and Uber drivers than they do for distant sweatshop employees they will never meet. In big ways and small, the fact that cities now matter economically, socially, and culturally amplifies the demands and claims of their citizens.

ECONOMIC JUSTICE AS ECONOMIC DEVELOPMENT

The economic transformation of U.S. cities upends old models of urban politics and urban economic development. Cumulatively, the long-run changes of post-Fordism, deindustrialization, and financialization have turned disinvestment into reinvestment and have shifted the economic base of cities from producing physical goods to producing services. We argue, simply, that these shifts create opportunities for local government bodies and community organizations that scholars previously understood as ineffective to contest growing inequalities. Seen narrowly, these opportunities influence who wins and loses in postindustrial urban economies. Yet the current political contest concerns the underlying mode of *economic development* as much as the post-hoc adjustment of economic wins and losses. This amounts to a shift from tasking after-the-fact redistribution with the cumbersome job of leveling off inequalities to imagining de facto *pre*-distribution: an economy that mitigates rather than amplifies social and economic inequalities as it grows (Imbroscio 2013). Scholars of economic development conceptualize the process as inclusive development that spreads the rewards of growth to historically marginalized populations (Lowe and Wolf-Powers 2018). We argue for a bigger, bolder imaginary.

Two recent lines of thought in economic development point to conceptual and practical paths forward. One is the groundbreaking work of Nobel laureate Amartya Sen, who argues for a "capabilities" approach (Sen 1990) that treats human fulfillment and the meeting of basic needs as indispensable building blocks of economic production and exchange. The human development approach reimagines equity and fairness as stimuli to growth, not threats. This approach is germane to questions about current urban politics and inequalities because it suggests that the political contest to ensure that work is rewarded is itself part of economic development. For the first time in a long time, the normative preference for less inequality overlaps with orthodox economic work warning that excessive debt leads to recessions (Mian and Sufi 2015), that mass incarceration spends public resources in order to waste human potential (Sykes and Maroto 2016), that starving households of income and health insurance poses a direct public health and economic threat to all (Madland 2015). The contest for equitable economic development is in many ways the decidedly old-fashioned contest to provide enough economic security for workers and their families to make future-oriented investments in themselves and their communities, which ultimately expands our collective capabilities (Feldman et al. 2016).

Second, our perspective aligns neatly with growing interest in treating the local "consumption base," the one-time afterthought of regional development theory, as a key source of economic growth and diversification (Markusen and Schrock 2009). This perspective inverts the traditional logic of urban economic development, which has historically maligned consumer spending and service industries as by-products of the manufacturing exports thought to drive economic growth. Public policy, collective bargaining, and powerful social movements can create local industries that pay their workers more, buy from other local industries, draw talented people to local economies, and eventually become exporting industries in their own right. Laws mandating higher pay, better working conditions, and employment opportunities for historically marginalized communities lead local industries to create many of the same wages, working conditions, and economic relationships that once characterized manufacturing industries. Focusing on services and consumption industries is also practical: hotels, restaurants, and security services cannot flee public policy by relocating.

Students of economic development spend a lot of time learning about tax incentives, job-training programs, revolving loan funds, and dozens of other innovations that have little demonstrated impact on growth and development. By contrast, the simple tool of requiring local government to favor minority and women-owned businesses in contracting proved effective from the start (Wiewel and Rieser 1989). The point is basic, but important: Even before the current era of urbanization tilted the balance of power toward cities, activists had spotted pressure points that urban locations provided. Today, activists can augment these changes to administrative actions with changes enacted through public policy. Regulating the economy writ large, rather than the actions of government agencies themselves, offers the promise of developing a broader and more effective response to the problems of inequality.

This provides a starting point of sorts for investigating how urban social movements put to use the power they have won with the urbanization of the economy. Our empirical chapters examine the spread of four representative policies that embody different reads on and approaches to the changing balance of power. The most visible response to cities' enhanced leverage, the $15 minimum wage, has more to do with the diminished threat of capital flight than with proximity, land, or city contracting per se. Targeted hiring programs, which require government contractors to hire and train from historically excluded populations and to pay at above market-rate levels, represent a clear and even simpler use of the power of local government. Our third major set of policies, work-home laws that ensure standards for paid time off, humane work schedules, child care, and other basic supports for social reproduction, respond in some measure to the challenge of escalating home prices and lengthening commutes. Finally, political action against austerity secures expanded public support for universal public goods—schools, dependent care, public services—that help working households achieve dignity and stability. Rather than systematically testing the types of leverage peoples' movements have won, our cases maximize difference and test responses to different facets of the problem of inequality: the shortage of high-paying jobs, inequalities in who holds those jobs, work that interferes with basic household duties, and fiscal austerity, which starves households of the basic services they need to make ends meet.

Casting this wide net has real advantages. Our most basic finding is that despite their many legal and discursive differences, these policies passed into law more or less through the same process. This surprised us: skepticism about using municipal power against inequality suggests that the minimum wage will be controversial simply because of the amount of money involved, that work-and-home policies will struggle to find a clear message or constituency and that targeted hire programs will diminish developers' interest in development. Recognizing the similarity of the processes through which these measures become policy points to an important development beyond the growth of leverage for cities. Specifically, it points to the growing power of urban social movements to write their visions of a fair economy into public policy. Accordingly, we shift our focus from the contest between cities and capital to the peoples' movements currently making demands of elected officials.

The challenges in making sense of these movements are immense. Studies of urban (electoral) politics and urban social movements address similar concerns yet speak to one another infrequently. Both bodies of research feature relatively few systematic, multisite studies. Notable exceptions, such as Savitch and Kantor's *Cities in the International Marketplace* (2002) and Pastor, Benner, and Matsuoka's *This Could Be the Start of Something Big* (2009), illustrate the rule. Overall, the information scholars fashion on urban social movements and urban politics provides little framework for a systematic investigation. Most focus on a single city, issue, or organization—often, all three. History, economic change, and changes in scalar relations—in the relative powers and weaknesses of cities vis-à-vis states and the federal system—rarely feature in such studies. We mount such criticisms in good humor and with real humility, since our own research embodies most of these limits (Schrock 2013; Doussard and Lesniewski 2017). In the next two chapters, we set out to overcome these barriers, first by making sense of significant changes in how urban activists organize themselves *within* cities, and second by providing a framework to make sense of how activism constitutes itself *across cities and scales*.

2

Economic and Racial Justice Coalitions

DIVERSE SOCIAL MOVEMENTS CHALLENGE INEQUALITY

The rise of unprecedented inequalities in cities has also fueled movements that work for justice. The growth and reorganization of these movements often goes unnoted in studies of city politics that focus on politicians rather than citizens. One cost of this focus is the general neglect of the people, institutions, and movements that make claims on officeholders. This has consequences, for urban social movements focused on economic justice have transformed as extensively as the cities they call home. In the mid-1990s, unions and community organizations began the work of building unified coalitions with a policy agenda focused on economic development and regional equity (Turner and Cornfield 2007; Pastor, Benner, and Matsuoka 2009; Dean and Reynolds 2011). Those movements have since matured into economic and racial justice (ERJ) coalitions—networks of unions, community organizations, and advocacy groups who push for policy intervention against economic inequality as part of the broader goal of addressing complex and multidimensional racial inequalities.

The scholarship of Manuel Castells noted this change in incipient form, as Castells progressed from analyzing place-based grassroots movements to networked economies and the movements they created (Castells 1983, 1996). Today, that shift is fully realized, and at scale. Urban social movements are uniting action against economic and racial inequality by drawing attention to their shared roots in racial capitalism (Robinson 2005). The movement participants we interviewed for this book do not use that term, but their actions and the discourses they use to build support for economic justice reflect an understanding that economic and racial inequality cannot be separated. Cedric Robinson's original work on the subject showed that from its early stages, capitalism relied on the creation and exploitation of racialized others to produce and extract value (2005). The implications of this insight for social movements are intuitive. As Ruth Wilson Gilmore argues, understanding capitalism this way obligates analysts to map both the racial and spatial differences in how the economy operates (Gilmore 2007).

This commitment to mapping racialized differences in the operation of the economy has led geographers in particular to ask how resistance and opposition to capitalism also takes on race- and place-specific forms (Bledsoe and Wright 2019). Studies of race- and place-based opposition to racial capital stand out for tying together diverse issues that Marxian political economists often address individually. For example, Clyde Woods's long-run study of racial capitalism in New Orleans put racism, economic vulnerability, and environmental vulnerability into a single conceptual frame, at a time when orthodox social scientists attempted to understand each subject individually (Woods 1998). Studying what McKitrick and Woods call the "situated" knowledge of communities of color thus steers our attention to movements, analyses, and critiques that address multiple manifestations of inequality at once (McKittrick and Woods 2007). This book makes a modest contribution to that goal by foregrounding the organizing techniques low-income communities and communities of color (who are often the same community) have adopted to impact public policy. Like the social movements whose efforts are the topic of this book, we use the language of racial capitalism sparingly. However, the broader commitment to understanding how the current economy produces systemic inequality, and identifying effective ways to counter that inequality, guides both the work of the movements we study and our own. Because the basic social, economic, and institutional building blocks of American life are all built on racist foundations, social movements that foreground racial critique have at their disposal messages, tropes, and networks that cut across domains of urban politics—in particular, work-based politics and a politics of home and collective consumption—that scholars of urban politics have long understood to work in isolation from one another (Castells 1983; Katznelson 1982). In other words, the language of racial justice reflects an analysis that more accurately conceptualizes the problems the poor and communities of color face. And that opens up new options unavailable to older instantiations of community-labor movements (Dean and Reynolds 2011; Pastor, Benner, and Matsuoka 2009).

We illustrate the transformation of urban social movements to act upon this problem with a snapshot that clearly encapsulates the stakes and challenges at hand. We focus again on Chicago, home to Saul Alinsky, the de facto founder of modern community organizing; Gale Cincotta, the activist behind the Community Reinvestment Act; and Harold Washington, the most visible progressive mayor of the 1980s. Each of those reformers represents a classic type, and those types have today been supplanted by newer, but equally innovative, forms of activism. Today, the socialist caucus on Chicago's City Council accounts for such a tenth of the body's fifty-person membership. Activist community organizations pushed conservative machine Mayor Rahm Emanuel to pass the nation's strictest wage theft law and a pilot universal basic income program. Today's reformers lack a recognizable figurehead like Alinsky, which is appropriate. Alinsky established the Industrial Areas Foundation [IAF] to disseminate his organizing model and link organizers across cities. The networks in which contemporary organizers now work are far denser and more complex—they span regions, neighborhoods, ethnicities, issues, and political scales, providing organizers the ability to move advocacy from site to site, problem to problem, and one political forum to the next. Their movement is strong for being synonymous with no single person or organization.

Today's activists organize themselves at the scale of the city. Neighborhood organizations remain politically active, but citywide advocacy proceeds through post-territorial organizations such as Grassroots Collaborative, who advocate on the basis of collective identity and class. A second difference: Grassroots Collaborative and its peers eschew the pragmatic, compromising language of prior reformers in favor of explicit, ideological critique: critique of the "1 percent," critique of systemic racism, critique of police budgets, critique of the service economy. Lots of critique, often overtly ideological. Notably, this critique, and the organizing that drives it, embraces the cause of antiracism—a cause that Alinsky, among others, did not engage as a structural problem. Antiracist messaging in Chicago both shapes the work organizers undertake and, as we will show in Chapters 4–7, makes that work more effective on its own terms.

A third major difference apparent in Chicago and elsewhere is that contemporary movements operate in networks: networks within the same city, networks between cities, networks between cities and state capitals. Grassroots Collaborative, for example, has eleven member organizations (one of which itself has many dozens of members). Grassroots Collaborative is at the same time a member of the Partnership for Working Families (renamed PowerSwitch Action as this book went to press), a national organization encompassing twenty urban affiliates engaged in organizing and policy. Decades ago, participants in the neighborhoods movement aspired to link cities together and to change policy in state governments. Linking urban organizers within national organizations, such as Alinsky's Industrial Areas Foundation or National People's Action, constituted a significant achievement. Today's organizations routinely work through multiple networks at a time, and new networks appear frequently. This makes the network structure of urban social movements an important feature of our study.

The differences between old and new urban social movements appear to lead to different outcomes. In the past, reformers succeeded in capturing elected office but struggled to establish their vision in public policy. The opposite applies today, both in Chicago and elsewhere. After the March 2019 elections, a bloc of progressive aldermen, including five Democratic Socialists, held nearly one-fifth of the City Council's seats. This legislative minority drives the agenda. Chicago continues to enact a string of laws favored by justice advocates: a $15 minimum wage, a comprehensive "fair workweek" law on scheduling, establishment of a citizen's police review board, and more. Yet despite the critiques of neoliberal capitalism that inform these renewed urban justice movements, their policy agendas do not fundamentally threaten the imperative of urban economic growth; rather, they seek to bend growth toward more distributively just outcomes. This enables advocates to advance their policies in surprisingly varied cities and political economies. Consider it a feature, rather than a bug.

Studies of urban politics focus far more attention on the state and on business interests than they do on peoples' organizations and movements. One reason for this is that urban justice movements are harder to study. Unlike a legislature or a chamber of commerce, their membership is fluid and unregistered, and the participants are difficult to identify and often too busy to interview. Another reason is that these movements historically operated individually, or in isolation from one another. Manuel Castells's landmark *The City and the Grassroots* (Castells 1983), the most detailed and revealing study of urban social movements, understood those movements territorially: they worked through urban space that empowered them yet simultaneously limited their focus. Today, however, multisited, multiscaled movements are everywhere. We need to understand them as such.

THE TASK AHEAD: UNDERSTANDING ECONOMIC JUSTICE MOVEMENTS' EVOLUTION FROM FORDISM TO THE SERVICE ECONOMY

We trace the evolution of community opposition through four key periods of action, closely matched to changes in the composition and operation of the economy. We focus on a subset of social movement actors whose work emphasizes economic fairness. We acknowledge that the term *social movement* promises a completeness that no analyst can really deliver. Activism for racial and environmental justice proceeded alongside, and sometimes in step with, economic justice activism. Our history of these movements centers actors focused on economic fairness, and emphasizes the growing integration of economic and racial justice movements over time.

Beginning with deindustrialization and the deep, prolonged recession of the early 1980s, neighborhood coalitions attempted electoral takeover of city government by uniting predominantly minority neighborhoods and white progressives (Bennett 1993; Kaufmann 2005). In the 1990s, citywide living-wage movements joined the remnants of this coalition to unions and issues-based organizers, seeking limited citywide legislation to mitigate the growth of service-sector jobs and working poverty. In the 2000s, these same movements turned to the goal of securing community benefits agreements—bespoke promises for the developers of large real estate projects to provide good jobs and mitigate negative impacts of new development. The community benefits movement failed to scale up but advanced the important work of linking campaigns for work to campaigns focused on housing and other problems. Following the Great Recession, community activism changed again, with organizers embracing messages, strategies, and tactics they had previously downplayed: racial and economic justice, public confrontation, multiorganization networks, and increasingly ideological critiques of capitalism and institutional racism.

The origins of these discrete campaigns, coalitions, and organizing strategies in longer-term concerns about economic and social inequality require us to conceptualize them as social movements. We use Castells's classic definition of urban social movements as collectives that (1) advocate for collective consumption (i.e., public services, goods, and support), (2) defend a particular community or culture, and (3) contest domination by the state (Castells 1983). The activists we study fit this definition well, particularly in the postwar era, when organizers often focused on halting the use of state power to clear purported slums, enforce segregation, and secure the property rights and rent collections of elites. Our interest in these movements more closely follows recent work by Benner and Pastor (Pastor, Benner, and Matsuoka 2009; Benner and Pastor 2012), Nicholls (Nicholls 2008; Nicholls, Miller, and Beaumont 2013; Uitermark and Nicholls 2017), Leitner (Leitner, Sheppard, and Sziarto 2008; Sheppard et al. 2015), and critical labor scholars (Brown 2018; Brady and Lesniewski 2018; Doussard 2015; Doussard and Lesniewski 2017) who ask how these movements reconfigure themselves to better contest contemporary problems of economic globalization.

We focus on the question of how formerly place- and territory-focused social movements built during urban disinvestment in the twentieth century evolved into multisited, multiscaled network movements that address a great variety of problems in a range of places and a multiplicity of political forums. Mirroring the insight that urban regions constitute the basic building blocks of the global economy, many studies of these diversified movements understand them as *regional* movements, engaged in a project of "regional power building" (Milkman and Ott 2014) that enables them to assemble political coalitions that favor action for the poor and communities of color (Benner and Pastor 2012). Many of the organizations this book engages with coordinate regional alliances and produce research using regions as the core unit of analysis. They have outwardly regional names, such as Seattle's Puget Sound Sage. Yet the regional scale provides few opportunities to enact policy. Accordingly, these organizations use the networks in which they participate to move policy making around horizontally, to different municipalities within a region or to different regions, and vertically, to different scales of state power. Pastor, Benner, and Matsuoka (2009, 13) noted this process a decade ago, observing that "the region can be an appropriate scale for forging coalitions and building power, which can then move policy as needed" within a given jurisdiction. Our immediate goal is to flesh out how these organizations evolved to develop such abilities.

We use three central choices in advocacy to define movements for justice over this forty-year period. First, justice movements had to find leverage with which to contest the strategies and choices—from businesses or the local state—that resulted in unjust outcomes for communities. The enterprise of passing municipal legislation to directly address those problems is a recent entrant to the agenda. Previously, activists turned to technical analyses of the economy to identify potential opportunities to intervene. In the neighborhoods era, emergent coalitions searched for pressure points they could use to keep workplaces and jobs and redistribute municipal resources to support neighborhood-based development. The trademark innovations of this era included the establishment of community development corporations to coordinate reinvestment in neighborhoods and policies designed to stop capital flight (Clavel 2010). The living-wage movement found leverage in municipal government, using city contracting and purchasing agreements to make businesses pay (slightly) above-average wages. In the current era, the service economy itself provides equity movements the leverage with which to make demands of firms that need urban locations and support from the local state.

Second, they must decide how to deal with the problem of racism. The current question about populist support for the Trump administration and its populist successors—does racism or economic fear motivate his supporters?—mirrors a question with which urban social movements consistently struggle. Economic precariousness and race overlap significantly in the United States. The labor movement historically simplified the problem by attempting to separate economic challenges from the problem of racism: unions focused on what was being distributed rather than to whom it was distributed. Community organizers simultaneously undertook sustained antiracist work targeted against agents of discrimination (Jayaraman and Ness 2015; Lesniewski and Doussard 2017), emphasizing the economic dimensions of discrimination only intermittently. After the Great Recession, participants in urban social movements began placing both on equal footing. The struggle to join appeals to racial and economic justice defines movements today and goes far in determining whom those movements include and the problems they address.

This ties directly to the third challenge, of building coherent messages and discourses that rival the simple imperative of growth. Economic growth is the language of public life in the United States: civics classes, political tropes, and the basic aspirations of an American life so thoroughly center economic accumulation that arguments for justice sound weak (compared to the masculinist discourse of growth, they are distinctly feminized) and *dissonant* (Logan and Molotch

1987). Equally problematic, arguments for justice complicate, while arguments for growth simplify. Thus, justice movements must develop clear, broad, and compelling messages in order to chart a viable path to materially changing the world—a difficult task! Today's emergent ERJ coalitions deal with this challenge by claiming the mantle of economic growth for themselves: rather than contest the primacy of economic expansion, they contend that distributive fairness boosts growth itself. Figure 4 summarizes this current form of advocacy and the way it fits with its predecessors.

MOVEMENT	IMPETUS	MECHANISMS	RESPONSE	LIMITATION
Neighborhoods movement (1970s/80s)	Urban disinvestment; urban renewal; and labor market dualization	Political mobilization to support progressive candidates; developing alternative policy	Community organizing for neighborhood development against downtown development; occasional/brief capture of city hall	Governing coalitions' ineffectiveness against growth coalitions; limited ability to engage across race and class
Living-wage movement (1990s)	Industrial restructuring; neoliberalization; privatization	Political mobilization to pass living-wage laws; developing national networks	Strengthening of Central Labor Councils to advocate for local living wages; service-sector unionization	Limited engagement on broader issues facing communities of color
Community benefits movement (2000s)	Urban reinvestment (private and public); racialized gentrification and displacement	Transactional organizing around targeted public works projects; developing national infrastructure	Organizing for agreements with developers and/or public sector agencies to mitigate impacts on community, e.g., often including living-wage and/or hiring provisions	Ad hoc character, rarely leading to sustained capacity; victories are often symbolic
Economic and racial justice (2010s)	Systemic gentrification and displacement; fiscal austerity; income and assets inequality	Networked organizing across neighborhoods and political scales; nationally networked organizations; focus on basic organizing in addition to mobilization and advocacy	Linked city and state policy campaigns: minimum wage, wage theft, fair workweek, universal prekindergarten, ban the box	Greater success in limiting economic than racial inequality; continued inability to address broader sources of growing inequalities

FIGURE 4. Four recent phases of urban economic justice movements

Rather than celebrate or reverse-engineer the fleeting successes of urban justice movements, we address underlying questions about how justice movements organize themselves, how they deal with the relationship between race and class, and how, discursively, they make claims. An honest appraisal of these coalitions is essential, for the simple reason that their frontiers—the limits of their social influence, political reach, and messaging—are the current limits of distributive urban policy.

THE NEIGHBORHOODS MOVEMENT: CONTESTING DISINVESTMENT, TARGETING CITY HALL

The neighborhoods movement, which came to fruition in the 1970s and 1980s, had multiple roots, all which were themselves rooted in the core problems of segregation, the uneven provision of public services, and uneven development. Community organizations and activists based in neighborhoods bulldozed for urban renewal, and neighborhoods neglected in order to free up resources for central business districts, responded by juxtaposing the interests of lower-income neighborhoods—"the neighborhoods," in the movement's vernacular—against downtown (Kain and Persky 1969; Hyra 2012; Mollenkopf 1983; Squires 1989, 1994). The central discursive trope of "neighborhoods" indirectly defined the movement's approach to the problem of racism: "the neighborhoods" were tacitly, and sometimes explicitly, neighborhoods of color. Many of the individuals and organizations that participated in the neighborhoods movement had previously developed their skills in past, race-focused campaigns for welfare rights, civil rights, and community control amid the scourge of urban renewal (Pastor, Benner, and Matsuoka 2009). The discursive container of neighborhoods placed racial difference in the same frame as economic difference, but subsumed the message of racial justice to the message of equitable investment. This approach constituted a tentative effort to countermand the overwhelming, layered ways public power wrote race into the built environment and the use of state power (Shabazz 2015; Jefferson 2020).

Neighborhoods also mapped onto wards and electoral precincts, and this in turn helped in drafting political allies and champions. In 1969, a vigorous neighborhoods movement in Cleveland convinced mayor Carl Stokes to appoint a planning department dedicated to steering "public resources to benefit those with few, if any resources" (Krumholz, Cogger, and Linner 1975). In the 1970s, the left-leaning mayor of Burlington, Vermont, drew on broad popular support to enact participatory budgeting and other experimental reforms (Clavel 1986). These electoral victories were isolated; analysts would not reach for examples from Burlington if progressive rule were commonplace.

Manufacturing job losses in the Reagan years added to the desperation of neighborhood movements. Cities, activists argued, had a duty to use their powers to limit job losses and secure well-paying work (Clavel 1986; City of Chicago 1984). This focus expanded the neighborhoods coalition by tying housing, public services, and investment to employment. Campaigning on promises of jobs and investment, Chicago's Harold Washington and Boston's Ray Flynn won elections with geographically broad majorities. They set about using public power to steer resources and jobs to neighborhoods punished by white flight and deindustrialization. In Chicago in particular, this drive was aided by not-for-profit organizations—the Chicago Association of Neighborhood Development Organizations, the Chicago Jobs Council, and the Community Workshop for Economic Development—that linked neighborhood organizations to policy makers (Clavel 1986, 2010).

These movements used remarkably blunt language that straightforwardly contrasted the needs of capital to those of citizens. *"Chicago Works Together,"* written by activist planning scholar Rob Mier, instrumentalized the symbolism of neighborhoods:

> This Plan sets forth measurable commitments for this next year: commitments to create and retain jobs, to rebuild neighborhoods, to renew housing and the City's physical assets, to aid businesses, and to inform and involve the public at every step along the way. Setting a new development course for a City of the size and complexity of Chicago presents an historic challenge. This is especially true when the course is to "work together" to invite and encourage the energies, talents and commitments of diverse citizens and neighborhood groups as development partners with business and the City. (City of Chicago 1984, 1)

Anticipating the later efforts of urban movements to recast themselves to negotiate across political scales, Washington and his activists identified the goal of shifting advocacy to political scales where the growth machine held less power and policy interventions could target the structural problems Chicago and its peers faced:

> The City has directed its representatives in both Washington D.C. and Springfield to work with other municipalities and states for new programs and resources to mitigate pressing regional and national problems... For example, the City's Springfield liaison is working with the Illinois Department of Transportation to ensure that Chicago receives its fair share of new State gas tax. City lobbyists also worked closely with the Illinois General Assembly as the World's Fair Authority Act was drafted and enacted, and will continue to actively fashion a World's Fair financing plan that will equitably distribute the costs of the 1992 exposition. (City of Chicago 1984, 19)

Expanding the remit of city power proved a popular winner but a policy failure. Washington and Flynn both earned reelection despite their limited policy track records. Chicago's Department of Economic Development in particular stands out for noble failure. It floated industrial revenue bonds, launched job-training programs, founded industry task forces led by accomplished scholars, and pioneered dozens of policies, programs, and forecasting models designed to limit job loss. They didn't work. A sympathetic analysis from Washington collaborator Wim Wiewel concluded that the city's economic development experiments yielded just a few hundred jobs (Wiewel and Rieser 1989).

The most effective remedies to the problems of disinvestment and job loss relied instead on cities' traditional power to control land use. In Chicago, the Washington Administration headed off residential encroachment on industrial land by designating a dozen Planned Manufacturing Districts in which land use could not be converted. Washington's eventual successor Richard M. Daley not only kept the program but expanded it (Hartley, Kaza, and Lester 2016; Rast 1999). Cities with robust private investment in downtown real estate were prime targets for progressive efforts. Boston's linkage fee ordinance attached high-dollar-value surcharges to the land use changes and permits developers needed to build skyscrapers in downtown and the Back Bay (Clavel 2010). This explicitly redistributed resources, dedicating surcharges borne by developers to affordable housing construction and community services. Developers and their allies called linkage fees a declaration of war on private business. They paid the fees nonetheless.

THE LIMITS TO CONTROLLING MUNICIPAL GOVERNMENT

Community organizations and urban social movements had previously been wary of attempting to seize the powers of city government. Welfare rights activists and racial integration activists built their movements around the exercise of power *outside* of municipal government: they sought to control elected officials, not become them (Piven 1970; Davidoff 1965).

When the neighborhoods movement installed its champions in office, results disappointed. Cleveland's pioneering reformers conceded that city government could do little to contest the structural problems of economic inequality and racism (Krumholz and Forester 1990). Operating from within government also compromised their bargaining power: making government a visible ally of reform movements led businesses to reflexively oppose city plans (Krumholz 1994). Both Washington and Flynn struggled with reelection, and the last neighborhood reformer to win election, San Francisco's Art Agnos, served a single term. The argument that mayors could not govern if they alienated private interests looked stronger than ever (Stone 2017; Reese, Sands, and Skidmore 2014).

The neighborhoods movement's discursive strategies limited the potential to build a larger and more powerful coalition that could compensate for these problems. Pitting outer-lying neighborhoods against downtown placed reformers who won power in conflict with the downtowns on which a path forward from deindustrialization depended. Championing "neighborhoods" underscored the zero-sum character of investment and provided abundant fuel for the growth machine's allies to argue that downtown investments were essential to a city's future economic growth.

After the 1994 elections removed the New Deal coalition from political power in Washington, and as the 1990s economy delivered growth without gains for low-income earners, activists would return to local policy advocacy as a tool of last resort. These efforts featured many veterans of the 1980s neighborhood movement, who began to strategically adapt strategies and techniques to their evolving political and economic problems. A key feature of their subsequent work would be to build and use national networks for exchanging strategies, tactics, and policies at a scale and level of intensity the neighborhoods movement did not reach.

THE LIVING-WAGE MOVEMENT: RIGHTS, ECONOMIC ADVOCACY, AND COALITION

The goal of a living wage expanded the scope of advocacy for social and economic equality. The institutional organization of the living-wage movement, which combined labor unions, community organizations, and activists rooted in low-income communities of color, broke the neighborhood movement's attachment to territory and built multi-organizational networks that would eventually gain the power to set the political agenda beyond the limited powers of city government itself. Much of the movement's potential and innovation, however, came from the service sector jobs on which it focused. Place-based service industries could not threaten to relocate like manufacturers, making them opportune targets for policy interventions. Because they disproportionately employed women and people of color, they also required explicit engagement with questions of race and gender. Living-wage ordinances themselves delivered disappointing returns, but the movement laid the groundwork for more ambitious organizing.

At the beginning of the living-wage movement, unions operated at a remove from local policy. Unions participated minimally in the neighborhoods movement, instead retaining their long-standing focus on Washington. In the 1990s, however, falling membership and growing organizing successes from the American Federation of State, County and Municipal Employees (AFSCME) and the Service Employees International Union (SEIU) led to a renewed focus on organizing for AFL-CIO-affiliated unions. These organizing efforts were boosted by the national AFL-CIO steering resources to numerous local Central Labor Councils (CLCs) charged with linking labor organizing to municipal policy (Ness and Eimer 2015; Dean and Reynolds 2011; Turner and Cornfield 2007).

Working effectively with community organizations required unions to overcome the extensive distrust they earned through their past racial discrimination (Lesniewski and Doussard 2017; Jayaraman and

Ness 2015). The increasing representation of people of color (and after 1986 many immigrants), in community organizations made this task particularly urgent. Out of necessity, community organizations serving low-income African American and immigrant populations devoted increased levels of resources to addressing the needs of the working poor—both on the job and at home, where insecurity and low pay caused problems for child rearing, financing planning and housing security (DeFilippis, Fisher, and Shragge 2010). Living-wage legislation represented a possible solution to these problems (Martin 2001; Luce 2004). First, it promised to directly raise pay for low-income workers in sectors and workplaces not covered by collective bargaining agreements.[1] Second, living-wage campaigns provided a shared goal around which labor and community organizations could begin to form working partnerships.

The diffusion of living-wage campaigns depended on another innovation: the organizational structure, resources, and planning of the Association of Community Organizations for Reform Now (ACORN). A descendent of organizations involved in the 1960s welfare rights movement and an agent in passing the 1978 Community Reinvestment Act, ACORN supplied a network to spread policy proposals (Reynolds and Kern 2001). Each city's ACORN chapter convened a coalition of community organizations, aggregating their individual interests into a citywide organization with the ability to convert individual neighborhood concerns into city-level problem definition and advocacy (Swarts and Vasi 2011; Luce 2017). Individual city-level ACORN organizations (in Baltimore, Chicago, and Albuquerque, for example) were themselves members of a national (and later international) ACORN organization that possessed infrastructure and resources for disseminating lessons about writing, lobbying for, and framing living-wage legislation. ACORN affiliates disseminated knowledge so effectively that several living-wage campaigns were eventually organized without ACORN participation. As the ACORN network diffused living-wage laws from their roots in large cities with left-leaning electorates, structural factors played a more important role than political opportunity. Cities with high poverty rates to motivate activists and well-funded community organizations to run campaigns were more likely than others to enact living-wage laws, regardless of the strength of organized business opposition (Martin 2006).

After winning ordinances in more than one hundred cities, living-wage movement members expanded the scope of their demands. The most ambitious of these efforts, a failed bill mandating a $10 hourly wage for employees in Chicago "big box" retailers, made clear the limitations to the living-wage approach. The Chicago bill only covered high-square-footage retailers who, like municipal contractors, had the sales volume and profit margins to cover higher wage costs with ease. However, this strategic cut-out—an attempt to preempt employer opposition—ultimately undermined the bill. Chicago's big box stores followed the industry model of locating in high-density (white) neighborhoods with high household income levels. Mayor Richard M. Daley justified his veto of the bill by alleging racism: living-wage activists, he argued, only protested low pay when retailers began to expand into poor and predominantly black neighborhoods (Doussard 2015). When the Great Recession began the following year, the living-wage model had no clear direction forward.

SMALL POLICY GAINS, BIG STEPS FORWARD: THE LIVING-WAGE MOVEMENT'S ENDURING INNOVATIONS

Reflecting on Chicago's first living-wage law in 1999, a long-time activist lamented to the authors that "we worked so hard for so little, and everybody was very tired." Nevertheless, disappointment with living-wage laws catalyzed several significant changes that remain influential today. These innovations center on the outsized influence ACORN wielded in organizing.

ACORN's participation in living-wage campaigns elevated the issue of racial discrimination. In order to organize the predominantly minority workers employed by the service sector, unions had to both change their current practices and overcome the distrust earned by prior, overt racism. For their part, the many community organizations that followed the tenets developed by Saul Alinsky avoided the issue of race in order to focus on simpler problems with more immediate solutions (Lesniewski and Doussard 2017). ACORN and its affiliates by contrast prioritized the issue of race, which featured centrally in their organizing techniques, political messages, and political coalitions (Luce 2004).

Directly engaging racism and racial and ethnic difference marked an important step for living-wage coalitions and the broader community-labor coalitions to which they belonged. After 1986, immigration to the United States accelerated significantly from the historically low levels of the postwar era (Massey, Durand, and Malone 2002); the jobs impacted by living-wage ordinances were held disproportionately by immigrants, workers of color, and women of color. Living-wage and related campaigns accordingly had to overcome mistrust earned by long-term racism within unions, particularly those in the trades (Jayaraman and Ness 2015). ACORN's historical development among communities of color and its skill in antiracist organizing paved the way for a rapprochement (Luce 2004).

A second significant contribution of the living-wage movement also bears ACORN's stamp: the blunt and direct way participants talked about both the economic and the social dimensions of inequality. Where the neighborhoods movement made limited and conditional claims about investment in particular places and industries, the living-wage movement invoked human rights. Today, rights-based discourses continue to provide an important tool for activists seeking to escape unfavorable tactical positions, often against well-organized political regimes (Moyn 2012; Dávila 2013). Rights-based language created alternative meanings, images, and alliances that allowed activists to stand for rights, as opposed to against economic growth.

FROM THE LIVING WAGE TO COMMUNITY BENEFITS

A final step toward the emergence of ERJ coalitions came from the attempt to transform campaigns for living wages into a movement for community benefits agreements. The community benefits movement itself has arguably been a transitional one, as campaigns succeed infrequently and few cities have political institutions receptive to the program. However, the drive to secure community benefits forced what had up to that point been labor-centric organizing and campaigns to interact with neighborhood movements focused on inequalities in housing, public resources and access to power (Cummings 2001, 464). The drive to unite these varied and related demands for equality continues—unevenly, but promisingly—today.

The neighborhoods and living-wage movements responded to city problems driven and accelerated by private- and public-sector disinvestment. By contrast, the community benefits movement responded to the increasingly pervasive problem of inequitable reinvestment, especially within neighborhoods that had experienced racialized disinvestment in earlier periods. Global cities including New York and Chicago had experienced waves of finance-led reinvestment since the early 1980s, and by the 1990s a broader trend of urban "renaissance" was evident. Parks and Warren (2009) describe the emergence in terms of a "new accountable development movement," led by groups such as local Partnership for Working Families affiliates. Community benefits agreements expanded the innovation of the linkage fee, developed by the neighborhoods movement in Boston but mostly forgotten afterward. Seizing on public support for large redevelopments, such as major housing construction, sports stadiums, and events centers, community organizations engaged sympathetic elected officials to attach a series of conditions to the planning approvals large development projects needed. Common conditions included agreements to use union labor, above-market minimum-wage rates, contributions to affordable housing funds, and support for job training programs (Wolf-Powers 2010).

City-based organizers secured more than a dozen community benefits agreements during the 2010s. The most ambitious and most successful came in Los Angeles, where the Los Angeles Alliance for a New Economy (LAANE), a crucial organization in the city's community-labor coalition, played a central role in helping an ad hoc coalition of neighborhood-based organizations secure promises for union labor, local hiring, and antidisplacement measures attached to the construction of the Los Angeles Lakers' new arena and associated entertainment venues. That agreement came closer to yielding the promised results than others. Community benefits organizers took advantage of a moment of instability in Los Angeles's political machine to win the favor of elected officials, and the agreement itself represented a qualitative step forward by attaching measures focused on displacement and residential housing to prescriptions for work rules (Saito and Truong 2015).

The Great Recession made clear the movement's limitations. When economic conditions worsened, developers and elected officials often backed out of the promises they made (Wolf-Powers 2010). The movement's innovation of targeting growth and investment rather than job retention also became a liability, as few new projects were built. Perhaps most problematic, community benefits agreements extracted marginal concessions on the edge of gentrification without providing grounds to challenge the broader dislocations of which gentrification itself constituted a principal part (Rosen and Schweitzer 2018; Marantz 2015). The push for community benefits agreements updated the goals of urban justice organizing, but the mechanisms it favored were inadequate to the task.

Despite its limitations, the community benefits movement made two important contributions to contemporary urban justice organizing efforts. First, it made use of the leverage we discuss in chapter 1 by zeroing in on places where private developers needed public approvals or subsidies to make projects work. These provided windows of opportunity to make development more distributively just. The fact that community members might show up at an otherwise sleepy public hearing and disrupt an economically and politically profitable development project changed political bargaining. Beyond simply protesting, community benefits organizers provided an answer to the problems they were creating, in the form of community benefits agreements. This strategy of escalating a problem and then supplying negotiators with a solution is now an important part of the repertoire of urban justice movements.

Second, the community benefits movement showed that even half-victories can build long-term power. Much like living-wage campaigns, community benefits organizing brought new and diverse actors together. The formal alliances were often ephemeral, but the relationships they created endured. Even where individual campaigns failed, the presence of citywide groups like LAANE made it easier to reassemble the community-based organizations and unions when the next development project or important city policy decision materialized.

ECONOMIC AND RACIAL JUSTICE COALITIONS

The 2007–2009 Great Recession upended living-wage and community benefits organizers' plans. First, rising unemployment hit low-wage employers and workers especially hard, increasing the need for policy action while diminishing the resources (i.e., stable work, housing, and incomes) that allowed rank-and-file workers to participate in organizing. Second, the racist structure of mortgage lending and bank-perpetuated mortgage fraud led to foreclosure, eviction, and collapsing housing values in poor and minority neighborhoods (Ashton 2009). Third, the financial crisis triggered a fiscal crisis, as cities faced falling sales, income, and property tax collections (Pagano

2013). They responded with fiscal austerity and reduced services. Ordinarily, community organizations would turn to donors and foundations to make up for losses in support from community development block grants and other forms of public support. But funders suffered enormous losses to their portfolios, leading them to scale back support for several years (Doussard and Lesniewski 2017). Adding to the movement's challenges, ACORN itself become a political target for a conservative Congress empowered after the 2010 elections (Dreier and Martin 2010).

A final and surprising challenge was the Obama administration itself. Urban community organizations nationwide devoted substantial resources to turning out voters in the 2008 election, and viewed the inauguration of the nation's first black president and a former community organizer with hope (DeFilippis 2016). A long-time organizer on Chicago's South Side summed up their ensuing disappointment:

> In the years right after the crash—around 2009, when I got involved—[it] become clear to a lot of leaders [that] we had this big change election in 2008, and Obama used this big change election to piece everything back together and keep everything the same. On the South Side, we had huge foreclosure rates, and a Black president who hadn't made huge changes. Just when I was coming on, there was a thought among leaders that we needed to move beyond short-term, small-scale victories: We could [still] do that, but we can't exclusively focus on the short-term when everything is crumbling down. (South Side Organizers quoted in Doussard and Lesniewski 2017, 625)

Just as the failures of actual living-wage laws spurred the movement to seek bigger goals, this disappointment with electoral politics itself generated important changes in how the movement approached politics. First and most significant, community organizations began to work through their local networks to cover for disappearing resources (Doussard and Lesniewski 2017). A Chicago labor activist explained that "austerity makes people network—it made them build relationships to keep funding. It was on some level good for the movement" (Doussard and Lesniewski 2017). Examples include neighborhood organizations referring members to the Fight for 15 minimum wage campaigns as a way to win income gains that would reduce neighborhood problems; worker centers drawing on the resources of food banks, ESL classes, and other basic services to ensure their membership was ready to organize; and unions and immigrant rights organizations devoting their resources to protests around school closures, infrastructure privatization, fiscal policy, and other issues they had historically considered to lie beyond their interests (Brogan 2014; Farmer and Poulos 2019; Doussard and Fulton 2020; Lipman 2013).

Working through networks started as a desperate response to funding cuts, but it quickly evolved into a means of reworking organizing. Organizations such as Make the Road New York, Chicago's Grassroots Collaborative, the Los Angeles Alliance for a New Economy and, Seattle's Puget Sound Sage drew on community and labor funding to provide citywide clearinghouses and coordination for economic activism (Milkman, Bloom, and Narro 2010; Milkman and Ott 2014; Reich, Jacobs, and Dietz 2014). Few of these organizations were new, but virtually all of them transformed their work after the Great Recession. For example, Denver's Front Range Economic Strategy Center, which had focused on community benefits agreements prior to the Great Recession, changed its mission and name to embrace grassroots organizing and to engage low-income communities of color (Doussard 2020). In smaller cities and cities with lower densities of community organizations, Jobs with Justice affiliates organized action on economic policy and substandard wages and working conditions in individual firms and workplaces (Cohen, Morris, and Gupta 2013). Other community network organizations include dozens of urban Interfaith Worker Justice chapters; faith alliances; worker centers devoted to specific communities, populations, or industries; and immigrant rights alliances. We provide an inventory of these organizations in Chapter 3. Significantly, most of these organizations are themselves embedded in national networks, a feature that systematizes the policy learning and coordinated advocacy that first appeared during the living-wage movement.

The second characteristic of ERJ movements after the Great Recession is their growing embrace of critiques of institutional and structural racism. Several developments propelled this change: the obvious racial inequalities of foreclosure and the housing crisis; the burgeoning racist backlash to the nation's first black president; the 2014 police shooting of Ferguson, Missouri, teen Michael Brown by police (and the subsequent growth of Black Lives Matter); and growing engagement between labor unions and urbanized immigrant communities (MacDonald 2017, 6). These developments sped community organizations' efforts to embrace race directly, both in their framing messages and in collaborations with antiracist organizers trained in techniques developed through decades of work conducted in parallel with economic justice organizing (Lesniewski and Doussard 2017). As one Partnership for Working Families affiliate explained to us, embracing race did not lead to the backlash they had feared: "We found that our funders liked it more when we talked about racial justice than when we talked about taking the wealthy's money."

Evidence of these changes is diffuse but systematic. The mission statements of a range of activist organizations prioritize racial justice in ways they did not before. A small sampling of mission statements from Partnership for Working Families affiliates, for example, reads as follows:

> EBASE advances economic, racial and social justice by building a just economy in the East Bay based on good jobs and healthy communities. (East Bay Alliance for a Sustainable Economy)

> ISAIAH is a vehicle for congregations, clergy, and people of faith to act collectively and powerfully towards racial and economic equity in the state of Minnesota. (ISAIAH Minnesota)

> United for a New Economy (UNE) envisions vibrant, strong communities where ALL community members have a voice in the decisions that impact them, access to economic security; which includes affordable housing and good jobs and the ability to live free of racism and fear. (United for a New Economy, Colorado)

Affiliates of Interfaith Worker Justice, which runs a series of dozens of worker centers nationwide, likewise foreground race at the beginning of mission statements that formerly focused on work:

> Greater Birmingham Ministries (GBM) was founded in 1969 in response to urgent human and justice needs in the greater Birmingham area. GBM is a multi-faith, multi-racial organization that provides emergency services for people in need and engages the poor and the non-poor in systemic change efforts to build a strong, supportive, engaged community and pursue a more just society for all people. (Greater Birmingham Ministries, Alabama)

> Pilipino Workers Center aims to secure the dignity and safety of the Pilipinx community in Southern California and build labor leaders in the domestic worker industry. (Pilipino Workers Center, California)
>
> WCRJ is staffed by a team of talented activists who offer a diversity of skills and experiences to help advance the movement for Black Liberation and racial equity. (Worker Center for Racial Justice, Chicago)

The overt embrace of racial justice stands front-and-center at the level of international labor unions. The SEIU, for example, identifies racial justice as a core goal alongside fair and reliable work. The message is clear: "We cannot achieve economic justice without racial justice" (Service Employees International Union 2021) Of course, talk is free. Resources speak more definitively to organized labor's stance toward racial justice. Here, all the available data point in the same direction. Unions began to prioritize hiring organizers of color, and later installing people of color into leadership roles, in the 1990s (McAlevey 2016). Politically active local labor unions, and especially effective ones, have changed leadership: the Chicago Teacher's Union, whose successful 2012 strike (and follow-up strikes) initiated a national wave of teacher strikes, earned its current authority in substantial part by electing a leadership representative of its members and Chicago's demographics (Farmer and Noonan 2019). The majority of the participants interviewed about the $15 minimum wage campaigns in SeaTac and Seattle, Washington, are people of color. Seattle's Central Labor Council, which coordinates activism and organizing for local labor unions, went so far as to rename itself MLK Labor.

We do not claim that a complete turn to racial justice has occurred, or that it is even possible for one to occur within existing institutions and norms. The work of racial justice in urban social movements remains contested, uneven, and intermittently developed. As current events and the current scholarly embrace of work on racial capitalism indicate, recognition of the need to prioritize race as a factor equally vital to class is increasingly widespread. But the adoption of race-forward organizing depends on the place, the organization, and the personalities (Woods 1998; Pulido 2017). What we can say with certainty is that coalitions that do prioritize race have at their disposal different networks, discourses, and strategic targets than do coalitions that continue to consign race to a secondary status. This marks an important development in its own right, and a significant addition to the conversation on how communities contest racial capitalism (Bledsoe, McCreary, and Wright 2019). We illustrate the point by returning to Chicago and the current work of an ERJ coalition led by the SEIU and Grassroots Collaborative.

FROM CLASS TO RACE: THE TRANSFORMATION OF CHICAGO'S GRASSROOTS COLLABORATIVE AND CHICAGO'S COMMUNITY-LABOR COALITION

To illustrate the impact of the long-term shift toward ERJ coalitions, we return to the current work of Grassroots Collaborative, the community-organizing organization we introduced at the beginning of this chapter. Grassroots Collaborative began in the late 1990s with two full-time staffers devoted to supporting organizing and policy on issues related to work (Tattersall 2013). It linked organizations that supported economic organizing and mobilized support for union-organizing campaigns and public policy issues, including Chicago's first living-wage law.

Grassroots Collaborative's conventional economic organizing work culminated in 2006, when the organization devoted its staff to supporting Chicago's expanded living-wage bill, which proposed a $10 minimum wage for large, "big-box" retailers. The eventual failure of the "Big Box" bill confirmed the need to emphasize race. During the short but intense campaign for the Big Box bill, "the faces of the people on the protests were black and Latino, but we didn't talk about race," executive director Amisha Patel explained in an interview with the authors. "And that left an opportunity for [Mayor] Rich Daley to talk about race."

Patel became the organization's leader in 2007, after securing a commitment from the board to address race more directly. The Great Recession and subsequent public austerity ultimately shifted Grassroots Collaborative's focus to public spending. The cuts that Daley and his successor Rahm Emanuel proposed cemented the organization's focus on race and finances, rather than traditional labor concerns around work and pay. Patel continues:

When [Mayor Rahm] Emanuel came into office in 2011, he clearly moved in on a neoliberal austerity budget. He closed half the mental health clinics, rolled back the head tax on large employers. Those two actions really set the stage for what was to come, which was to go hard after unionized teachers and to go hard after public schools themselves. So, this set us up to go for progressive education organizing from the point of revenue, and for black and Latino kids, who are 90% of the school district.

School funding in particular intersected with Chicago's many social, economic, and racial inequalities in ways that conventional labor organizing campaigns, or even citywide wage laws, could not. The organization's focus on finance accelerated in the first years of the Emanuel administration, when staff organizers began using finance and public-spending decisions as ways to talk about race and public policy. Grassroots Collaborative's work emphasized race more in subsequent years, and it did not do so alone. Both the older, white-led community organizations and a newer cohort of race-focused organizations had begun to push racial inequalities to the front of their agendas (Lesniewski and Doussard 2017).

In addition to addressing the problem of fiscal austerity, organizing around public finance had significant practical advantages. First, the breadth of Chicago's real estate subsidies and deals (Weber 2015) provided numerous organizing targets: construction on the lakefront, residential property conversions, tax increment financing subsidies to developers. Second, finance helped the organization to develop connections across political scales. The 2014 election of antiunion Illinois governor Bruce Rauner elevated Grassroots Collaborative's alternative vision of a "People's Budget" based on progressive income taxes and investment in disinvested communities. This led the organization to the old idea of Chicago uniting with other cities. The executive director explains, "We talk about *cities* doing collective bargaining, a string of cities getting together and going to banks and saying, 'I'm not going to do business with you.'"

Perhaps the easiest way to assess the changes to Grassroots Collaborative's mission and work is to consider the endpoint. In the late 2010s, Chicago passed a string of workplace-focused laws that exceeded anything organizers could have imagined in the 2000s: a $13 minimum wage, then a $15 minimum wage, earned sick time, and fair workweek bills. Grassroots Collaborative supported the campaigns for these laws without focusing on them. In the months before the Covid-19 pandemic, and later the mass protests of policing after the murder of George Floyd, Grassroots Collaborative was beginning to organize campaigns for investment in public health and to cut policing budgets. The embrace of race is notable in the changing membership and leadership of community organizations and local labor unions (Fulton, Oyakawa, and Wood 2019; Larson 2016), in the incorporation of racial justice messages into economic organizing campaigns, and, less visibly, in the steady redirection of organizational resources toward delivering services to, and organizing, minority populations facing multiple barriers to participation in activist movements (Lesniewski and Doussard 2017). These changes represent important, and still incomplete, accommodations of strategy and tactics to raced practices that shape investment, work, politics, and public service delivery.

CONCLUSION

Community activists and organizers in U.S. cities have changed their approach to advocacy in ways that are nearly as drastic as the concurrent reorganization of capital and investment. Responding first to deindustrialization, and later to the normalization of inequitable growth and the calamity of the Great Recession, organizations that initially focused on neighborhood territory and incremental bargains with businesses and local government built citywide networks. They nest those networks within national policy and advocacy organizations, and pressure city councils to pass economic legislation of a scope far beyond what urban scholars long assumed to be possible. They achieved this transformation in part by foregrounding racial and social inequalities that previous generations of union and economic justice–focused community organizers typically deemphasized. The result is the ERJ coalition—a network of activists who contest economic and racial inequalities at the same time.

Like scholars, organizers historically faced the choice of foregrounding either economic or racial inequality—the achievements of Cesar Chavez and Ella Baker in combining the two stand out today, but they were outliers in their own time (Ganz 2000). Like most scholars, their peers emphasized either class or race, and frequently emphasized class *over* race. As a racial capitalism analysis urges, ERJ coalitions attempt to erase the distinction. Both in their visible public advocacy and in the membership building, direct organizing, and education that underlie that advocacy, they treat economic and racial inequalities as manifestations of the same problem. Closing arguments for workplace-focused legislation commonly drop the racial justice component of their messaging at the end. Yet the determination to foreground race has transformed organizations' goals and abilities. This shift is evident in the ways that ERJ coalitions realize the organizational goals of their predecessor movements: finding leverage, incorporating racial justice into advocacy, and developing resonant organizing messages.

Admonitions for urban social movements to avoid municipal public policy stemmed from the belief, wholly justified at the time, that activists lacked the leverage to enact the changes they desired. Racial justice organizers in particular commonly fought *against* the state and its policies. The neighborhoods movement's response to deindustrialization and rising economic inequalities appeared to confirm the warnings about limited city power. When activists won political office, they attempted to use city power to stop manufacturing disinvestment and job loss—and lost. The movement's most durable innovation, attaching linkage fees to large-scale property redevelopments, appeared to constitute only a small victory at the time. But then the living-wage movement found leverage by targeting the service economy itself. Efforts to unite the living-wage movement with linkage fees through the innovation of community benefits agreements, however, did not scale: activists quickly determined that the project of winning equity one labor-intensive protest at a time was not viable.

ERJ coalitions address the scale problem by using the city itself as leverage. They accept the growth of the service economy by making demands that key on the significant place attachments of retail, personal services, and advanced services firms. In doing so, they act on the understanding, now commonplace in economic development, that high-performing firms need urban locations. More simply, developers, financial firms, and the new class of elite businesses do not directly employ many low-wage workers themselves, and thus pay comparatively little for distributive economic legislation. Most of the firms who pay the cost of employment policy changes profit as much from where they are as what they do.

Second, ERJ coalitions solve the practical problem of how to incorporate race into organizing by foregrounding it. Participants in the neighborhoods movement used the imaginary of the neighborhood itself to suggest investment in communities of color, while rarely making the point explicitly. The living-wage movement was visibly run by and for low-wage workers of color, who subsumed any message about racial justice within a broader discourse of human rights and dignity. Foregrounding race as ERJ coalitions have done does not just correct for the ethical problem of relegating one manifestation of inequality to a secondary status. It actually makes all types of justice organizing more effective. Foregrounding race improved working relationships between community organizations and unions (Lesniewski and Doussard 2017). It expanded the network of organizations involved in organizing, both in terms of horizontal territory and in terms of vertical political scale. Finally, as Grassroots Collaborative's experience suggests, prioritizing race simplified forms of organizing that were previously too complicated.

ERJ coalitions' more expansive approach to leverage and race was also supported by (and supportive of) a broader framing of the coalitions' demands. The neighborhoods movement employed a narrow discourse about investment in particular places, one which placed the goals of neighborhoods at odds with downtown investors who held power. The living-wage movement expanded from space to work—a less restrictive focus, but one that still emphasized narrow policy measures (small minimum wage increases for city-contracted firms) and the morally deserving status of low-wage workers. By contrast, the discourse of ERJ coalitions is expansive. As we write this, major service sector unions are arguing, writing, and tweeting that racial justice is economic justice, investments in health care are investments in work, workers' rights are everybody's rights. Many of them are arguing for budget cuts—to the police.

ERJ coalitions in their current form face many challenges. Their leverage on property investment stems from the extensive resources and influence local states devote to serving investors, a reality that constrains the amount of financial support available to neighborhood organizing and service delivery (Ashton, Doussard, and Weber 2016; Weber 2015). Enforcing newly passed employment standards also presents a problem for cities, which lack states' labor law enforcement capabilities. And state and national laws themselves increasingly pose threats to economic justice coalitions. States with unified Republican control continue to pass laws that preempt local employment standards and so-called Right to Work laws that drain union finances (Peck 2016). We will deal with these and other challenges in time. We design our analysis to make sense of the *underlying bargaining dynamics* that shape the contest over work, economic fairness, and urban politics. Our analysis of targeted hiring programs, wage legislation, and social legislation will identify the ways in which particular issues and types of reform complicate, transform, and tilt these general bargaining dynamics. Justice movements negotiate these challenges by drawing on the resources of national networks of activists, researchers, and policy development organizations.

3

Urban Policy Entrepreneurs

NETWORKED POLICY CHANGE FROM THE GRASSROOTS

How do workers, community organizations, and citizens take advantage of the political opportunities the current moment provides them? Scholars typically answer this question one city and issue at a time (Logan and Molotch 1987; Stone 1989; Rast 1999). To take a canonical example: Harvey Molotch and John Logan, substantiated growth machine theory in part through the example of a successful anti-growth campaign in Santa Barbara, California (Logan and Molotch 1987). That seminal account showed that luck—mainly an oil spill that galvanized proenvironmental sentiment—rather than bargaining position drove successful opposition to growth. This is a common lesson from single-site studies, which tally case-specific details in ways that emphasize the sheer improbability of reproducing successful organizing campaigns for other issues or in other places.

Both this conclusion and the way it was reached seem out of place amid contemporary, multisited activism. How can we be confident that successful equity campaigns are the product of luck rather than design without scrutinizing activists' efforts to replicate campaigns? This chapter undertakes the work of building a multisite perspective on advocacy, movement development, and policy. We evaluate city-level organizing and policy campaigns as strategic contests within a national network of campaigns. At stake is the potential for urban justice movements to replace the unreliable fuel of luck with the more dependable materials of strategy, design, and learning. Furthermore, moving policy across cities is a staple of contemporary urban politics (Peck and Theodore 2015). From living-wage laws to the minimum wage, participatory budgeting, and affordable housing trust funds, policies that began with a single victory eked out by exhausted organizers increasingly proceed to sweep across U.S. and world cities. Understanding how activists move policy proposals, advocacy techniques, and campaign messages across jurisdictions will allow us to address bigger questions about why advocacy succeeds or fails.

Evaluating networked advocacy campaigns requires us to resolve a classic dilemma about how to study urban politics across cities and political scales. Many current studies of urban politics only engage the interplay between global economic structure and local agency deterministically, because they focus on single cities in which structural forces and local particulars cannot be reliably separated. We propose studying not cities but rather urban policy entrepreneurs (UPEs): activists who work through coalitions to shop for political venues with favorable bargaining terms, and who experiment systematically with both legislation and techniques to win support for their projects. These policy entrepreneurs work and share members with the economic and racial justice (ERJ) coalitions we outlined in chapter 2. They include leaders in community organizations and labor unions, and policy analysts scattered across research organizations, think tanks, and universities. Policy entrepreneurship provides a multisite, multi-issue object of study through which we can systematically evaluate politics within and across cities and policies.

We build the idea of UPEs from the political scientist John Kingdon's (1984) classic study of Washington-based policy entrepreneurs. Kingdon's approach combines structure and agency without according too much power to either. We argue that political conditions in cities enhance policy entrepreneurs' control of the policy process. Urban space, networks, and political institutions give them power to shape the way problems are defined, incubate policy alternatives, and apply political pressure in ways that lead to change.

ANALYZING URBAN POLICY CHANGE: FROM REGIMES TO RELATIONAL POLITICS

Theories of urban politics in the United States say little about the mechanics of passing public policy. As cities lack formal power and fiscal independence, scholarship has focused on *limits*: limits on the exercise of public power, and limits on the political ambitions of the regimes that struggle to remain in power (Hackworth 2007; Markusen 1980). Due to fiscal austerity in particular, cities function as the guarantors of last resort for the provision of basic and essential public services (Wen et al. 2018; Xu and Warner 2016). They rarely occupy an economic position that lets them plan and build systematically for the future.

The recent, widespread success of economic policies long deemed unrealistic has prompted urban politics scholars to recalibrate their ideas to incorporate the reality of equitable development. Stone (2015), for example, argues that the growth politics of the post–World War II "redevelopment era" are still powerful but no longer hegemonic, and that the dynamics of urban governance are more "fluid" than before. This fluidity characterizes an evolving "urban political order," where political change "does not follow a single logic but consists of a success of configurations" (Stone 2015, 109). Weaver (2021) argues that an "egalitarian political order," led by unions, community-based organizations, and political parties like the Democratic Socialists of America constitutes a counterweight to the "neoliberal" (growth-oriented) and "conservative" (social order–oriented) political orders. Weaver observes that typologizing cities as "progressive" or "neoliberal" misses the political hybridity of governing arrangements, such as the common coexistence of progressive regimes with neoliberal, growth-oriented support for development, and openly racist policies (e.g., stop-and-frisk policing).[1]

Our own efforts to make sense of the living-wage movement and current advocacy coalitions point to three key challenges in understanding how political pressure becomes public policy: (1) explaining the success and failure of policy proposals on different issues, (2) illuminating social movements with the same precision as governing regimes, and (3) understanding how the multisited character of organizing and advocacy shapes the political agenda. Activist coalitions tailor their tactics to the social, economic, and political particulars of individual cities, and they build and execute strategy through networks. In the process, they move policy, ideas, and personnel both *horizontally* across cities and *vertically* from cities to counties and states. Focusing on single sites ignores a wealth of information that comes from movement and change within activist networks.

TRAVELING POLICIES: WHICH IDEAS LAND ON THE AGENDA?

Two strains of thought in urban politics offer insight into the success of particular ideas and policy proposals. Studies of *discourse coalitions* assess activists' efforts to constitute political coalitions and messages that build support for their causes (Fischer 2003; Hajer 2009). This research follows the scholarly innovations of Frank Fischer (2003), who showed that activists' choices of discursive themes, images, and tropes shape their networks. Discourse coalitions succeed when they assemble networks of political actors under a common message that transcends differences in their material interests. This resembles the concept of "collective action frames" in the literature on social movements (Benford and Snow 2000). Messages about equality and justice, for example, are most effective when wedded to clear images and compelling rhetorical tropes (e.g., "We are the 99%"). The discourse approach also emphasizes the cause-and-effect arguments embedded within effective policy discourse—the basic requirement that a policy in fact addresses a mutually recognized problem (Ganz 2000).

Policy mobilities scholars examine these questions by scrutinizing the travel and transformation of policies across jurisdictions (Peck and Theodore 2010, 2015; McCann 2013). By focusing on the elite networks and the inelegant trial and error through which model policies move and change, policy mobilities provide a way to make sense of traveling and dynamic policy. In the form of traveling technocrats, it also provides an object of study. A key limiting factor to this approach, however, comes from the central research focus on elite organizations and elected officials (with the significant exception of Peck and Theodore's account of Porto Alegre activists driving that city's fabled participatory budgeting process; see Peck and Theodore 2015). Questions about mobile policies typically consider elite actors' agenda-setting activities, leaving open the questions of how nonelite actors shape that agenda. Discourse coalitions and policy mobilities provide ways to identify ideas, messaging, and complexity as key elements shaping the propensity for a policy to become law. Both perspectives, however, deemphasize the advocacy coalitions that push for public policy reform, and the question of how actors within those coalitions identify, exploit, and sometimes create openings for change.

POLICY ENTREPRENEURS: STRUCTURED CONTINGENCY IN THE POLICY PROCESS

Our approach to understanding urban policy change begins with the political scientist John Kingdon, who elevated the figure of the policy entrepreneur. In his slender, seminal *Agendas, Alternatives, and Public Policies* (1984), Kingdon developed the "multiple streams approach" (MSA)[2] to public policy. Scholars in this vibrant tradition (Cairney 2013; Cairney and Jones 2016; Zahariadis 2014) reverse-engineer rare instances of substantial policy change in the United States in order to disaggregate luck from skill. The approach provides satisfying, complete accounts of the two-step process by which the political system comes to focus, and then act, on a given problem. Kingdon studied Washington, D.C., where the size and complexity of the political system makes opportunities to enact major change quite rare. The framework can easily be modified for cities, where it highlights the extra resources and capabilities policy entrepreneurs enjoy in setting the agenda and winning votes.

MSA understands agenda setting and policy passage as activities constrained by ambiguous information, the public's perception of problems, and the limited time, resources, and political capital of the political system. Policy entrepreneurs and other actors in the process enjoy discretion in framing and interpreting problems, but the policy process itself is neither linear nor "comprehensively rational" (Cairney and Jones 2016, 39). This imparts *structured contingency* to the policy change process: multiple but finite outcomes are possible from any given starting point. Policy change is more likely under certain circumstances, but it is never a given. Agency matters, but agency is also constrained.

MSA centers the figure of the *policy entrepreneur*, an individual who nurses a pet idea or proposal, which she eventually yokes to an opportunity for reform. Policy entrepreneurs use power in ways overlooked by studies of politics that privilege elected officials themselves. They

> are not necessarily found in any one location in the policy community. They could be in or out of government, in elected or appointed positions, in interest groups or research organizations. But their defining characteristic, much as in the case of a business entrepreneur, is their willingness to invest their resources ... in the hope of a future return. (Kingdon 1984, 122)

Kingdon and his successors situate the work of policy entrepreneurs within three "streams" that must align for a major policy to pass into law: *problems, policy,* and *politics*. These streams operate semiautonomously, coming together through "coupling events" that open windows of opportunity for policy change. The policy entrepreneur plays a distinctive role in each stream.

The Problem Stream: Chance and Skill Drives Public Attention

The problem stream determines which of the innumerable number of potential problems become objects of political attention. Political systems rarely address more than a few major problems concurrently, due to scarce time and complex bargaining dynamics. Potential problems most commonly become publicly acknowledged problems due to an exogenous focusing event (Cairney and Zahariadis 2016). Examples include the 2008 financial crisis steering attention to financial regulation; the September 11, 2001, attacks creating consensus for the Patriot Act; and the Covid-19 pandemic paving the way for the CARES Act and American Rescue Plan. All these events compelled swift policy action that overwhelmed the normal barriers of the political system.

But sometimes a problem becomes a *recognizable* problem when policy entrepreneurs frame the issue in a way that commands public attention. Rebranding the estate tax as a "death" tax during the George W. Bush administration led the public to ease opposition to exempting wealthy earners from inheritance taxes. The Affordable Care Act emerged, not from an acute health insurance crisis, but rather from political candidates prioritizing reforms to chronic underinsurance. Policy entrepreneurs were not solely responsible for these issues becoming acknowledged problems, but they contributed significantly. We will demonstrate below that the features of urban space and urban life significantly enhance policy entrepreneurs' problem-defining abilities.

The Policy Stream: Policy Entrepreneurs Incubate and Propagate Models

To compel action on their problem, policy entrepreneurs need to deliver credible solutions, ideally through prevalidated policies. Thus, policy entrepreneurs incubate policy frameworks and proposals as they wait for focusing events. Policy think tanks left, right, and center coordinate this work. The area of economic policy, for example, features the left-leaning Economic Policy Institute, Center for American Progress, and Washington Center for Equitable Growth; the right-wing centers Cato Institute and Heritage Foundation; and the centrist Brookings Institution. Each maintains or backs networks of academics who generate supporting research, and coordinates with sympathetic elected officials and agency staff through white papers, conferences, and shared publicity. Kingdon captures policy entrepreneurs' professional fluidity well, writing that "certain kinds of researchers have regular and intimate relationships with those in government, sometimes on the payroll as consultants, other times testifying before congressional committees, and often in more informal capacities" (1984, 45).

Policy entrepreneurs often scan for policies they can adapt from elsewhere, by making the case for importing "successful" models. Policies move frequently between countries, but belief in American exceptionalism makes the United States an infrequent importer. The geographic origins of a policy—the imagined body politic from which it originates—shapes its palatability in each jurisdiction. Policies from the United Kingdom are easier to import than those from continental Europe, the cities of the Sunbelt rarely look to the Rustbelt for solutions, and so forth.

The Politics Stream: When Problems Become Political Concerns

Elections, rather than the efforts of policy entrepreneurs, drive the politics stream. The perennial need for politicians to run campaigns predisposes them to pursue solutions to problems they see as potential electoral threats. This can mean issues that impact their electoral base or that create openings for political challengers who respond convincingly to a political problem. Elections heighten this ever-present attentiveness, particularly when public sentiment and interest groups intensify the focus on a problem.

The wake of elections also matters. Elections provide discursive and political capital for their victors to cash in, particularly after partisan turnover. Large partisan shifts lead to significant policy change, such as the 2008 election eventually paving the way for the Affordable Care Act, the 2016 elections leading to upper-class tax cuts via the Tax Cuts and Jobs Act of 2017, and the 2020 election leading to the $1.9

trillion American Rescue Plan. Elections and contested reelection campaigns reliably elevate select issues to public attention.

Agenda Windows: Policy Entrepreneurs Solve Political Problems

Policy entrepreneurs incubate ideas for years or decades—then spring into action when an *agenda (or policy) window* opens. Studies of policy entrepreneurs emphasize two crucial points about policy windows: First, they are rare and ephemeral. Second, they develop through forces policy entrepreneurs themselves cannot control.

Policy windows originate in either the problem stream—through focusing events—or in the political stream through elections (Herweg, Zahariadis, and Zohlnhöfer 2017, 26–27). When windows open, policy entrepreneurs seize the opportunity to "couple" the streams, presenting their policy as a solution to the problem, or to the politician's need to appear attentive, or both. Where conventional studies of legislation focus on vote counting, horse trading, and how bills become laws, studying policy entrepreneurs privileges the often-overlooked process of *agenda setting*—a clear advantage given our focus on social movements that themselves work to change agendas. Our approach conceptualizes policy change as the de facto end game to a long-run strategic process that begins with building movements and creating broadly acknowledged problems to which the political system must respond. In other words, the skilled work of passing laws only arises when the crucial work of steering the agenda to a policy bears fruit.

URBAN POLICY ENTREPRENEURSHIP: HOW THE STREAMS OF CHANGE DEVELOP IN CITIES

Scholars of the MSA have speculated that policy entrepreneurs should enjoy greater control over agenda setting and policy enactment when the arena shifts from Washington to states and localities (Cairney and Jones 2016). Adapting the policy entrepreneurship framework to city politics helps to identify distinct and to this point unappreciated powers held by urban policy entrepreneurs (UPEs).

We argue that both the city itself and the strategic configuration of ERJ coalitions provide powerful resources with which UPEs can steer the problem, policy, and political streams (Figure 5). Urban policy

STREAM	KEY EVENT	URBAN RESOURCES
Problem stream: The set of all possible problems policy can address	"Focusing events" steer public attention to a specific problem that cannot be ignored. *Federal-level policy entrepreneurs wait for the exogenous shock of a focusing event.*	Cities provide visible platforms for protest Problems of inequality are highly visible amid urban renaissance, making framing around equity hard to ignore Local media easier to access, especially with use of digital media
Policy stream: The set of tested or validated solutions to the problem	Policy entrepreneur uses the window of opportunity to attach a solution to the problem. *Federal-level policy entrepreneurs introduce policies they developed over time.*	Large number of peer cities provide numerous opportunities for network dissemination Low legislative volume, unicameral structure, ease of access simplifies legislative access Diverse number of legislative scales permits "scale shopping"
Political stream: The set of problems to which politicians respond	Elections or shifts in public opinion create pressure to address the problem. *Federal-level political stream follows electoral cycle and major unexpected shocks (i.e., Covid-19).*	Large urban public investments and development projects provide visible targets for organizing campaigns Low cost of municipal elections allows activists to field successful candidates

FIGURE 5. Urban resources for policy entrepreneurship

entrepreneurship is not simply a miniaturized version of the federal process—it differs in ways that put policy entrepreneurs in control.

Identifying urban policy entrepreneurs as collaborators with ERJ coalitions also provides insight into the strategies coalitions use to win policy victories (Figure 6). ERJ coalitions work the "outside game" of applying pressure: their protests, campaigns, and members push inequality and social justice onto the agenda. UPEs complement them by playing the "inside game" of technocratic policy design—converting political pressure into actual policy reform. No bright line separates the two groups of actors; in practice and in spirit, many UPEs participate vigorously in advocacy coalitions. Their powers to shape and negotiate policy, however, are highly specialized. The combination of outside pressure from coalitions and inside expertise from UPEs creates windows of opportunity for policy change.

STREAM	ERJ COALITIONS	URBAN POLICY ENTREPRENEURS
Problem stream	*Community organizing*: Develop interest, messages and community leaders *Organize protests*: Drive attention to inequality *Launch media campaigns*: Take advantage of organizational ties to media and elected officials	*Research*: Develop data, measurement techniques, and reports to make problems concrete *Testimony*: Lend credibility to organizing actions and legislative hearings
Policy stream	*Couple policies to problems*: Move policies into the political stream *Outside game*: Apply pressure to working groups and elected officials to ensure follow-through on policy promises	*Tailor policies to local conditions*: Adapt model legislation to specifics of state, county, and municipal law *Policy development*: Adjust policy mechanics during negotiation *Expert testimony*: Measure benefits of legislation, dispel fears about its "fiscal note" and potential side-effects
Political stream	*Apply pressure through friendly incumbents*: Movement allies call hearings, issue reports, file bills *Rival candidates*: Support or threaten to support challengers friendly to movement goals *Ballot initiatives*: Use or threaten referenda to compel political attention to the issue	*Limited role*

FIGURE 6. The inside-outside game: Divisions of labor in policy campaigns

Finally, scrutinizing policy entrepreneurship brings into focus extensive collaboration between UPEs based in specific cities and national-level policy entrepreneurship networks that work to develop and circulate policy (Figure 7). Just as ACORN's Living Wage Resource Center circulated model legislation across local living-wage campaigns (chapter 2), these national networks provide resources, expertise, legal advice, and expert testimony that UPEs cannot fashion by themselves. UPEs tailor these resources to their locales by providing place-specific data, testimony, and legal solutions.

STREAM	NATIONAL POLICY ENTREPRENEURS	URBAN POLICY ENTREPRENEURS
Problem stream	Use national media to elevate issue awareness Coordinate research across cities, engage national funder networks	Work with national and local media to publicize research, ground in local vernacular and history Connect/validate research with local activists and communities
Policy stream	Develop model legislation, provide testimony and expertise Promote policy models and frameworks	Adapt national models to local conditions Serve on study committees or task forces Monitor policy implementation
Political stream	Funnel resources into local campaigns	Write op-eds, testify Act as resource for local media Use ERJ connections to get a legislative audience—"on-call answer person"

FIGURE 7. National and urban policy entrepreneurs—Roles in the three streams

The city itself, as well as the resources of community organizing networks, provide distinct advantages to UPEs in each step of the process. It is important to itemize these advantages in detail, because they cumulatively suggest that policy entrepreneurs have greater flexibility and more power at the urban scale.

Problem Stream: UPEs Use the City to Focus and Frame

UPEs can shape the problem stream in ways that Kingdon's policy entrepreneurs rarely do. First, the smaller size and distinct political economies of cities provides the opportunity to *make* focusing events. Occupy Wall Street achieved symbolic importance and steered attention to the problem of economic inequality with the fundamentally *local* maneuver of occupying Zuccotti Park near the literal Wall Street. Subsequent Occupy marches across dozens of cities put inequality in the headlines and helped to make it a recognized national problem. The basic Alinskyan repertoire of marches, sit-ins, occupations, and public confrontations functions as a de facto toolkit for commanding the public's attention on neighborhood and local issues.

The point also resonates at the level of theory. Political economists and scholars of social movements prize "the urban," however conceived, precisely because it provides "trenches" for collective action and supplies ready-made outlets for grassroots movements (Katznelson 1982; Castells 1983; Sites, Chaskin, and Parks 2007). The glaring inequalities of contemporary urban life provide fertile soil in which campaigns against inequality easily take hold. For example, the global scale of gentrification consistently creates activism flashpoints around building demolition and developer subsidies (Sites 2003), public school closures and openings (Lipman 2013; Farmer and Noonan 2019; Doussard and Lesniewski 2017), and community responses to urban renewal (Hyra 2012).

Local media provide another advantage for policy entrepreneurs. Unions, community organizations, and activist politicians tend to have strong connections with local media outlets, who have many hours and pages to fill from limited possibilities for source material. Thus, causes driven by unions and community organizations are likely to win coverage (Doussard and Fulton 2020).

UPEs also work strategically with national-level policy entrepreneurs to coordinate and package localized protests. The Fight for $15 campaign, for example used concurrent local strikes to create national media coverage that amplified the effect of local actions. Working in the other direction, UPEs make abstract, national problems concrete by reframing them in terms of local impact. Directly and indirectly, through symbols, space, and social ties, cities provide activists a range of tools with which to set the political agenda.

Policy Stream: UPEs Network across Cities

UPEs operate through complex networks that span multiple issues, cities, and political jurisdictions. These networks provide multiple capabilities that Washington-based policy entrepreneurs often lack. Equally important, the presence and reliability of network ties allows UPEs to develop strategies that take advantage of their network resources. Just as the resources of the internet make it possible for scholars to routinely execute research of previously unimaginable complexity and volume, the resources of these networks and the focus of those networks on city politics allow UPEs to do much more than their peers in Washington.

First, multicity networks expand the range of model policies, research, and testimony on which urban policy entrepreneurs draw. The large number of U.S. cities and counties makes available plentiful policy experiments, models, and evidence upon which to draw. Policy entrepreneurship networks disseminate this legislation across political scales and jurisdiction. Second, the diversity of subnational legislative forums also opens the process to new ideas and participants. Rather than locking onto a single opportunity to enact a new law, policy entrepreneurs can shop for opportunities in multiple cities, counties, and states, running several campaigns at once (Karch 2007; Hertel-Fernandez 2019).[3] The victories these campaigns win are likely to be, well, bigger than those available in Washington. The general left lean of urban electorates reduces conservative opposition to economic bills to just a handful of city council members, with the result that distributive economic legislation in cities rarely contains the kinds of compromises that water down federal legislation. Equally important, the small number of elected officials a city bill needs to please (just a dozen city council members in many large cities) makes it possible for ambitious and complicated bills to survive negotiation intact. The delivery of $15 minimum wages in cities while the national minimum remains stuck at $7.25 makes the point.

Third, the strategic and networked character of UPEs also makes clear that their opportunities to contest economic inequality are systematic. This provides an important counterpoint to single-site studies of successful progressive policy, which attribute reform to epiphenomenal chance or individual skill (Saito 2019; Darrah-Okike 2019; Molotch 1976; Clavel 2010). We believe that this approach can shift the debate away from big-picture questions such as "Is resistance possible?" to smaller, more practical questions about how resistance works and how it can expand.

Politics Stream: Activists Apply Pressure

Cities offer two distinct advantages to UPEs and the activists with whom they coordinate. First, the urban real estate investment boom creates numerous opportunities for intervention, often from the multiple public approvals relating to funding, zoning, site assembly, and local law. Despite the best efforts of planners and politicians to obscure those approval processes, they represent visible targets for well-organized campaigns to force or block action. Spicer and Casper-Futterman (2020) characterize these efforts as "exactive/concessionary," in that activists use their power to compel private developers, contractors, and public authorities to "pay up" on behalf of marginalized communities. The economic and political importance of the projects themselves sustains the political stream in this case, as mayors seeking to deliver "wins" may be compelled to bargain with communities to secure those victories.

Second, municipal elections provide opportunities to escalate pressure to address a problem. This marks a significant departure from the role of elections in national policy entrepreneurship, where a change in party control is one of the few events that can overwhelm the system's barriers to bold policy. In cities, election campaigns provide leverage in the policy stream by generating a series of events that give justice coalitions the opportunity to apply pressure. The major economic policy reforms we evaluate in chapters 4–7 respond to these political pressures: mayors signed off on high minimum wages either to ward off their electoral opponents (Doussard and Lesniewski 2017) or to deliver on promises that political pressure had made central to their campaigns (Rolf 2015a). These events did not just happen, and they were not distributed randomly or incidentally across U.S. cities. Instead, activists and policy entrepreneurs *manufactured pressure* on elected officials by targeting their campaigns or supporting challengers.

Steering the politics stream to a given issue often requires just a single politician or candidate, whose voice can easily rise about the crowd in small media markets and small political institutions. The U.S. Congress has 538 members. The Seattle City Council, for example, has nine. These shifts in attention can happen quickly. In the early 2000s, for example, politics in Chicago and Washington, D.C., swerved to the issue of economic inequality after city council members introduced living-wage bills (Doussard 2015). From participatory budgeting (Gilman 2016; Russon Gilman and Wampler 2019) to universal basic income trial programs (Mitchell 2019), radical economic policy proposals can take over formal politics with the actions of just a handful of individuals.

Several additional features of urban political institutions enhance access for activists. Without major exception, city councils face re-election every four years, making them more accountable to public opinion than the U.S. Senate. Low barriers to entry and the absence of gerrymandering in the style of the U.S. Congress also make races for city council more contested: candidates need less funding to enter races and only rarely compete in bespoke districts gerrymandered to geographical extremes. In fact, many cities limit campaign financing and/or provide public financing, opening the door to less-resourced candidates. Many others allow ballot initiatives, a legislative mechanism that outsiders use to pressure elected officials. And municipal elections are often held on "off-cycle" dates, resulting in relatively low turnout that can benefit well-organized campaigns.

Unlike the problem or policy streams, where they can maneuver capably by themselves, UPEs require the assistance of ERJ coalitions in the politics stream. Elected officials may occasionally agree to entertain a new policy on the merits alone, but they are much more likely to do so when social movements have established a credible threat in an upcoming election. Once social movement actors manufacture the need for elected officials to act, UPEs have the opportunity to persuade by mobilizing positive policy examples from other cities as a form of peer pressure for local action.

The easy access activists enjoy to the urban political agenda also allows these actors to strategize in ways that national-level actors do not. The organizers, unions, and activists we interviewed for this book talked as much about their efforts to shape *politics* as to enact policy. In one particularly memorable example, organizers in Chicago casually summarized the three-year plan they put in place to "define the narrative [mayor] Rahm Emanuel would have to run against." The negative public image that organizers shaped for Emanuel became a major factor in his decision to support a $13 minimum wage and other measures that could help him shed the label "Mayor 1%."

Moving between Streams to Create Windows of Opportunity

In Washington, the work of policy entrepreneurs requires an almost Zen-like calm:

> When you lobby for something, what you have to do is put together your coalition, you have to gear up, you have to get your political force in line, and then you sit there and wait for the fortuitous event. (Anonymous policy entrepreneur quoted in Kingdon 1984, 165)

This quote speaks to the semiautonomous, nonlinear, and contingent character of the streams: policy entrepreneurs incubate their pet ideas and groom their political alliances, while the dynamics of problem salience remain out of their hands. UPEs, however, frequently do not need to wait. In contrast to their counterparts in Washington, they can make their own luck.[4]

UPEs have the ability to open agenda windows, which they then couple opportunistically with policy ideas. Thus, they use the problem and politics streams strategically and tactically. For example, the inaugural success of contemporary community-labor organizing, the Los Angeles–based Justice for Janitors campaign, used immigration marches to focus public attention on janitors' pay and working conditions (Milkman 2006); shopped around for public authorities willing to entertain legislation on the issue; brought *other* public authorities into the mix when the L.A. City Council developed cold feet; and finally used the neighborhood-based political connections of community organizations to win the votes it needed. Dozens of other campaigns followed this template (Aguiar and Ryan 2009; Archer et al. 2010; Milkman, Bloom, and Narro 2010; Broxmeyer and Michaels 2014; Clawson 2003).

We expect participants in ERJ coalitions, including UPEs, to shape the local politics and problem streams by staging protests, introducing legislation, and shaping the political narrative through door knocking, social media, public events, and the other vernacular work of organizing. Following research on discourse coalitions, we anticipate that such organizations will set the policy agenda more effectively when the problem they articulate is simple: the themes of inequality and racism should impact agenda setting more than housing justice or sexual harassment at work. Similarly, we expect simple issues with precedent in federal law, such as the minimum wage, to enter the problem stream more readily than comparative abstractions, such as wage theft or predictive scheduling laws. We also anticipate limited instances—namely, the appointment of a working group tasked with drafting a bill—in which agenda windows open before a policy has been proposed. In these instances, the mission of the UPE is speed: they work to secure an agreement before politics and other issues close the window.

These observations about how activism and agenda setting in cities differ from Washington lead to simple and useful comparative questions. Our case studies of the minimum wage (chapter 4), targeted hiring (chapter 5), and policies advancing social and economic justice beyond the workplace (chapters 6 and 7) use these direct comparisons between federal and urban policy entrepreneurship to answer detailed questions about how, why, and where activism for particular policies succeeds and falls short.

MAKING SENSE OF URBAN POLICY CHANGE: OUR RESEARCH APPROACH

Why and when does activism for social and economic equity translate into new policies? We answer this broad question through smaller questions focused on the where, why, and how of urban policy entrepreneurship.

Problem Stream

Urban activists should have latitude to set the public agenda. Studies of organizing suggest a number of simple mechanisms, including protest, relationships with elected officials, research, direct action, and the skillful use of media campaigns, through which activists shape what politicians and the public think of as pressing problems (Doussard and Fulton 2020). The first and most basic task for our case studies is to explore these mechanisms: *Who uses them, when and why do they work, and what other strategies do they support or conceal?*

This leads to a second question about the problem stream: *Which issues are more likely to become generally acknowledged problems?* Drawing on the discourse coalitions tradition, the odds of an issue becoming a generally acknowledged problem should increase when the issue is broad. When the issue is narrow, we expect that simple issues are more likely to draw attention. For example, we expect "inequality" to gain more traction than "low-wage work," and "low-wage work" to gain more traction than paid time off, predictive scheduling, or the very real threat of sexual harassment on the job.

Politics Stream

Recent studies of community and labor organizing identify a handful of tools UPEs use to influence the politics stream. First, many coalitions nominate their own candidates for city council or mayor and use the candidacy as leverage to elevate issues. Second, uniquely skilled politicians can use the persuasive powers of their office—the so-called bully pulpit—to steer attention to a problem. Third, some activists use ballot initiatives to create or document a threat to current officeholders. The brevity of this list in comparison to the list of tools that can shape the problem stream is very much the point: the legal and procedural rules that shape electoral politics channel action to specific times in the electoral cycle (Karch 2007; Hertel-Fernandez 2019), a reality that inevitably restricts effective advocacy to certain points on the calendar.

Policy Streams and Windows of Opportunity

The technical components of policy creation play a relatively minor role in our analysis, not because they are unimportant but rather because they appear to be less variable. City policies need to pass a few basic hurdles to become viable. First, lawyers must establish that cities have the authority to regulate the issue and that no state or federal law preempts local policy. Second, potential laws need clear enforcement mechanisms, a reality that undermined most early-2000s economic legislation (Gleeson 2016; Reich, Jacobs, and Dietz 2014). However, in some cases, policies require adaptation to fit with local institutions, adding to the complexity of the work in the policy stream. This can slow the process in ways that offer opportunities for political opposition to mount or attempt to water down or undermine the policy.

Following past successes against urban growth machines and the discourse coalitions tradition in politics, we expect mechanically and discursively simple policies to pass more easily. Both of those characteristics overlap with problem definition: narratively simple problems should enter the public agenda more readily *and* lead to policy solutions with a comparatively high rate of uptake. We further expect the multisited organization of advocacy networks to play a central role in diffusing and refining policies. This can work in several ways. Most simply, past policy success creates a kind of track record and proof-of-concept to lessen mayors' and city councils' hesitation to act (Martin 2001; Peck and Theodore 2015). More significantly, the national network provides constant data, analysis, and ideas through which to refine both the policies themselves and the surrounding messages, actions, and campaign necessary to create a window of opportunity. For this reason, we expect the process of policy adoption to grow shorter, simpler, and less contested as the number of jurisdictions that pass the policy expands.

FOUR CASES AND THREE STREAMS OF ACTION: POLICY ENTREPRENEURSHIP MEETS CITY HALL

We focus our analysis on four policy domains that represent steps toward the long-term social and economic goals of urban social movements. We expect the three streams of problems, politics, and policy to yield different results for each. We focus primarily on the top-level comparison: How does advocacy for pay, advocacy for inclusion at work, and advocacy for other types of social and economic equity lend itself to successful policy entrepreneurship? This basic comparison proxies as a comparison of the other differences between cases. For example, we expect campaigns for the minimum wage—a simple, easily quantifiable measure with long-term precedent in labor law—to be easier to organize than campaigns for fair workweek policies, police reform, and other measures that have no obvious prior analogue in the public's lived experience.

Minimum Wage

Two factors weigh heavily on assessments of the prospects for successful minimum wage campaigns. On the one hand, organized business interests have a long and fierce tradition of opposing the minimum wage, whose symbolic value as direct regulation on the terms of employment overshadows the often-tiny increases that minimum wage laws stipulate. On the other, almost all adults work or have worked, making hourly pay a kind of lingua franca for comparing jobs and their merits. We expect these latter realities to lower the bar policy entrepreneurs need to clear: once organizers move the problem of low wages onto the agenda, the policy remedy will raise few eyebrows or questions.

The Fight for $15, which has driven advocacy on the minimum wage nationally since 2012, created broad consensus to raise the minimum wage. We expect increases to happen in places where organizers can inject the issue into the political stream, either by supporting candidates or by using (or threatening) a ballot initiative. Seen this way, we expect the limits of the minimum wage to be the limits of current political geography: double-digit minimum wages should become law except in places where state-law preempts local action, where local politics skews right or ballot initiatives are viable as neither reality nor threat. To contemporary readers, these might appear to be dog-bites-human conclusions. However, as recently as 2013, those preconditions failed to secure even small city minimum wage ordinances anywhere.

Targeted Hiring

Efforts to redirect employment opportunities toward disadvantaged populations, especially communities of color, date from civil unrest in the 1960s. These efforts meet resistance on two fronts, especially when they compel, rather than incentivize, employers to hire from outside of their traditional "labor queue" (Thurow 1975): one, from businesses who anticipate mandates to hire workers inadequately prepared for the job; and two, from working-class white communities and labor unions, especially within the construction trades, who see a threat to their power and privilege.

Targeted hiring programs thus have multiple barriers to overcome. As with the minimum wage, these organizing efforts would need to overcome the interests of businesses, and to identify politicians attentive to their interests. They would also need to forge cross-racial alliances with labor unions to build power. Additionally, they need a high level of technical capacity to participate in the development of targeted hiring policies, which can be complicated to implement. We expect to see success on targeted hiring where organizing efforts succeed in engaging and building power across racial divides and where technical capacity exists within ERJ coalitions to work out detailed targeted hiring policies and agreements. These would enable those coalitions to respond in situations when window-opening events—usually in the form of large, public, job-creating project investments—occur.

Justice beyond Work

This category is necessarily messier than the others. The strength and limits of advocacy for better conditions on the job come from paid work comprising a single, highly regulated portion of life. City and household problems are by contrast more expansive. We select four sets of such policies to investigate, and we analyze them sequentially, moving from policies that use the workplace to enact changes aimed at life outside work to policies focused on social reproduction and public space. Given that advocacy on these issues is a work in progress, we selected policies that our research subjects could address in detail because they were currently working on them.

Home-and-Work Policies

Since 2014, more than a dozen cities and several states have enacted paid time off legislation, which provides for sick days, vacation days, and other forms of time off that federal law does not require. More recently, cities have turned to what advocates label "fair workweek" legislation, which addresses the problem of consistently variable and unpredictable work schedules that make planning for childcare, education, and other life basics impossible for low-wage workers. Like the minimum wage, these measures regulate the employer-employee relationship by requiring fixed conditions of employment. Unlike the minimum wage, they have little or no precedent in federal law and, crucially, they aim to improve employees' lives *outside the job*. For these reasons, home-and-work policies represent a real effort to expand justice at work to reach outside the workplace.

Where minimum wage campaigns could draw on past activism around the minimum wage and familiarity with the one-size-fits-all job quality measure of hourly pay, these measures do not clearly attach to any established discourse about work and economy. We expect this to put work-and-home policies in a weak position, from which activists cannot credibly attach them to established messages about growth. However, we expect activists to compensate for these feebler messages by using the resources available to them in the political stream—essentially, passing paid time off and fair workweek measures through the same process and pressure that generated the minimum wage.

Public Goods and Austerity

After the Great Recession, austerity dominated the daily work of ERJ coalitions. Yet when organizers began to turn toward the issue of public finance in the mid-2010s, they did so out of desperation more than fit. Forty-plus years of taxpayer rebellions had made messages in favor of raising taxes and increasing public spending at best nonstarters and at worst completely dissonant to the public and elected officials.

As a result, justice activists began near zero. The politics and policy streams had few solutions available to them. Out of necessity, activism for equity in public spending operated at the level of the problem stream. Over and over, organizers asked themselves: How can we dramatize austerity? How can we reduce a complex problem to simple proposals? Race and racism played a surprising role in the answers. While talking about tax increment financing, bonding, debt swaps, or other important finance issues resonated with neither movement constituents nor the press, labelling the entire enterprise of austerity as racist did. This led to a result that previous generations of organizers could not imagine. By foregrounding questions of racism they were supposed to avoid, ERJ coalitions gained real traction on what had been an intractable problem.

OUR RESEARCH METHODS

Our research covered parts of fourteen years from 2006 to 2019. Over that time period, we conducted more than 270 interviews with participants in social movements and policy entrepreneurship, as well as with low-wage workers, elected officials, and outside observers who became involved in the policy process. Most of the research took place in Chicago, which features in each of the three cases as a kind of methodological through-line. We conducted more than 150 interviews in Chicago, with particularly high counts in 2006, 2013, 2017, and 2018. Our analysis of Chicago, however, conceptualizes the city and its social movements as a node in a network. That network contains more than 120 interviews, many conducted elsewhere during long-term research engagements, including St. Louis (30 interviews), Indianapolis (30 interviews), and Denver (18 interviews). We wish we could say that we selected and ordered our studies as part of a carefully measured research strategy, but the truth is rather less elegant. Our research sites came about via a mix of careful selection, happy accident, and pure opportunism.

Chicago is both a key site of meaning making in urban studies and, no less significant, the de facto back yard of both authors for most of that period. We added research in St. Louis and Indianapolis to determine how models developed in Chicago diffused to smaller cities in politically conservative states (Doussard 2016). Portland and Seattle were the backyard of Greg Schrock after 2010, Marc Doussard spends a month every year in his hometown of Denver, and New Orleans represents a site of strategic opportunity due to the development of vigorous equity policy under Mayor Mitch Landrieu (2012–2018). What these sites lack in ideal research design, they make up for in volume, diversity, and long timeframes.

Interviews provide the backbone of our analysis, but we supplement them with several additional primary and secondary data sources. Participant-observation in community and labor organizing, and direct observation of marches, protests, and strategy meetings in which we participated, provide a lot of valuable information we used to test, refine, and substantiate our conclusions. We have written many reports for community and labor organizations in these coalitions. We have additionally acted as sounding boards, provided advice when asked, run numbers, pulled data, and answered technical questions for a range of activists. Without overstating the impact of these relationships, we believe they gave us access to a level of strategic thinking that helped to fill gaps from the interviews. We also developed or used a range of secondary data sources, including a database of wage theft laws (Doussard and Gamal 2016) and inventories of minimum wage (UC Berkeley Labor Center 2019), earned sick time (A Better Balance 2018) and fair workweek laws (Cooke 2019). Finally, we made extensive use of the University of Washington's Minimum Wage History project, a digital archive of over fifty long-form interviews with participants in the SeaTac and Seattle minimum wage campaigns.

Rather than probe for systematic variations to some kind of new universal rule of urban politics in the United States—a rule we would greet with considerable skepticism—we set out to build viable explanations of why equity campaigns succeed where they do, where they fall short, and how they are attempting to expand the pursuit of justice at work to encompass justice beyond work. The end result is a comprehensive, networked analysis of research locations that already appear frequently in scholarship on community and labor organizing.

Activism on these issues remains a work in progress. In the mid-2000s, activist coalitions engaged in employment had begun to experiment with support for sentencing reform and other small measures related to criminal justice. As we write this, protests following the police murder of George Floyd in Minneapolis have elevated police spending to the level of a publicly acknowledged problem, and the American Rescue Plan has written into law dozens of measures supporting the goals of urban social movements. Our investigation of these issues focuses on identifying the basic strategies activists used to unsettle public consensus so thoroughly that recently unimaginable reforms of this type seem not just possible, but inevitable.

4

Organizing for Better Jobs

THE FIGHT FOR $15 TRANSFORMS URBAN POLITICS

Low minimum wage rates seemed a permanent feature of the U.S. economy at the turn of the twenty-first century. Congress rarely raised the federal minimum wage (just $5.15 at the time), few states had their own minimum wages, and city-level minimum wages simply did not exist. Today, most states have minimum wages, more than a dozen have set minimum wages higher than $10, and the list of cities with $15 minimum wages continues to grow. Popular accounts of the turnaround of the minimum wage rightly acknowledge the skill of the Fight for $15 movement in reversing public sentiment on the subject. However, the Fight for $15 movement itself developed by capitalizing on the three major transformations we have documented so far in this book.

First, the Fight for $15 used the leverage of the city itself. Minimum wage campaigns originally feared capital flight: set wages above the market rate, and mobile investors might move where labor is cheaper. Current minimum wage activists find opportunity in deindustrialization, for their policy targets customer-serving retail and consumption businesses that can rarely relocate. Second, the movement's members build their campaigns on the backbone of mature community-labor alliances and a field-tested repertoire of campaign strategies and tactics. Finally, participants in individual, local minimum wage campaigns draw on the resources of a national, entrepreneurial network of policy activists to improve and to standardize campaigns for fairness on the job.

The minimum wage provides campaign participants the reward of clear, direct movement toward the abstract goal of economic justice. But winning a $15 minimum wage does not conclude the coalition's work. To the contrary, the coalitions that pass minimum wages in U.S. cities quickly and repeatedly return for more. Follow-up campaigns typically target county- or state-level minimum wages, wage theft laws, the establishment of local labor standards offices, legislation mandating paid time off work, and, most ambitiously, laws to standardize radically flexible, "just-in-time" work schedules. No less important, running multiple campaigns has the immediate effect of strengthening the coalition itself. As unions, community organizations, researchers, advocacy groups, and think tanks work toward the goal of passing ambitious local policy, they develop routines, relationships, and network assets that tie advocacy for fairness at work to other kinds of struggles.

We assess the minimum wage's expansion in three steps. First, we chart the movement's growth in terms of political jurisdictions, political scale, and policy outcomes. Second, we isolate ten campaigns that entail significant steps forward for minimum wage politics, beginning with the first successful $15 minimum wage ordinance and ending with the groundswell of state $15 minimum wage laws in early 2019. Reviewing these cases indicates distinctive shifts in both scope and strategy: campaigns for a $15 minimum wage have moved from small cities to large ones to states, and they have traded the labor-intensive work of counting votes and winning commitments from public officials—what Imbroscio (2006) memorably termed the "inside" game of urban politics—forstrategies that use broad grassroots support to pressure politicians everywhere.

These insights lead to the third step, of detailed case studies of the successful SeaTac, Seattle, and Chicago campaigns. We analyze the campaigns in terms of (1) the changing economic structure of cities, (2) the changing composition of social movements, and (3) the rise of urban policy entrepreneurship. These individual campaigns illuminate the current wave of state-level minimum wage laws, which apply the innovations of city-level minimum wage campaigns to other political scales. Policy networks and peer learning, we show, have transformed minimum wage campaigns from intensive, risky struggles to off-the-shelf solutions to longstanding problems. The active question is less where the minimum wage will appear next, than what kinds of politics, policies, and campaigns will follow it.

DESPERATION AND DEVELOPMENT: THE FIGHT FOR $15 IN THE 2010S

Ten years ago, no U.S. city had its own minimum wage. Today, more than fifty-five cities and counties have not just passed minimum wages but set them at or near $15 per hour. Even though the federal government has not raised the minimum wage since 2007, most of the U.S. population now lives in cities and states with wage floors above the federal base (Table 1).

To better understand the evolution of these campaigns, we used

Table 1. Diffusion of the minimum wage

YEAR	LOCALITIES	STATES
2013	Bernalillo County, N.Mex. ($8.50)	
	Prince George's County, Md. ($11.50)	
	Richmond, Calif. ($13)	
2014	Chicago ($13)	Connecticut ($10.10)
	Las Cruces, N.Mex.($10.10)	Delaware ($8.25)
	Oakland, Calif. ($12.25)	Hawaii ($10.10)
	San Diego ($11.50)	Maryland (10.10)
	San Francisco ($15)	Massachusetts ($11)
	Santa Fe County, N.Mex. ($10.66)	Michigan ($9.25)*!
	Seattle ($15)	Minnesota ($9.50)
	Sunnyvale, Calif. ($9)	Rhode Island ($9)
	Washington, D.C. ($15)	Vermont ($10.50)
		West Virginia ($8.75)
2015	Bangor, Maine ($9.75)	
	El Cerrito, Calif. ($15)	
	Emeryville, Calif. ($15)	
	Los Angeles ($15)	
	Los Angeles County ($15)	
	Mountainview, Calif. ($15)	
	Palo Alto, Calif. ($15)	
	Portland, Maine ($10.68)	
	Tacoma, Wash ($15)	
2016	Berkeley, Calif. ($15)	Arizona ($12)*
	Cook County, Ill. ($13)	California ($15)
	Cupertino, Calif. ($15)	Colorado ($12)*
	Flagstaff, Ariz. ($15.50)	Maine ($12)*
	Los Altos, Calif. ($15)	Washington ($13.50)*
	Malibu, Calif. ($15)	New York (NYC $15)

(continued on next page)

Table 1. Diffusion of the minimum wage (cont.)

YEAR	LOCALITIES	STATES
2016 (cont.)	Pasadena, Calif. ($15)	Oregon ($14.75/$12.50)
	San Jose ($15)	
	San Leandro, Calif. ($15)	
	San Mateo, Calif. ($15)	
	Santa Monica, Calif. ($15)	
2017	Belmont, Calif. ($15.90)	Rhode Island ($10.50)
	Milpitas, Calif. ($15)	
	Minneapolis ($15)	
	Montgomery County, Md. ($15)	
2018	Alameda, Calif. ($15)	Arkansas ($11)*
	Redwood City, Calif. ($15)	Delaware ($9.25)
	St. Paul ($15)	Massachusetts ($15)
		Michigan ($12.05)!
		Missouri ($12)*
2019	Fremont, Calif. ($15)	Connecticut ($15)
	Chicago ($15)	Illinois ($15)
		Maryland ($15)
		New Jersey ($15)
		New Mexico ($12)
2020		Florida (15)*

Source: UC Berkeley Labor Center 2020. *: Law passed via ballot initiative. !: State legislature later weakened resulting law.

news accounts, legislative records sources, and our own field interviews to compile brief summaries of campaign milestones, goals, and outcomes. We then narrowed this inventory of campaigns to ten corresponding key developments in the minimum wage movement (Table 2).

Both the campaigns and the coalitions conducting them grow simpler by the year. For example, early campaigns in Washington State consumed the efforts of dozens of highly involved community organizations and local unions. Subsequent campaigns in smaller Midwestern cities involved just a small handful of unions and community organizations. By the time most minimum-wage advocacy had moved to the state level, successful campaigns were run by small cadres of

Table 2. Key minimum wage campaigns

JURISDICTION	RESULT YEAR	STATE UNION DENSITY	KEY COALITION MEMBERS	NOTABLE CHARACTERISTICS
SeaTac, Wash. ($15)	2013	20%	Puget Sound Sage; Service Employees International Union locals	First U.S. $15 minimum wage. Passed via ballot initiative that included action on wage theft, earned sick time, targeted hiring.
Seattle, Wash. ($15)	2014	20%	Puget Sound Sage; MLK Labor	First $15 minimum wage in a large city. Both mayoral candidates in general election supported the law. A mayor-appointed working group drafted the final bill.
Chicago, Ill. ($13)	2014	14%	Service Employees International Union, Grassroots Collaborative	Mayor Rahm Emanuel reversed his opposition to the bill. A mayor-appointed working group drafted the law.
St. Louis, Mo. ($13)	2015	9%	Service Employees International Union, Missouri Jobs with Justice	State legislature preempted local minimum wage legislation; voters passed a $12 state minimum wage in 2018 elections.
Washington D.C. ($15/$12)	2016	10%	Maryland Working Families, Progressive Maryland and CASA.	Hybrid local-state campaign combined minimum wage for District of Columbia and Surrounding Counties. Organizers used Chicago campaign's tactics.
Denver, Colo. ($15)	2019	11%	Colo. AFL-CIO, United for a New Economy, Denver Area Labor Federation	City council passed $15 minimum wage bill after new Democratic legislative majority repealed a minimum wage preemption law.
Indianapolis, Ind. ($10.10)	None	9%	American Federation of State, County and Municipal Employees, Community Faith-Labor	Small minimum wage increase for hundreds of city employees survived state preemption law.
Ark. ($12)	2018	5%	Arkansans for a Fair Wage: Minimum wage, Little Rock Attorney David Couch	Ballot initiative won with little coalition action or funding.
Conn. ($15)	2019	16%	AFL-CIO, Raise the Floor	Early 2019 legislative priority in state with narrow Democratic control.
Ill. ($15)	2019	14%	AFL-CIO, Raise the Floor	Early 2019 legislative priority in state with Democratic supermajorities.

Source: Authors' calculations from news reports and Current Population Survey data.

think tank employees and state organizations. They involved selective testimony and research, rather than the labor-intensive work of organizing workers and lobbying politicians one by one.

We selected three campaigns from this list for further, in-depth analysis: the 2013 $15 ballot initiative in the small Seattle suburb of SeaTac, Seattle's own campaign for a $15 minimum wage in 2014, and Chicago's successful campaign for a $13 minimum wage that same year. Each of these campaigns developed the movement's techniques in a clear way. SeaTac, the first campaign, established proof-of-concept at a great resource cost. Moving advocacy to Seattle required organizers to build an experimental campaign around outside pressure from community organizations and the public. Finally, Chicago's minimum wage campaign used a national advocacy network to adapt techniques developed in Seattle to Chicago's strong mayor system of government and strong mayor Rahm Emanuel. The national Fight for $15 campaign itself learned and adapted by assessing the rapid development of tactics and strategies within this short window of time.

ACTIVISM EVOLVES FROM LIVING WAGES TO THE MINIMUM WAGE

In the 2000s, members of the living-wage movement began experimenting with state-level legislation. Those state-level campaigns entailed significant innovations, including the development of statistical methodologies for establishing the minimum wage's limited impact on job growth. In 2010, a landmark study took advantage of the natural experiments created by uneven minimum wage levels across the country in order to establish the negligible long-term impact of the minimum wage on employment levels (Dube, Lester, and Reich 2010). Subsequent research led many economists to reverse long-held opposition to minimum wages.

State-level minimum wage campaigns also piloted the use of ballot initiatives in the 2006 elections (Sonn and Luce 2008). Ballot initiatives subsequently played a major role in 2010s campaigns, both as a way of taking the issue directly to voters and, in more sophisticated iterations, as a mechanism for compelling legislators to act. State-level minimum wage campaigns also convened new coalitions that subsequently drove action on the minimum wage and related employment issues (Doussard and Gamal 2016). State AFL-CIO federations, individual unions engaged in low-wage worker organizing, antipoverty organizations and politically engaged urban community organizers all began to make joint trips to state capitols in this period. These organizations appear recurrently in subsequent advocacy campaigns.

These 2000s-era campaigns built a national network of organizations, organizers, and researchers with expertise on city and state minimum wage issues. This network included the National Employment Law Project; the Economic Policy Institute; several state-level affiliates of the EPI-sponsored Economic Action Research Network (EARN); economic policy staff at the Service Employees International Union and other union internationals; scholars at the UC Berkeley Labor Center; and a continuously expanding network of organizers, campaign operatives, and researchers who had experience with lobbying, media, and organizing. These national policy entrepreneurship resources supported local campaigns lead by economic and racial justice coalitions and urban policy entrepreneurs.

CHRONOLOGY OF THE MOVEMENT

The campaign to raise the minimum wage spread from a trio of improvised strikes in 2012 to cover hundreds of U.S. cities and multiple countries a few years later. This spread happened deliberately: the campaign's initial organizers planned to expand from fast food to retail, from McDonald's franchises to the McDonald's corporation, and from early demonstration sites to cities and states spread throughout the United States. From the first attempts to expand living-wage laws into something more substantial to current campaigns targeting job problems that stretch far beyond low pay, the policy entrepreneurs at the movement's center worked to create the political "problem" of low-wage work—a problem to which the $15 minimum wage provided a field-tested solution.

The idea for the Fight for $15 emerged from the shock of the Great Recession and union leaders' recognition that campaigns for small living and minimum wage increases promised an unfavorable ratio of risks to rewards (Rolf 2015a). One of the Fight for $15's first advocates in the labor movement explained the reasoning bluntly:

> We talked about doing it [advocating a $15 minimum wage] in the run-up to the 2012 election. Conditions were so bad. We looked

around and said, "If we're not going to lead the fight for pay, then who is?" (senior labor official)

The first Fight for $15 strikes were designed as experiments to test the viability of staging campaigns in varied industries and cities (Rolf 2015b). On the prime retail Black Friday after Thanksgiving, retail workers in Manhattan and Chicago and fast food workers in Detroit walked off their jobs. Labor officials conceived of the Black Friday ministrikes as demonstration projects to validate the viability of a resource-intensive nationwide campaign (Rolf 2005). But the scaled-down test strikes by definition could not justify a campaign for $15, which would have to begin with a leap of faith. Amid preparations for the first national strikes in early 2013, a high-ranking organizer made his nervousness clear to the authors: "I'm not really sure we know what we're doing, or that $15 isn't going to get us laughed out."

The Black Friday strikes worked in the narrow sense that workers commanded public attention without losing their jobs. Organizers responded by scheduling a second, larger New York strike for April 4, 2013—the anniversary of Martin Luther King Jr.'s assassination. Messaging around the strike drove home the point that civil rights necessitate economic rights: "We believe that it's a continuation of a civil rights fight against low wages and for Martin Luther King's movement to win dignity and living-wage jobs," explained Jonathan Westin, director of a New York community organization network that supported the strikes (Greenhouse 2013a).

Campaign architects chose the next cities to organize with an eye toward demonstrating the ubiquity of workers' discontent with their jobs (Doussard 2016). The May 9 and 10 strikes took place in St. Louis and Detroit, sites laden with symbolic meaning. They had large populations of black workers, who make up a disproportionate share of low-wage earners; they were in states that had recently passed antiunion right-to-work legislation (Michigan) or were threatening to (Missouri); and they indicated the movement could work in smaller cities. Collectively the strikes built national support for the idea of a high minimum wage. Individually, they spoke to local symbols and concerns. In a nod to historical efforts to integrate African Americans into the local United Auto Workers, St. Louis organizers chose the slogan "$15 and a union." The Detroit campaign sometimes appended

$15 to the iconic "I have a dream" slogan and placed the D from the Tigers baseball team caps next to "$15."

The first coordinated national strike took place the Wednesday after Labor Day in 2013 with workers in more than 150 cities walking off their retail and fast food jobs (Greenhouse 2013b). Additional strikes in December 2013; April, September, and December 2014; and April 2015 continued to expand the campaign's scope.[1] Domestically, the strikes pulled in workers from an increasing array of low-wage sectors, including airport workers, home health workers, security guards, and adjunct university faculty.[2]

Viewed from afar, the selection of SeaTac, Washington, as the first site to attempt a $15 minimum wage appears confusing. Viewed within the broader project of testing methods for winning minimum wage policy campaigns, however, SeaTac had significant advantages: activist local labor unions with experience organizing low-wage service workers, and easy mechanisms for forcing a vote on the minimum wage.

FROM VOTE COUNTING TO MASS MOVEMENT: THE BIRTH OF THE $15 MINIMUM WAGE IN THE PUGET SOUND

Voters in SeaTac, Washington, made it the first U.S. city to approve a $15 minimum wage when they ratified Proposition 1 in the November 2013 elections. The campaign to pass Proposition 1 demonstrated the viability of the policy of a $15 minimum wage, but did so without developing techniques to address the other core requirements of passing legislation via policy entrepreneurship. The national Fight for $15 movement had established low-wage work as a generally recognized problem, but using the mechanism of a ballot initiative allowed activists to bypass the challenges of moving that problem to the center of local politics (the problem stream) and making the problem one that politicians could not ignore (the politics stream). Proposition 1 passed into law without establishing an obviously replicable approach for other jurisdictions.

No national organization or labor union designated SeaTac as the first experiment with a campaign for a $15 minimum wage, yet the Service Employees International Union (SEIU) local (Local 775) that coordinated the campaign was part of a union that had previously seeded national experiments with food, service, and retail worker organizing. When a long-term campaign to organize workers at the city's eponymous airport stalled on routine employer opposition in early 2013, the union's leadership turned to the SEIU-supported national fast food strikes for ideas. The president of an involved SEIU local explains:

> After a couple of years of banging their heads against the wall asking to have either Alaska Airlines or the Port of Seattle impose union neutrality on the subcontracted economy, workers at the airport just got fed up and said, "OK wait a second, they're striking for $15 [in New York]. There is a strike for $15 in Seattle and St. Louis and Detroit, why are we not doing this ourselves?" . . . We looked at SeaTac and said, "OK, if we can't actually get living wages, good benefits, paid time off and sick leave, and stop employers from stealing tips through bargaining a union contract, let's just write the union contract into law." And that's what we did. (Rolf 2015b)

The campaign in SeaTac built on several long-term initiatives designed to deepen relationships between Puget Sound unions and community organizations: multiple living-wage campaigns in the 1990s; expanded policy advocacy by the powerful King County Labor Federation in the late 1990s (Ness and Eimer 2015), a series of campaigns to organize airport staff and service workers (Rolf 2015b), a successful 1998 Washington State ballot initiative that raised the state's minimum wage to what was at the time the highest rate in the nation, and in 2011, the SEIU's "Fight for a Fair Economy" initiative, which steered resources into basic community organizing and relationship building (Luce 2015; Dean 2012). As one of the lead SEIU organizers in SeaTac explains, Fight for a Fair Economy

> was a national campaign that we started here in the King County area. . . . What we did is we went to knock on more than a hundred thousand doors. . . . One of the goals is to increase prosperity and decrease inequality for working people. So that means that we want to link everybody up, not only homecare workers, nursing care workers. That was the decision that the board made when we start[ed] the fight for fair economy and when we started thinking about that. (Rivera 2015)

SeaTac's small size (2010 population: 26,900) and the availability of ballot initiatives made the task of passing Proposition 1 simple, but difficult. The simplicity came from organizers using the ballot initiative to take the campaign directly to the city's small population of registered voters. The difficulty came from the labor-intensive get-out-the-vote process vital to passage. SeaTac has far more socioeconomic variance than news accounts of the campaign suggested, including a large bloc of high-income voters who opposed the bill and significant demographic divisions between the low-wage workers the bill would benefit:

> [SeaTac has] a huge differential in economic mobility and economic status. We have Angle Lake; that is the nice part of SeaTac. Quarter-mile driveways, views, homes that have been owned for quite some time.... And then 200th [street] is a completely different world. It's all apartment complexes. It's Somali families, Eritrean families, Amharic speaking families, upwards of six people in a two-bedroom, three-bedroom apartment. Everyone that is of working age has multiple low-wage jobs.... From every imaginable angle you could take a look at a community, this one was a diaspora. No two doors that are alike. (Thomas 2015)

Campaign organizers reached community members through the city's incumbent community and labor organizers, who knocked on doors and visited churches, mosques, hometown associations, and other organizations that helped to build trust across SeaTac's population. These techniques were not new—the civil rights movement and NAACP used them to organize across scales in the 1960s (McAdam, Tarrow, and Tilly 2003)—but they were novel within the context of a union-backed campaign to turn out voters.

The campaign's potential to deliver proof-of-concept on a municipal $15 minimum wage helped to command the resources necessary to persuade residents to support and vote for the initiative. Private citizens, union members, and political activists from the Seattle region volunteered and knocked on doors. Unions flew in dozens of organizers for a preelection organizing "blitz"—a standard union-organizing technique designed to reach workers at home, and quickly. The campaign timed the blitz to coincide with the date King County delivered ballots to voters, who in Washington State vote only by mail. That created another problem:

> I remember that super clearly—October 16th or 17th—because we had these people flown in from all over the country! . . . And then there were no ballots. We had this 300-person canvas set up to get the vote out over four days with people from all over the country and there were no fucking ballots. . . . So we ended up chasing mailmen because we just wanted to know. (Thomas 2015)

The ballots finally came, and Proposition 1 passed by just seventy-seven votes. The victory established the viability of the $15 target, but the resource-intensiveness of the campaign, combined with the slender vote margin, argued against using the same techniques elsewhere. The SeaTac campaign had operated like an old-fashioned union organizing blitz. The use of a ballot initiative mostly sidelined local and national policy entrepreneurship networks whose efforts would be vital to reproducing the campaign elsewhere. Thus, even though the next minimum wage campaign took place in Seattle, the move fifteen miles up Interstate 5 was effectively *a national move* in which the Fight for $15 campaign deliberately tinkered with SeaTac's techniques in order to produce a model that would scale elsewhere.

SCALING UP THROUGH THE OUTSIDE CAMPAIGN: POLITICAL PRESSURE DRIVES THE LANDMARK SEATTLE MINIMUM WAGE

The Seattle $15 campaign began in earnest in early 2013 and moved slowly because it was burdened by the problem of scale: no realistic organizing plan could involve knocking on every door in a city of 600,000. The resources of the city itself ultimately provided a solution. Seattle's strong protest culture and vigorous left-wing movements drove popular attention to low-wage work (the problem stream) as both a real problem with significant practical impact, and as a symbol for the ills of a city increasingly skewed by wealth and inequality. That same movement created the successful city council candidacy of democratic socialist Kshama Sawant, whose attention-grabbing campaign made the $15 minimum wage a central issue for which all candidates in the election were accountable (the politics stream). Using this small but vigorous cohort of activists to drive the policy agenda, participants in the Fight for $15 then used the novel forum of a working group convened by the mayor to negotiate final support for the policy (the policy stream). Here, urban policy entrepreneurs played a direct role in securing a law that avoided major compromises and concessions to employers.

These contributions evolved accidentally, half-accidentally, and piecemeal from a campaign whose principal actors often improvised. The first hurdle campaign organizers faced was internal, the challenge of persuading themselves that $15 was not just a dream:

> [We] were really antsy about putting "$15" on our signs, honestly.... It seemed kind of ridiculous, it just seemed like a little bit of an absurdist kind of demand. It just seemed too much, and kind of random.... We had an internal struggle, "Should we even put $15 on these things?" Then we did. As it turned out everything was fine, nobody listened to me. (Wilson 2015)

External events ultimately settled the question, when democratic socialist Kshama Sawant seized on the $15 minimum wage to dramatize her campaign for one of Seattle's nine city council seats. Sawant's campaign manager explains:

> In the 2012 campaign, $15 an hour wasn't the centerpiece of our campaign, but it was a part of it. It didn't catch on fire or turn the world upside-down at the time, but we got a good response.... Kshama got 29% of the vote, which was much higher than expected, and was the highest vote for someone running as a socialist in many decades in the US. And on the basis of that we decided to run Socialist Alternative and Kshama, through discussions and debate. We agreed that Kshama would run again in 2013, this time for a city-wide position for City Council. (Locker 2015).

Sawant's forceful endorsement of the $15 minimum wage throughout the 2013 campaign "made it the critical issue in the 2013 [Seattle City Council and mayoral] elections that other candidates, including the mayoral candidates, had to start addressing" (Locker 2015). As the campaign continued amid a series of pilot fast food and retail strikes,

SEIU Local 775 decided to use the pending election to drive the minimum wage to the center of Seattle politics:

> We said, "OK, we are going to organize not just our strike, but everything else: mayoral debates, boycotts, civil disobedience, direct actions." A whole summer and early fall of activity, mainly by fast food workers, some by others, around $15 an hour. (Rolf 2015b)

The combination of strikes and activist participation in campaign events created what political scientists term "positive feedback" effects around the minimum wage. Alerted by the success of SeaTac Proposition 1, the national and local press covered the Seattle campaign frequently. The sheer density of events—fast food strikes, campaign stops, mayoral town halls, debates, protests—gave the issue a momentum of its own.

> I really enjoyed the mayoral town hall that we did about a month after the first strikes.... There were a lot of people running for mayor at that time in Seattle in June of 2013. We all had them come in, and we had them sit up on a panel. But we also had a worker panel where workers would share their stories, and I think two of the four people were fast food strikers. They got so much applause and they were just really excited about it. But they shared their stories and asked questions of the panel and really asked, "Are you willing to commit to 15?" It's interesting because at that point none of the candidates had committed to 15.... When you fast-forward... you see candidates tripping over themselves to be the person. You see now-Mayor [Ed] Murray coming out first in support of 15, I think, a month or two later. Then-mayor [Mike] McGinn saying at least 15, if not more. So we see candidates tripping over themselves to be better on worker issues—and on the issues that are led by fast food workers, of all people. (Parikh 2015)

Murray won the November election and pledged support for a $15 minimum wage law. With newly elected council member Sawant threatening in late 2013 to introduce a bill to immediately raise the minimum wage to $15, Murray adopted a minimum wage increase as his first priority. He soon named a working group of twenty-three business, labor, and public sector representatives, charged with delivering a bill that labor and businesses could both accept. The final minimum wage bill was shaped by an inside-outside pressure campaign reminiscent of a good-cop, bad-cop routine from the movies. Outside the working group meetings, organizers maintained pressure by attending public events and filing a ballot initiative to immediately increase the Seattle minimum wage to $15 for all workers. Backed by a clear majority of would-be voters, the ballot initiative compelled Murray to increase pressure on the committee and business representatives to make a deal. One of the restaurant owners' primary representatives explains the clear calculus involved:

> All the research, the market research, the voter research that we had done . . . indicated if this measure went to the ballot, it would pass with overwhelming numbers. 68 to 80% of the voters in Seattle supported going to $15 now. (Donegan 2015)

Pressure inside the working group came from the King County Labor Council's David Freiboth, whom one business representative labeled a "crazy, angry guy . . . making facial contortions and waving his arms about" (Feit 2014). Confrontation and political arm twisting punctuated the process, with the inside and outside pressure from organizers counteracting organized business's demands for a slower phase-in and greater cut-outs for small businesses (which business representatives first defined as having up to five hundred workers). The pressure provided opportunity for consensus-building within the working group (Houser, Thomas, and Page 2017). Union and community participants in the working group used economic and legal analyses developed by the national policy entrepreneurship network, including several studies from the Berkeley Labor Center, to convince business participants that the minimum wage represented a significantly smaller threat to their businesses than they anticipated.

The research they channeled was compelling in its own right. Following the turn to large-N natural experiments, economists who compared employments across state borders with uneven wages had found that employment growth did not differ in higher-wage states (Dube, Lester, and Reich 2010; Schmitt 2013). Howard Wright, the representative of hospitality employers on the panel, describes the learning process as one of personal conversion:

I was not well-informed about this subject, so I first thought, "Wow, [$15 is] crazy." And as I learned more and more about it, I had thought, "Well I think there is some validity to this." And then, by the time I embraced it, it reminded me—I don't know, ten years ago, marriage equality was at the forefront of the discussions in Hawaii and everybody looked at Hawaii and thought, "Wow, people of same sex are allowed to marry? That's way out there." And by the time it got here I totally embraced it. So I guess it shows when you become better educated, more informed, you can change your opinion and be open to new ideas. (Wright 2015)

In June 2014, the Seattle City Council passed unanimously the working group's proposed bill. The Seattle model appeared to be more scalable and transportable than the exacting work of SeaTac's ballot initiative. Yet the individual ground conditions that aided organizers in Seattle—an extremely liberal electorate, a socialist city council member, a relatively weak mayor, the threat of a ballot initiative—applied to only a few U.S. cities. Collectively, no other city had all these factors. Thus, expanding the movement from Seattle required adopting the campaign's techniques to other, less hospitable climates.

CHICAGO: POLICY ENTREPRENEURS ADAPT THE SEATTLE MODEL TO LESS FRIENDLY CIRCUMSTANCES

Chicago reached a $13 minimum wage through careful adaptation of the techniques developed in Seattle. The electoral popularity of Mayor Rahm Emanuel made the task of problem definition especially important for Chicago's economic and racial justice coalition. Local and national policy entrepreneurs played a smaller role in the campaign due to Seattle's first-mover status, which reduced policy makers' worries about the final details of the eventual law. Yet Chicago's minimum wage campaign does not constitute a straightforward triumph of national policy entrepreneurship networks transferring a policy directly. The innovations enacted by organizers were effective because Chicago activists had seized on the city's school system to make inequality a broadly recognized problem the mayor and his allies could not ignore.

Chicago's national image as a center of Democratic and progressive politics stands at odds with its long history of machine political control and extraordinary racial segregation. Alliances between a strong mayor, developers, and city council members rooted in white-majority neighborhoods, gerrymandering[3]—and, crucially, aldermanic control over public spending in their home wards—made progressive policy rare in a city with high union density, thick networks of activist community organizations, and a left-skewed electorate (Judd and Simpson 2011; Lester 2014; Doussard 2015).

When Chicago activists searched for ways to convert the Fight for $15 strikes into policy, they faced limited options. A labor-intensive mass-mobilization campaign like the SeaTac campaign was out of the question: organizers had already played and lost the conventional game of winning over voters and politicians one at a time in order to pass a scaled-down living-wage bill in 2006 (Doussard 2015). The Seattle minimum wage campaign offered a prospective model, but required adaptation. First, Chicago had a less vigorous protest tradition with which to compel the public's attention. Community development corporations, one of the innovations of the neighborhoods movement in the 1980s, had steered organizations toward bargaining and incremental demands, rather than mass protest of the kind that elevated the minimum wage in Seattle.

Second, Chicago's ballot initiatives were not legally binding. Third, the pending mayoral election in March 2015 offered little raw material for the campaign. Incumbent mayor Rahm Emanuel, a strong opponent of organized labor, faced a relatively unknown challenger in community organizer Jesus "Chuy" Garcia and had no obvious reason to negotiate with activists.

Chicago's eventual passage of a $13 minimum wage followed the same general process as Seattle's, but the details reflected the Second City's unique features. Where Seattle's Fight for $15 campaign drew on the city's vigorous tradition of public protests, the Chicago campaign was propelled by the successful 2012 Chicago Teachers Union strike, an *endogenous* outgrowth of changes in the city's community and labor organizing (Farmer and Noonan 2019; Doussard and Fulton 2020). The campaign capitalized on opposition to inequality with a series of innovative techniques that amplified the threat the voters, unions, and Garcia presented to the Emanuel administration. The eventual minimum wage increase Emanuel signed only went to $13. When viewed in light of the barriers to activism in Chicago and the comparatively small amount of effort organizers spent on the minimum wage campaign, the law's passage suggests the maturation of the

Seattle model into a flexible framework for controlling the problem and politics streams in other cities.

The Fight for $15 campaign evolved with and alongside the Chicago Teachers Union's own maturation as a political power. After winning the 2011 election with a diverse coalition and wide margins, the Emanuel administration proposed closing a string of public schools on the black South and West Sides, as a prelude to replacing them with charters (Lipman 2013). To the surprise of activists and elected officials alike, the Chicago Teachers Union, a one-time machine ally recently reinvigorated by a takeover of rank-and-file educators, rallied broad public opposition to the closures. In fall 2013, the Teachers' Union went on strike, winning concessions from Emanuel on wages, working conditions, and policy. Activists note the transformative effect the strike had:

> The takeover of that union by people who cared mattered so much. I still remember going to my first meeting at a school [before the takeover]. A big car pulled up, and these people got out in *fur coats*. They walked through the place like they owned it, they didn't say anything, and they left. Afterwards, I'm like "Who's that?" "That's the CTU!" (Senior organizer, community organization)

In addition to seeding the transformative Chicago Teachers Union Strike, the planned public-school closures also unsettled organizational alliances, priorities, and dispositions toward the neighborhood territory central to organizing in Chicago (Doussard and Lesniewski 2017). An organizer from a Northwest Side organization changed the way he framed issues, built alliances, and lobbied elected officials as the result of *winning* a campaign to prevent a school closure in his neighborhood:

> We saw that our win meant they didn't get [to keep] their schools on the South Side and the West Side. So schools were an issue that got us to broaden out. We went from labor, to schools, to class and race justice. And part of that was shifting from transactional to transformative approaches to our work. (Senior organizer, Northwest Side community organization)

The question of how to drive forward a minimum wage bill, however, initially lacked a clear answer. Organizers used two resources to propel the $15 minimum wage to the center of politics. First, they seized on Garcia's candidacy, and the newly popular epithet "Mayor 1%," to compel Emanuel to soften his image.[4] Second, they seized on that vulnerability by placing a nonbinding vote in favor of a $15 minimum wage on the ballot in strategic wards and precincts during the March 2014 elections. The ballot initiative allowed organizers to pressure city council members and the mayor *without the cost of running an old-fashioned vote-whipping campaign*:

> We would have liked to go citywide. But the resources to get it on the ballot in 105 precincts were immense. So we chose precincts that were representative of key demographics and voters, and we spread it out over the North, South and West Sides' (Senior organizer, labor organization)

> Look, there's an election coming up, and Emanuel wants to push a bit to the left. The ballot initiative was important—it documented the demand for the minimum wage. Also, as a lot of people have noted, it provides Emanuel cover, lets him tell businesses that he'd love to listen to them, but the voters have tied his hands. (Senior activist, policy organization)

More than 80% of voters approved the nonbinding $15 minimum wage referendum. This show of support allowed organizers to control the politics stream by treating the referendum as a symbol of the popular sentiment politicians needed to address:

> Aldermen will sign anything that sounds good. So our strategy is to use the Aldermen to move the mayor *symbolically*. It's not about vote-counting; it's about moving the debate. (Senior organizer, labor organization)

As the March 2015 mayoral election drew near and Garcia remained within 10 percentage points of Emanuel in the polls, Emanuel established a working group comprising city council members, workers, employers, and not-for-profit organizations to develop a minimum wage proposal. Like their peers in Seattle, Chicago's community and labor participants on the task force equipped themselves with studies from the National Employment Law Project and Economic Policy Institute, testimony from national analysts, and related resources from the national policy network in which they worked. The outside pressure and Seattle's prior vetting of the policy had worked so effectively, however, that Emanuel's representatives were eager for a deal:

> The task force really made a difference—once it was set up, it was for real, not theater. It didn't really have labor representatives, which in context, helped. It was all of the pols figuring out what they could live with. (Senior activist, policy organization)

The ensuing bill to raise the city minimum wage to $13 by 2019 fell short of the goal of $15, but significantly exceeded the goal organizers set at the beginning of the process. Reflecting on the campaign, organizers note that importance of outside pressure on incumbent politicians: "Look, everyone knew Chuy was going to lose. But nobody was afraid of Rahm backing down, and that's because of the minimum wage referendum" (Senior activist, policy organization).

Chicago activists had at their disposal the decidedly inferior materials of a nonbinding ballot initiative and a political challenger who never threatened to win, but won their goal by using those resources to shift the problem and politics streams.

$15 GOES VIRAL

The Seattle and Chicago minimum wage campaigns established the viability of symbolic politics that circumvent the labor-intensive work of counting votes and commitments with elected officials. The visibility of the Fight for $15 movement itself, and carefully arranged reminders that the public overwhelmingly supported the law, sufficed as leverage to win votes. This approach provided economies of scale in reproducing the campaign. In the subsequent five years, minimum wage policy campaigns consumed progressively fewer resources, took less time, and faced small odds of failing. In the process, they extended the $15 minimum wage from a handful of large cities with politically and economically favorable conditions to smaller cities, cities facing population loss, and to states—including many states with politically conservative legislatures.

After Florida voters ratified a $15 minimum wage in the November 2020 election, approximately one-third of the U.S. population lived in places schedule to adopt a $15 wage floor (see Table 1). Each of these victories keyed in its own way on the distinguishing features of the nationally networked set of local Fight for $15 campaigns: the popularization of the $15 minimum wage, the ability of local minimum wage campaigns to make inequality a formal problem that legislators had to address, and the circulation of discourses, tactics, and expertise through a national network. Labor and community activists sustained popular support for these measures, but played a limited role in their realization. After 2018, city-level minimum wage legislation was replaced by state-level laws driven by national policy entrepreneurship networks.

Fifteen-dollar minimum wages in California, Connecticut, Florida, Illinois, Maryland, Massachusetts, New York, and New Jersey represent the biggest policy impact of minimum-wage coalitions. However, success in a pair of highly unlikely municipal campaigns better illustrates the movement's scope. In a first example, Indianapolis activists succeeded in winning a $13 minimum wage for city and county employees—a small but notable victory in a politically conservative state with right-to-work legislation and an outright ban on local living and minimum wage laws (Briggs 2017). The Indianapolis measure covers just 365 public employees who did not previously make $13. It stands out for the routine way in which it passed after Democrats won the mayor's office and a majority of seats on the city-county council. As the municipal minimum wage expanded, contestation over individual laws diminished. This dynamic is highlighted in Chicago, where new mayor Lori Lightfoot signed in 2019 a law to raise the city's minimum wage from $13 to $15—without a concerted campaign from organizers.

A second pair of successful local campaigns in Missouri shows the movement's ability to bring public support for higher pay to bear in unlikely forums. In 2015, St. Louis and Kansas City both passed bills to raise the minimum wage to over $10, but immediately saw the policies undone, first a by a St. Louis County judge who blocked the law's enactment, then by the state legislature preempting municipal minimum wages. Adding to the challenges that organizers faced, the state's new Republican governor signed a right-to-work law within a week of taking office in January 2017. In broad outline as well as detail, these events follow the familiar script of organized scale-jumping by business interests (Lafer 2017; Kim, Aldag, and Warner 2020; Aldag, Kim, and Warner 2019): political control and superior financial resources allowed opponents of labor legislation to venue shop until they settled on an authority that would change the rules in their favor.

However, the events of the next two years undercut the familiar, gloomy story of preemption and venue shopping. The St. Louis–based community-labor coalition used the popularity of the $15 minimum wage, and Missouri's ballot initiative system, to overturn both measures. Voters rejected Proposition A, to keep the right-to-work law, by a two-to-one margin in a special election in August 2018; three months later, they supported Proposition B, for a $12 minimum wage, by nearly the same margin. Reported expenditures by Proposition B's supporters totaled just under $7 million, making the ballot initiative cheap relative to its impact.

After Minneapolis and St. Paul passed $15 minimum wage laws in early 2018, municipal policy proposals slowed (Table 1). Instead, campaigns moved to ballot initiatives in the 2018 elections, and to legislatures with unified Democratic control in 2019. The 2018 ballot initiatives in Michigan, Missouri, Arkansas, Colorado, and Arizona stand out primarily for producing binding votes on minimum wage laws in states where Republican control of some or all of government deterred legislation. More subtly, and perhaps more important, these campaigns were small, informal, and relatively low in terms of required funding. For example, Colorado Families for a Fair Wage, which coordinated the campaign in support of the successful Amendment 70, had a budget of just under $5 million, derived primarily from cash support and in-kind support from unions. The campaign to collect signatures to place Amendment 70 on the ballot, however, was decentralized and grassroots-led (Doussard 2020). After July 2018, Colorado Families for a Fair Wage employed four staff members and drew principally on volunteers (Doussard 2020). The resulting minimum wage law covered 150 times as many workers as SeaTac's Proposition 1—a good result for total campaign spending just four-and-one-half times higher than in SeaTac. Similarly, Arkansas Issue 5 came to voters due primarily to the efforts of activist Little Rock Attorney David Couch, and passed on a campaign budget of $1.5 million. These ballot measures drew indirectly on the Fight for $15, converting broad public support for higher wages into electoral success.

Activists typically trade a lower minimum wage for public support when they introduce ballot initiatives. Near-consensus support for a $15 minimum wage among campaigning and elected Democrats makes such trade-offs unnecessary when the legislative path poses no barriers. Passing a $15 minimum wage was a first order of business for new Democratic majorities in Illinois, New Jersey, and Connecticut in 2019. These campaigns stand out for the comparative lack of organizing they entailed. The lead-up to the adoption of a $15 minimum wage in Illinois entailed one major day of legislative debate by the House labor committee (the first author testified during the hearing). Plans to recall major witnesses in advance of the full house vote never materialized because they were unnecessary: the bill passed both chambers with minimal testimony, and the governor quickly signed it into law. The $15 bills in New Jersey and Connecticut followed a similar process, and Maryland's law differed only because both legislative chambers overrode the Republican governor's veto of the bill. This caps the minimum wage's transformation from controversial, labor-intensive policy to routine business.

MINIMUM WAGE POLICY ENTREPRENEURSHIP AND THE CURRENT HORIZONS OF ELECTORAL POLITICS

The national Fight for $15 campaign uses a template uniquely well suited to the task of moving policy at the state and local level. Based in cities, the Fight for $15 movement builds *national* awareness about the problems of working poverty and low pay. Symbolic strikes and protests in Chicago, New York, and other large cities simultaneously targeted local elected officials and the broader attention of the public and policymakers. Drawing upon this national focus and a set of general discourses about low-wage work, activists selectively localize political struggle and contest (Figure 8).

The current horizons of minimum wage activism are effectively the horizons of electoral politics: minimum wage campaigns succeed where elected officials face electoral incentives to raise the pay floor. The geographic unevenness of these horizons may at first appear to constitute a drawback. In reality, the ability to move minimum wage policy in most receptive legislative arenas constitutes a remarkable victory for community and labor organizers long shut out from activism at the federal scale.

	SEATAC 11-2013	SEATTLE 6-2014	CHICAGO 11-2014
Background	SeaTac Airport union organizing campaigns (2000s, 2010s) Community outreach and door knocking under Fight for a Fair Economy (2000s, 2010s)	Community outreach and door knocking under Fight for a Fair Economy (2000s, 2010s) Protests, including 2000 WTO protests and annual pride parade	Failed 2006 living-wage law Postrecession networking among unions and community organizations Chicago Teachers Union organizing
National policy entrepreneurs	National Employment Law Project, Economic Policy Institute, Center for Economic Policy Research, Service Employees International Union, UC Berkeley Labor Center, Interfaith Worker Justice		
Key local policy entrepreneurs	Working Washington, Puget Sound Sage, United Food and Commercial Workers Local 21, Service Employees International Union Local 775, Service Employees International Union Local 6, Teamsters Local 17, Honest Elections Seattle	Working Washington, Puget Sound Sage, Casa Latina, SEIU Local 775, Socialist Alternative, city council candidate Kshama Sawant, Fair Work Center, $15 Now	Grassroots Collaborative, Women Employed, Brighton Park Neighborhood Council, Just Pay for All Coalition, Action Now, SEIU Healthcare Illinois-Indiana
Problem stream *Activists drive attention to economic inequality*	National Fight for $15 campaign Low wages and working conditions at SeaTac airport (the largest employer) Problem definition circumvented by ballot initiative	National Fight for $15 campaign Local Fight for $15 strikes Growing income and housing inequality Democratic Socialist city council candidate Kshama Sawant champions $15 minimum wage	National Fight for $15 campaign Chicago Teachers Union strike Fiscal austerity; growing work and housing inequalities
Politics stream *Activists compel elected officials to act*	Circumvented by ballot initiative Required voter signatures and high voter turnout	Threat of legally binding ballot initiative predisposes elected officials to bargaining Sawant's candidacy steers attention to minimum wage Fight for $15 members organize mayoral town halls and speeches Organizers force mayoral candidates to publicly address minimum wage	Non-binding ballot initiative documents broad popular support for $15 "Mayor 1%": Long-term organizing makes inequality a liability for Rahm Emanuel Pending 2015 election forces Emanuel to address his weakness

	SEATAC 11-2013	SEATTLE 6-2014	CHICAGO 11-2014
Policy stream *How commitment to act becomes legislation*	Circumvented by ballot initiative	Mayor-elect Murray establishes working group National policy organizations draft legislation and testimony Organizers maintain outside pressure Unions threaten binding ballot initiative if working group fails Business representatives on working group negotiate with "radical" and "moderate" labor factions	Emanuel establishes large working group with little labor representation Working group holds public meetings; workers and community organizations testify Fight for $15 continues outside pressure: Reports, strikes, events Emanuel's representatives see high minimum wage as competitive win
Policy result	Comprehensive law: Two-year phase in to $15 minimum wage Earned sick time standards Anti-wage theft measures	Two-tier minimum wage: For employers of 500+: Four-year phase-in For employers of <500: Six-year phase in; tips and health costs count towards wage	Lower minimum wage with food service cut-outs: Phase in to $13 by 2019 Tipped wage rises to half value of the full minimum wage Amended to $15 by 2021 after Emanuel leaves office
Reproducible campaign components	Ballot initiative	Campaign drew on popular discontent with inequality Campaign used elections to make candidates accountable	Symbolic pressure: Organizers converted non-binding ballot initiative and weak mayor candidate into threats Working group with public forums Use of worker testimony to push opinion
Barriers to reproduction	Resource-intensive campaign Circumvents rather than controls the three streams Requires binding ballot initiative	Required the threat of a binding ballot initiative Benefited from epiphenomenal Sawant candidacy	Few obvious barriers to reproduction

FIGURE 8. Policy entrepreneurship in the Fight for $15

Understanding the Fight for $15 movement as a case of policy entrepreneurship helpfully draws attention to the movement's strengths and achievements, and to the potential to expand minimum wage advocacy techniques into other arenas. Several innovations underpin the movement's success. First, the national fast food strikes gave popular discontent with economic inequality a focus and an outlet. The campaign's second innovation was to support a network of city- and state-level campaigns capable of making the minimum wage a *political* problem for elected officials. The most common mechanism here was the election cycle. Just as national policy entrepreneurs use turnover in electoral control to generate momentum for their proposals, economic justice coalitions used mayoral races to push candidates to endorse the minimum wage. This simple tactic represents a significant innovation: as recently as the mid-2000s, economic justice themes featured either rarely or not at all in municipal elections. By 2014, every mayoral candidate in a large U.S. city voiced support for a double-digit municipal minimum wage.

Those minimum wage proposals often became law thanks to the campaign's third major innovation, the development of a national policy network. During the neighborhoods era, early municipal reformers faced the daunting task of developing from scratch policy proposals to use limited municipal powers for economically distributive ends. Minimum wage activists instead drew on shared national resources. The National Employment Law Project, Raise the Floor chapters, affiliates of the Economic Policy Institute's EARN Network, and other national-level resources provided draft legislation, legal advice, and testimony. The involved task of lobbying city council members benefited from the SEIU's coordination of the national Fight for $15 campaign, which allowed union organizers and researchers to systematically learn lessons from both failed and successful campaigns.

Together, these innovations provided the Fight for $15 with strategic options and tactical availabilities that go far beyond those charted for national-level policy entrepreneurs. At the federal level—the level from which virtually all scholarly knowledge about U.S. policy activism originates—the three streams of policy entrepreneurship operate independently of one another (Cairney and Jones 2016; De Leeuw, Hoeijmakers, and Peters 2016; Jones et al. 2016). Building a national network of urban coalitions helps minimum wage activists to control all three streams. They used the strikes to set the agenda, local coalitions to support progressive candidates who injected minimum wages into municipal politics, and their national policy network to supply bills and testimony.

The Fight for $15 campaign itself required substantial resources, and it cannot drive change in regions lacking the institutions, voters, and cities that give it strength. Yet the campaign provides infrastructure, tactics, and models for addressing economic inequality at the level of cities and states. High minimum wages draw the most attention from the press and the public, but activists have increasingly moved to address other, more complicated economic issues, including wage theft, paid sick days, universal prekindergarten, and fair scheduling legislation. Advocacy for these issues draws on the same basic template as the Fight for $15, but faces additional challenges in messaging, coalition building, and policy development. The minimum wage now succeeds where the coalitions who support it are strong, but effective advocacy on these other measures requires additional campaign innovation—innovation that remains in process, incomplete, and to date little documented.

5

Good Jobs for All

TARGETED HIRING FIGHTS RACISM AT WORK

The details of structural racism have evolved, but not the issue's fundamental obduracy. Racial inequality remains one of the constants of urban political economy (Massey and Denton 1993; Wilson 1996; Sugrue 1996). Thus, organizing for good jobs in communities of color has been a nearly constant struggle since the Great Migration. Civil rights organizers focused their energies on desegregating public employment and creating affirmative action programs to remedy historical disparities in the good jobs of the Fordist era. In the wake of civil unrest of the late 1960s, community-based organizations experimented with new approaches to community economic development that leveraged federal and philanthropic resources to make investments where banks would not (Halpern 1995, chap. 2). War on Poverty organizations in their various incarnations also sought to build the employment skills of inner-city residents to address their limited credentials and perceived deficiencies in the labor market (Weir 1992).

In more recent years, organizing efforts have linked economic justice and racial justice, from living-wage campaigns to "Ban the Box" measures. The locus of jobs-based organizing has shifted as the character of the "good jobs" problem has evolved, and as new institutional levers for influencing access to those jobs come into sight. Efforts to prioritize marginalized populations—especially communities of color—for new jobs resulting from public actions are a through-line of this work. *Targeted hiring* policies move local governments from passive to more active roles in the labor market, using the *quid* of their public construction, contracting, and economic development activities to achieve a *quo* of job creation for their structurally unemployed residents. Targeted hiring policies take a variety of forms, from procedural requirements to use local employment services to outcomes-based goals and mandates for local residents or marginalized

APPROACH	ELEMENTS
First source hiring	Requires employers to recruit from publicly funded employment services on a "first source" basis, usually for a limited duration
Opportunity plans	Requires employers to specify actions, and often targets, to support person of color, women, and local worker hiring
Local hire	Requires employers to achieve a defined share of jobs/hours worked by residents of the local jurisdiction
Priority hire	Requires employers to achieve a defined share of jobs/hours worked by residents from disadvantaged/underrepresented populations or geographies

FIGURE 9. Principal targeted hiring approaches

populations (Figure 9). As such, they pose a different set of challenges to urban policy entrepreneurs.

How do organizers and urban policy entrepreneurs translate chronic conditions of racialized labor market exclusion into windows of opportunity to institutionalize policy change? We show that policy change around targeted hiring can occur when economic and racial justice (ERJ) coalitions expand the discursive frames around access to good jobs to forge broader alliances, and when urban policy entrepreneurs leverage investment and job creation opportunities to pressure political leaders into action. In comparison to the minimum wage, targeted hiring policies demand more local customization and implementation, which has caused them to fall short in practice. Still, where the stated ends of target hire policies often disappoint, they provide a means for building power to press local governments to move on two of the long-run goals of urban justice movements, dismantling racist labor market structures and reversing community disinvestment. Successful organizing for targeted hiring requires opportunistic mobilization within the political stream to attach a viable local policy solution that satisfies the demands of a mobilized community seeking justice at work.

TRANSLATING ORGANIZING INTO ACTION: THE RISE AND FALL OF CHICAGO FIRST

Organizing efforts to expand access to good jobs must navigate extremely difficult conditions in order to achieve policy change. Not only must organizers name and take on the powerful institutions and actors that perpetuate racist labor market outcomes, but policy entrepreneurs need to offer effective policy models that will bend job creation and distribution toward more just outcomes. To do so, they must combine "outside game" strategies to build power with "inside game" strategies to meaningfully change institutions.

Chicago's experiment with targeted hiring policies in the 1970s and 1980s illustrates both the possibilities and constraints. The four-and-a-half-year tenure of Mayor Harold Washington from 1983 to 1987 (see chapter 2) originated in organizing around jobs and economic development. Propelled by a multiracial coalition allied with reform-oriented white progressives, Washington's campaign drew upon a neighborhood-based movement for community economic development that had emerged over the preceding decade, challenging the downtown-, real-estate-oriented growth coalition with an equitable development platform that emphasized neighborhood development, industrial retention, and workforce investment (Clavel 2010; Alexander 2007).

"Local hiring" was a central pillar of the Washington administration policy platform. The second policy listed in *Chicago Works Together*, the administration's guiding policy document, was "Local Preference in Buying and Hiring," calling for the creation of a "First Source" program. His administration justified the policy in race-neutral terms, emphasizing return on public investment:[1]

> Chicago's development activities should benefit the City's own businesses, workers, and neighborhoods first. Jobs are retained and created for Chicagoans when investments, purchases, and training resources assure that a substantial portion of their rewards will remain in the City. (City of Chicago 1984, 7)

The Washington administration launched a "First Source Task Force" in 1985 led by the Chicago Jobs Coalition (CJC), which represented community-based employment and training programs around the city. Over the course of 1985 and 1986, the task force studied policy models in other cities. The task force report, issued in late 1986, recommended a two-pronged policy: one part would cover "permanent" jobs supported by economic development incentives and city contracting activities, and a second would focus on construction jobs tied to city-assisted projects. The particularities of construction labor markets—the transitory, project-based nature of work, federal and state mandates for "prevailing" wages on publicly funded projects, the governance of skill formation and labor market entry through registered apprenticeships connected to building trades unions, and importantly, its extreme histories of racial and gender exclusion (Sugrue 1996; Baran 2018, 306–19)—made interventions in this sector highly complicated and contested. For this reason, when the "Chicago First" program launched in January 1987, it focused initially on permanent (nonconstruction) jobs, such as jobs with airport vendors.

The proposal for a Chicago First construction jobs hiring policy drew fierce opposition. Construction contractors called the requirements "official intimidation" of employers, saying the proposal was bureaucratic and wasteful in light of their own outreach and diversity efforts with construction trade unions.[2] Chicago's construction trade unions had their own history of excluding black workers, leading to multiple civil rights complaints in the 1970s and 1980s. Faced with this opposition, the Chicago First Construction Jobs program never got off the ground. The death of Harold Washington in fall 1987 dissipated whatever momentum existed toward the program. Meanwhile, the remainder of the Chicago First program operated under the city's Mayor's Office of Employment and Training until Mayor Richard M. Daley's administration quietly killed it in 1991. Concerned advocates working through advocacy organizations like CJC attempted throughout the 1990s to rebuild elements of Chicago First, drawing considerable foundation interest and support to experimental models of neighborhood-based hiring networks and workforce development (Schrock 2015). The rise and fall of Chicago First illustrates the importance—but in this case, also the inadequacy—of organizing and advocacy in compelling institutional change.

LESSONS FROM FIRST-WAVE TARGETED HIRING

Chicago's experience with targeted hiring highlighted several key challenges that would burden future attempts to build successful programs. The first was the search for successful models in other cities to address local problems. Beginning with Portland, Oregon, in 1978, progressive mayors had experimented with targeted hiring as a way to address the chronic need for good jobs within communities of color

(Schrock 2015). In the 1970s, many cities sought to connect their federally funded employment and training programs more directly to job creation efforts (Van Horn, Beauregard, and Ford 1986). Others sought to address the collapse of Nixon-era construction industry affirmative action initiatives through more blunt policy tools (Baran 2018). Boston's Resident Jobs Policy, initiated in 1979 by Mayor Kevin White as an executive order and later passed as a city ordinance, required 50 percent of construction hours on city-funded projects to be worked by city residents, 25 percent by racial minorities, and 10 percent by women. But compared to other policy areas discussed in this book—or later models discussed in this chapter—these policy innovations diffused informally, through localized search processes conducted by advocates or mayoral task forces.

The second challenge was the amount of energy consumed by the policy implementation apparatus around targeted hiring. Effective implementation required a robust public-sector labor market intermediary that could credibly identify and prepare workers for job opportunities, while at the same time linking back into disadvantaged communities who were most often left behind by job creation efforts. This work consumed scarce local government resources. The architects of Chicago First recognized the challenge and advocated placing the program inside the city's Private Industry Council to foster the "image and reality of a private sector guided program"[3] with potential to raise private sector resources to augment public funds.

Finally, Chicago's experience demonstrated the resistance targeted hiring faced from employers and often construction trade unions. Resident hiring policies in Boston and Camden, New Jersey, faced vigorous Supreme Court challenges based on Commerce Clause and Privileges and Immunities Clause[4] concerns (Baran 2018, 343–57). Furthermore, the Supreme Court's 1989 *Croson* decision invalidated set-asides for minority business enterprises (Baran 2018, 333–42), which impacted cities' use of race in their targeted hiring programs. Although a few cities like Boston, Cleveland, and Washington, D.C., managed to keep their resident hiring requirements, by the 1990s most cities had either abandoned their targeted hiring policies or substantially defanged them in favor of process-based language that simply asked employers to make a "good faith effort" to utilize local hiring programs. Scholars argued that this fated policies like first source hiring to become a "dead letter," nominally on the books but without meaningful municipal support, staffing, or, critically, community support (Douthat and Leigh 2017). In more recent years, targeted hiring policies have become targets of state-level preemption efforts, part of the broader conservative assault on local policy autonomy.

GET IT IN WRITING: THE COMMUNITY BENEFITS AGREEMENT MODEL

In the 2000s, the community benefits movement revived targeted hiring in direct response to the frustration felt by low-income communities to the weakening of first-wave policy efforts (see chapter 2). Renewed private investment in central cities created jobs—usually, low-wage service-sector jobs—while employers continued to shut out local residents for the limited number of good jobs they created. Community benefits organizers also addressed the related problem that new developments displace long-term residents.

The model of community benefits agreements (CBA) demanded that developers compensate community residents for projects that received public subsidies or land-use approvals, and win the consent of impacted local communities. By negotiating directly with developers, community members could sidestep legal restrictions facing local governments to hold developers accountable for outcomes. Targeted hiring was one among many typical provisions in a CBA (Gross, LeRoy, and Janis-Aparicio 2005, 10). Others included (1) living-wage requirements for new jobs created; (2) community social space, such as child-care centers or parks; (3) mitigation of environmental impacts; and (4) affordable housing.

This breadth expanded the range of potential allies for CBA organizing. For example, living-wage provisions helped to engage labor unions, especially service-sector unions that were actively fighting the erosion of job quality in retail and hotel sectors while looking to expand into other areas like security and janitorial services. This model of raising the floor while expanding access to the pool of improved jobs through targeted hiring is one that later coalitions would successfully emulate.

Unlike first-wave targeted hiring policies, CBAs did not require sympathetic leadership in city hall. In fact, they emerged as a response to entrepreneurial state strategies that made aggressive use of tax increment financing and other public finance tools to stimulate reinvestment. Well-organized community benefits coalitions identified the important leverage points in the development process, applying pressure strategically on elected officials and members of key boards to build power to bring developers to the table.

Despite these benefits, the clear limits to the CBA model have limited its diffusion. First, agreements require significant organizational resources to complete, especially when the question of who represents the community invites conflict. Second, negotiating terms with developers, and achieving necessary public approvals, can take months or years, elevating organizational exposure to risk: interviewees with advocacy organizations in both Seattle and Denver recounted their organizations spent over a year working to build momentum on a CBA for a development project that ultimately collapsed with the 2008 recession. Although the process served to build power and organization within the community, it nonetheless consumed an unsustainable amount of time and energy on the part of community members.

CBAs thus require an organization with the capacity to negotiate with developers. Without an umbrella organization such as the Los Angeles Alliance for a New Economy (LAANE), individual community-based organizations or coalitions have to scale up their work to manage a community benefits agreement—a rare feat that requires significant financial and staff resources. Since the mid-2000s, the Partnership for Working Families (PWF, recently renamed PowerSwitch Action) has been the primary institutional mechanism for diffusing the CBA model. As of today, there are PWF affiliates in more than twenty cities, many of which are active in CBA organizing efforts.

Finally, the institutional structure for local development impacts communities' capacity to build sufficient power to compel developers into CBA negotiations. Chicago's political structure, for example, gives local elected officials and appointed boards almost unchecked authority over development. As a result, community organizing efforts around large new developments are often undermined or co-opted. The Gateway Project, a large mixed-use development connected with the Illinois Medical District (IMD) on Chicago's Near West Side, illustrates the problem. In 2014, the Community Renewal Society (CRS), a membership organization of churches and other faith-based and grassroots organizations, began working with West Side organizations to make good jobs available to long-term unemployed residents of high-poverty, high-unemployment neighborhoods.[5] CRS and its

West Side Community Benefits Coalition partners first asked IMD board members to insert community benefits language in the project's pending RFPs. When that failed, coalition members showed up unannounced and with local media in tow to a public hearing in September 2015, with plans to pressure elected officials about the use of TIF funds on project construction. IMD responded by suspending the public hearing and proceeding to finance the project without TIF support. An independent public authority, IMD green-lit the project without land use approvals from the City—excising one of the community advocates' main leverage points in the process. The coalition then shifted focus to a county hospital redevelopment on the Illinois Medical District site. They were thwarted when a county commissioner *who had initially encouraged them to organize* called a press conference to announce that he himself had negotiated a CBA on behalf of the community. This reversal highlights the common problem of politicians co-opting CBAs (Wolf-Powers 2010).

"FAILURE OF GOOD FAITH": SAN FRANCISCO ADVOCATES PUSH BACK ON LEGAL CONSTRAINTS

By the late 2000s, the CBA movement had reinvigorated grassroots organizing campaigns to intervene on behalf of communities of color and was recording numerous victories. But those victories needed to be continually negotiated, as opposed to being codified in local policy—policy that required enforcement and accountability. A breakthrough solution to this challenge came in San Francisco, through intersectional organizing around the needs of low-wage workers in an increasingly unaffordable city, and communities of color who were not sharing in the boom. The conditions driving this boom—new private investment, which helped to support new public investment—offered policy entrepreneurs pathways to drive policy change that were lacking in first-wave cities like Chicago.

On paper, San Francisco did not need a new law. It had both a 1990s-era First Source Hiring program for entry-level jobs in economic development and construction projects, and a Local Hire policy that pledged to achieve 50 percent resident share of job hours on public infrastructure projects. But like many such policies from that time, they were toothless and weakly enforced. In September 2010, Chinese for Affirmative Action (CAA) and Brightline Defense (BD), an advocacy group focused mostly on environmental justice issues, issued a report showing that the City had achieved less than half of that goal. It argued in stark terms:

> The "good faith efforts" approach has clearly failed to achieve the City's local hiring goals, and targeted hiring mandates are a *legal and powerful* tool for San Francisco to utilize going forward. (Chinese for Affirmative Action and Brightline Defense Project 2010, 2, emphasis added)

Undertaking these efforts in the wake of the Great Recession was noteworthy for several reasons. First, local governments seeking stimulus prioritized capital projects with the potential for construction jobs. The 2009 American Recovery and Reinvestment Act (ARRA) had funded state and local governments for projects in areas like clean energy, which in some places had stimulated local organizing efforts around "green-collar jobs" (Ho and Hays 2011). The CAA/BD report called attention to the fact that the City of San Francisco had plans for $27 billion in investment in its 2011–20 Capital Plan, which it cited as an "extraordinary opportunity" to address deepening poverty and unemployment in the city's disadvantaged communities.

But the timing also complicated efforts to win construction trade union support for inclusionary hiring efforts. Recession-induced unemployment in the trades made hiring mandates particularly controversial. San Francisco's trade unions featured less racial conflict than their Eastern and Midwestern peers, but many remained "old school" in their hiring networks, as one organizer indelicately put it.[6] Yet thanks to City-led efforts to build preapprenticeship networks during the 2000s, some unions were open to local hiring mandates.

In the policy stream, convincing the City's legal staff of the legality and defensibility of the local hire mandates was a bigger challenge. As the organizer put it, "The usual response from the city attorney's office to the idea of setting enforceable limits was 'We can't do that.'" Indeed, the coalition's analysis found that City attorneys had been removing even the weak "good faith" language from many public works contracts over fear of court challenges (Chinese for Affirmative Action and Brightline Defense Project 2010, 17). CAA/BD proposed an alternative: the City could establish and enforce local hiring mandates based on its role as a "participant," rather than a regulator in the construction market

WAVE	KEY ELEMENTS/ DRIVERS	CONTRIBUTIONS	TENSIONS/ LIMITATIONS
First wave policies 1970s/1980s	Context of urban disinvestment Civil rights organizing Progressive mayors Informal diffusion	Linkages to federal employment programs	Legal challenges leading to "dead letter" policies Construction unions as opponents
Second wave 1990s/2000s	Context of urban reinvestment Community benefits organizing Entrepreneurialist mayors Diffusion through Partnership for Working Families networks	Focus on organizing, coalition building Focus on enforceability and accountability	Resource intensity of CBA organizing Potential for co-optation
Third wave 2010s	Targets public investment Racial justice organizing Neoprogressive mayors Semiformal diffusion through localized search	Institutionalization within local governments Nuanced targeting approaches Construction unions as partners	Local implementation capacity State preemption threat

FIGURE 10. Waves of targeted hiring policies

(Cantrell, Jain, and McDaniel 2013; Baran 2018). This persuaded several members of the Board of Supervisors (San Francisco's City Legislature), who passed the Mandatory Local Hire ordinance in 2011. It went into effect without the signature of then mayor Gavin Newsom, who organizers described as "tepid" about the law. Despite its origins in these unique circumstances, the decision to enforce hiring standards through the city's role as a participant in the construction market made the San Francisco model ready for export (Figure 10).

TARGETED HIRING AS ADAPTABLE LOCAL POLICY RESPONSE

San Francisco's passage of Mandatory Local Hire reignited targeted hiring as a progressive policy tool. In one sense, it was a classic policy stream innovation: San Francisco's actions created a model ready for travel across urban policy networks, much like the minimum wage. The policy's actual diffusion, however, was more limited and less formal. Although national organizations including PolicyLink heralded the ordinance, the San Francisco campaign organizers were more often contacted by individual activists than organizations working through national networks. Baltimore was one such city; in 2013, its city council passed a local hire ordinance, over the objections of city attorneys and over the mayor's veto. New York City followed a year later with an executive order creating the HireNYC program. But rather than copying and pasting, each city adapted the targeted hiring approach to reflect the contours—and in many cases, the capacities—of the local context. San Francisco's model depended on having a City-level agency that was committed to robust implementation, with the resources to monitor and report detailed, project-level outcomes. An agency official in Baltimore described their approach as "raw" in comparison, owing in part to their inability to track certified payroll from contractors.[7]

The multiple streams framework of policy analysis emphasizes that a new policy innovation is on its own neither necessary nor sufficient to spur action. Urban policy entrepreneurs, working in and with ERJ coalitions, need to take strategic action in both the problem stream and political stream in order to create "coupling events" that unlock windows of opportunity to move legislation (Figure 11). In the problem stream, their task is to take a chronic issue whose problem framing seems relatively straightforward, albeit stubbornly so—racial disparities in access to "good jobs"—and build some sense of urgency to find an answer. In some cases, this means building out complementary problem framings that link the racial disparity problem to broader problems of job quality (e.g., the linking of living wage and targeted hiring), suburbanization, or environmental sustainability. This has the effect of bringing new allies into the coalition, and allowing advocates to make arguments based on more than just appeals to racial justice.

Forcing action within the political stream becomes the necessary piece of the puzzle for organizers. For organizers working in communities of color, the potential benefits in terms of jobs and incomes need to be tangible in order to muster a requisite optimism that new coalitions and new organizing strategies might transcend legacies of disappointment, broken promises, and community mistrust. Organizers rarely have the ability to call forth such targets on their own, but their

	ROLE OF UPES	NEW ORLEANS – HIRE NOLA	SEATTLE – PRIORITY HIRE
Problem stream	Data analysis to demonstrate need Alternative/complementary problem framings	Data center analysis driving "black jobs crisis" narrative STAND "Black Workers Matter" campaign	City-funded data analysis showing low share of city residents on projects Sustainability framing to engage white liberals Analysis of long-term construction labor shortage
Policy stream	Identification of existing policy models Adaptation to local conditions and institutions	Mayoral task force examining models from other cities PolicyLink, Emerald Cities Collaborative as policy intermediaries	City council task force to analyze policy tools and past outcomes Local PWF affiliate, UCLA Labor Center as intermediaries
Politics stream/key coupling events	Organizing around large projects, especially public investments	Airport project as organizing device—Community RFP process	Rainier Beach park project as organizing device for community coalition Major infrastructure projects, including Elliott Bay Seawall Replacement

FIGURE 11. Urban policy entrepreneurship in New Orleans and Seattle targeted hiring campaigns

responses when such opportunities do arise are critical to the political stream. In that light, case studies of cities where organizing has resulted in targeted hiring gains need to be understood as contingent outcomes that reflect a combination of local conditions of possibility, and strategic action on the part of actors on the ground. We turn to those cases now.

HIRE NOLA: COMMUNITY ORGANIZING FORCES NEW ORLEANS MAYOR'S HAND

New Orleans is renowned for its rich history and unique culture; unfortunately, persistent, racialized inequality is a deeply entrenched part of both (Woods 1998). Once a vibrant port, New Orleans now thrives on tourism, with low-wage service jobs in restaurants and hotels shaping a dualized labor market exhibiting one of the highest rates of income disparity, both vertically and by race, in the United States. This context of chronic racial inequity across multiple dimensions of urban life serves as an important backdrop for community organizing around ERJ. The passage of the City's "Hire NOLA" program in 2015 illustrates how organizers can use data and public investment opportunities to build pressure for local officials to act on chronic problems.

The inflection point was Hurricane Katrina. The resulting devastation, which disproportionately impacted New Orleans' black neighborhoods, gave way to a contentious, decade-long process of reconstruction, one that attracted billions of dollars in new public, private, and philanthropic investment, and drew idealistic young professionals (Ehrenfeucht and Nelson 2013) and immigrant construction workers, who disrupted the equilibrium state of racial inequity. Katrina's aftermath also saw new community organizing through organizations like ACORN (Whelan and Strong 2018) and the New Orleans Worker Center for Racial Justice (NOWCRJ), which was founded in the wake of Katrina to organize day laborers (Keegan 2020). NOWCRJ serves as an umbrella organization for several ERJ projects, including Stand with Dignity (STAND), a grassroots organization of black workers and families.

By the early 2010s, Mayor Mitch Landrieu, who fashioned himself as a white progressive concerned with racial justice, was talking about a "New New Orleans" built on inclusive development. But the data and lived experience of communities of color belied the claim. A 2013 report showed that 52 percent of working-age black men were unemployed or out of the labor force (Sams-Abiodun and Rattler 2013). That statistic, combined with rising violent crime in 2014, fueled discussion of a "black jobs crisis." In response Landrieu unveiled, with support from national foundations, an Economic Opportunity Strategy with provisions for anchor institution engagement, new workforce intermediaries, minority entrepreneurship, and business development resources—but no proposal for, or commitment to, targeted hiring.

But ERJ coalition members sought to ensure that targeted hiring remained on the agenda, with their organizing focused on new public investment. In 2014 the City undertook an expansion of Louis Armstrong Airport. After a contested RFP for a half-billion dollar construction contract led the New Orleans Aviation Board to reassess the project in 2014, a coalition of community groups led by STAND launched their own "Community Evaluation Commission" composed of fourteen individuals from community and labor organizations across the city. They held a public hearing in August of that year, in which the two lead bidders for the airport project were invited to respond to a questionnaire about their track records and plans for community benefits (which came to be called the "community RFP" process). Neither participated, so the Community Evaluation Commission proceeded with its own assessment of the bids on community-friendly criteria, scoring contractors for "commitment to community targeted hiring," setting a goal that qualified local residents would work 40 percent of all hours. The list of qualifying criteria was expansive: receiving public assistance, living in public housing, having low income or a criminal record, or being un- or underemployed (New Orleans Airport Expansion Community Evaluation Commission 2014, 35). The winning bidder committed to invest $2 million into workforce training programs, but with no guarantee of work at the end (McClendon 2014).

Landrieu's initiative, announced just a month later, did not commit to targeted hiring. But his administration established a task force to explore a local hiring policy, which included representatives from STAND and other coalition members, as well as construction trade unions. The decision to exclude targeted hiring from the mayor's initial strategy likely reflected anticipated concerns over local businesses' response. The Landrieu administration focused instead on improving the workforce training and intermediary system serving the construction industry, a way to prepare for inevitable claims from (white) contractors that job-ready (black) workers were unavailable.[8] But the community RFP process was important in focusing political attention on the issue. Building off the emergent Black Lives Matter movement in late 2014 and 2015, STAND began using "Black Workers Matter" as a rallying cry to build momentum around their agenda for ERJ (Keegan 2020). The pressure that STAND and their coalition brought was focused on ensuring that whatever programs or policies emerged would be more than symbolic politics, delivering meaningful opportunities to black communities that had been consistently shut out from the city's reconstruction.

Nearly a year later, in fall 2015, the Landrieu administration unveiled the "Hire NOLA" proposal, which included provisions for oversight and enforcement that community groups sought, provisions for living wages and apprenticeship utilization that construction trade unions sought, roles and resources for workforce providers, and importantly, negotiation over hiring target levels that businesses and the community felt they could live with. The program drew on national organizations like PolicyLink and Emerald Cities Collaborative to learn from models in other cities. By the time the Hire NOLA proposal reached the New Orleans City Council in December 2015, it had been through the sausage grinder of bargaining. In testimony to the city council, STAND members expressed qualified support for the proposed ordinance, while raising deep concerns about the need to strengthen enforcement and accountability (Williams 2015). Despite those concerns, Hire NOLA passed unanimously.

Hire NOLA began in January 2016, and applied to all City-funded construction or economic development projects exceeding $150,000. It combined multiple targeting elements—a "local hire" requirement of 40 percent, a "priority hire" requirement of 20 percent disadvantaged workers (defined by income levels or barriers to employment),[9] as well as a "first source" requirement obligating contractors and subcontractors to utilize City-funded workforce development providers as a first source on new hires. Hire NOLA was paired with a Living Wage Ordinance that applied to City contractors related to both construction and nonconstruction activities, which broadened the political coalition driving it.

Hire NOLA faces challenges from both without and within. In 2017, organizers mobilized successfully to stop a legislative attempt to preempt the law; preemption remains an ongoing threat.[10] But the lack of clear accountability mechanisms impedes advocates in monitoring outcomes. STAND's influence has not extended to other employment policy goals. As in many Southern states, Louisiana's legislature thwarted local policy efforts, something that the community and labor groups behind Hire NOLA are seeking to address through their "Unleash Local" campaign.

SEATTLE'S PRIORITY HIRE: ORGANIZING RESPONDS IN A DIVERSE, INEQUITABLE BOOMTOWN

Whereas New Orleans conforms to conventional scholarly understandings of racial inequality—black central city, white suburbs—that prevailed in the decades of "urban crisis," Seattle corresponds to a different manifestation of racial capitalism against which organizing efforts take place. Seattle, like New Orleans, experienced significant growth and new investment during the late 2000s and after the Great Recession. But unlike New Orleans, Seattle's growth was heavily fueled by the technology sector, which brought waves of capital investment and highly educated migrants to the region. The city of Seattle experienced rapid population growth during the 1990s and 2000s, with accompanying displacement of low-income communities of color, especially in South Seattle (Gibson 2004; Houston 2019). These developments helped to fuel a revitalized labor movement to contest this inequality (chapter 4).

Seattle has complex racial dynamics, and inequalities (Hwang 2020). The region's initial white settlement in the nineteenth century coincided with immigration by Asian and Pacific Islanders. Those communities have further diversified, but also polarized, through the more recent in-migration of highly educated technology workers from East and South Asia. Black migration to the region began in the 1940s to support military production, and is now supplemented through international migration from Africa. In this century, continued expansion in manufacturing, service, and construction has drawn Latinx migrants. And Native American and Alaska Native tribal communities have long comprised a small but significant share of Seattle's population. By 2010, 32 percent of Seattle's metropolitan population identified as nonwhite, with no single racial/ethnic group representing more than half of that share. This diversity meant that organizing efforts had to engage across race and class, often on the ground in low-income neighborhoods and inner suburbs.

Seattle's construction trades had their own long history of racial exclusion. Immigrant communities find work in lower-wage residential construction, but high-wage unionized construction trades remain white dominated. Early organizing efforts in the 1990s and 2000s sought to build workforce training pipelines into the construction sector through preapprenticeship programs. However, the limits of these supply-side interventions were clear: they contained no requirements for contractors to hire from these training providers.

The political importance of environmental sustainability created openings for organizers to build power by linking targeted hiring into a movement for "green-collar jobs" in the late 2000s. In 2008, a longtime community activist and union electrician, Michael Woo, started the organization Got Green as a project of a community-based organization in South Seattle, and began organizing to access employment opportunities in the emerging residential energy efficiency market (Got Green Project 2010). The City of Seattle was using a portion of its ARRA funding in 2009 and 2010 to support residential energy efficiency retrofits. Energy efficiency work was historically low paid and exempt from federal prevailing wage requirements, and among the construction trades, the Laborers Union became very engaged in efforts to organize and win "community workforce agreements" with local governments that would ensure union-scale wages in exchange for inclusionary hiring provisions. The boom was short lived. Federal incentives and funding support for energy efficiency initiatives diminished by 2011 and 2012, leaving many of the newly trained workers unemployed and underemployed. This outcome reinforced the narrative that interventions on labor supply would not work without mandates for inclusionary hiring.

Woo's coalition, the Construction Jobs Equity Coalition, turned its attention to the lack of diversity in publicly funded construction work. They drew media attention to the lack of neighborhood residents and Seattle workers employed on a City-funded park renovation project in Rainier Beach, a racially diverse, low-income neighborhood in the city's South End (Minard 2013). From 2012, the coalition lobbied members of Seattle's City Council for local hire provisions resembling those recently passed in San Francisco. At the time, the city council was dominated by "white liberals" whose support for business interests could be tempered by appeals based on environmental sustainability. An early supporter on the city council, Mike O'Brien, told a local newspaper "Local hire is an environmental issue. It reduces commutes and improves urban sustainability" (quoted in Minard 2013). And as in San Francisco, major pending public infrastructure investments, such as the $200 million Elliott Bay Seawall Project, provided a focal point for organizing.

Their organizing coalition combined three key organizations: Got Green, Laborers Local 242, and Puget Sound Sage, the local Partnership for Working Families affiliate.[11] Woo and Got Green were the operational center and public face of the initiative, capable of turning out community residents for rallies and protests. Sage had a citywide constituency and technical capacity to bring policy knowledge to the table through its connections with partners in the Bay Area and Los Angeles, where community benefits organizing and targeted hire efforts had been advanced.[12] Both organizations depended on the Laborers, who brought an ability to work the inside game within the building trades, to overcome resistance to policy measures that would operate alongside Project Labor Agreements (PLA) between the trades and the City to provide additional layers of accountability.

The City Council responded by creating a Construction Careers Advisory Committee task force in September 2013, which brought various public-sector, community, labor, and industry stakeholders together to analyze the problem and review potential approaches.[13] Much like the minimum wage, the push for targeted hiring used the so-called Seattle process to produce a consensus policy that could achieve legislative approval. Elected officials wanted answers to several basic questions, including the outcomes of previous city construction projects and the number of new workers the trades were likely to need in the near future. These questions shaped the problem framing. On the first point, the analysis by UCLA Labor Center (2014) found that only 6 percent of hours worked on City-funded projects were completed by city residents, and only 3 percent by residents of low-income communities in Seattle. This finding reinforced the narrative that City funds were "leaking" out to suburban communities, a race-neutral problem framing that helped sell the idea with white constituencies. Meanwhile, a separate analysis of the construction workforce "pipeline" projected significant workforce shortages in the construction trades in the years to follow. This finding helped to allay concerns, especially within the building trades, that new targeted hire requirements on City projects would come at the expense of opportunities for existing construction trades workers. What resulted was a more durable problem framing that allowed organizers and advocates to make the public case for targeted hiring along multiple discursive lines that were less dependent upon normative appeals to racial justice.

Overcoming contractor opposition to targeted hiring required effectively countering the Associated General Contractors, the trades' main lobbying arm. The contractors argued that targeted hire requirements would actually *limit* contractors' ability to hire a diverse workforce, by limiting their ability to draw on their own apprenticeship and training programs.[14] But their opposition carried little weight on its own. More troublesome was the opposition of the minority contractor community. Although they were initially part of the coalition, frictions emerged during the task force over PLA requirements to work through union apprenticeship programs, many of which had spotty track records of bringing in and retaining workers of color, especially African Americans.

The task force completed its work in 2014 and introduced a "Priority Hire" bill in the Seattle City Council. It required all City-funded construction projects of $5 million or greater to achieve a minimum of 20 percent of hours worked by "priority workers," which were defined as geographies (ZIP codes) of economic distress (i.e., low incomes, high poverty rates, low educational attainment) within the city of Seattle and King County. This definition was necessary because of state constitutional limitations on affirmative action in public sector hiring and contracting passed in the 1990s. The bill established aspirational but essentially unenforceable goals for hiring women and racial minorities.

A crucial piece of the Priority Hire bill was a Project Labor Agreement provision that required signatory unions and nonunion contractors to prioritize workers from "priority" geographies. For construction trade unions in particular, this upended seniority-based dispatching rules that worked against women and workers of color. The trades disliked the exacting detail on hiring, but community members successfully pushed back on any effort on their part to water down the language, recognizing it was important to "get it in writing."[15]

Even as the bill came to vote in January 2015, final negotiations continued over key provisions. One particular sticking point was the number of core workers that nonunion contractors could bring onto jobs before going through union dispatch procedures. The figure in the bill—five core workers—was higher than activists wanted, but revisions reduced it to three, with two apprentice-level workers coming from priority geographies, approved preapprenticeship programs, or "an individual who furthers the City's aspirational goals for women and people of color."

In comparison with the New Orleans case, the Seattle Priority Hire program has achieved greater community involvement and transparency in program implementation. Unlike Hire NOLA, the Seattle Priority Hire Advisory Committee includes significant representation of community advocates, including lead organizer Michael Woo and a staff member from the Rainier Beach Action Coalition. The City publishes detailed reports of project-level hiring outcomes annually.

DIFFERENT GROWTH, DIFFERENT OUTCOMES

Economic growth and real estate investment shaped the targeted hiring campaigns in both New Orleans and Seattle. However, differences in the *type* of growth led to different framing messages, advocacy coalitions, and policy results. In New Orleans, deep-seated, historical racial disparities were exacerbated by waves of post-Katrina public and private investment, with organizers countering a narrative that the city was rebuilding itself into a new, more inclusive economy and community. At the same time, groups like STAND successfully leveraged Mayor Landrieu's stated commitment to racial inclusion to create policies to hold white-dominated businesses and institutions accountable, in a context where trust on the part of the black community over the delivery of results—i.e., jobs—was understandably lacking.

In Seattle, waves of investment from the city's extended tech boom were prompting uncomfortable questions about the racialized dimension of inequality in the region. In the early 2010s, Seattle and King County were among a vanguard of local governments that were prioritizing racial equity as a lens for their policy work, which likely increased the efficacy of racial justice appeals, especially among liberal and progressive white officials. As an organizer involved in the Priority Hire campaign described it:

> I would say that (racial justice) was absolutely central (as a narrative).... Unions don't always use a racial justice analysis or focus. It was not a campaign about union jobs.[16]

By calling out the institutional racism that was embedded in the City's public works construction program, the coalition was able to bring local government officials and reluctant construction trade unions to the table to negotiate for meaningful language around inclusion. The sophistication of Seattle's targeting language, which also prioritized low-income communities in inner-suburban jurisdictions, represented a meaningful acknowledgement of how central city gentrification had impacted displaced communities of color, and demonstrated solidarity with those communities in ways that further the cause of racial justice.

CONCLUSION

"Good jobs" will continue to serve as a rallying cry in marginalized communities, even as issues at work compete with police violence, gentrification, food security, and other crises. Restricted access to the limited supply of jobs that provide income, dignity, and stability stands alongside residential segregation as one of the main mechanisms through which the United States creates separate and unequal societies. Yet a good job cannot undo generations of systemic racism. In that sense, targeted hiring can be understood as a limited, tactical response to a broader problem of racial inequality in contemporary cities, one that attempts to leverage the modalities of real estate and infrastructure-led growth toward less disparate outcomes.

How this chronic condition of racialized employment disparity rises to the top of the agenda for organizers—and ultimately for public officials—is the subject of this chapter. Periodic commitments by local officials to target employment opportunities to historically marginalized groups have invariably resulted from organizing efforts in those communities. Yet historically, those commitments were often more symbolic than substantive, and rarely challenged the power and prerogatives of businesses or trade unions that controlled access to those jobs. Where communities did push, white interests sought recourse in racist legal structures that denuded the power of local governments to regulate economic activities toward antiracist ends.

The emergence of ERJ coalitions has fostered a reemergence of organizing around good jobs, one that brings the institutional power and resources of labor unions together with the grassroots energy of community-based organizations. The CBA model responded to the failures of first-wave targeted hiring policies by recentering organizing efforts and demanding accountability for outcomes, but implicitly let public officials off the hook to demand results themselves. The move to reinstitutionalize targeted hiring that began with San Francisco's 2011 Mandatory Local Hire ordinance placed pressure squarely on mayors, city councils, and agency officials to be accountable for breaking down institutional racism and delivering ERJ through their public investments.

Despite the elegance of "local hire" as a rallying cry, the policy tools in support of targeted hiring are invariably complicated, and off-the-shelf models from one city need considerable adaptation to the political and institutional environment of another city. In both New Orleans and Seattle, local task forces labored to learn the intricacies of how existing programs elsewhere worked, and how to implement them in ways that met the demands of local advocates while avoiding excessive legal exposure for local governments. In both cases, advocates inside City Hall who were committed to racial equity goals served as critical allies to ERJ coalitions, helping them to overcome internal resistance and external opposition, and ensuring successful implementation within public sector agencies.

As with the Fight for $15 movement, "winning" at City Hall on targeted hiring does not always serve the ultimate goals of building and sustaining community power. To put it bluntly: promising good jobs and delivering good jobs are not the same thing. Even where local officials are publicly committed to using the tools of local government to redistribute opportunity to marginalized communities, they are almost equally allergic to opening themselves up for accountability to outcomes. And it is just as difficult for communities themselves to stay at the table, especially where no table is established for communities to engage agency officials, contractors, and labor organizations.

At the same time, targeted hiring represents a renewed platform for challenging the long-term impacts of public investment (and disinvestment) on communities of color. Targeted hiring organizing efforts make affirmative demands of local governments to take responsibility for their own agency and complicity in reproducing racist labor market structures that reinforce disparate access to good jobs in the urban environment. By linking up with labor unions, they expand the conversation beyond a scarcity framework, by expanding the pool of good jobs. And fundamentally, they invite a conversation about *who benefits* from public investment that challenges a liberal consensus about the "limited interest" of cities in promoting growth.

6

Justice beyond Work

SICK DAYS, FAIR SCHEDULES, AND THE
POLITICS OF SOCIAL REPRODUCTION

The devastating economic contraction from 2007 to 2009 goes by the shorthand "Great Recession" in popular parlance. That name belies the pain it caused. To low-income communities, communities of color, and activists engaged in the work of justice, the Great Recession wasn't just deep, but functionally intersectional. The direct economic impacts of the recession were by themselves devastating: the economy shed a greater share of its jobs than at any point since the Great Depression, and it did so after six years of economic growth that delivered gains to investors at the expense of workers. Yet statistics about work and income fundamentally mischaracterize the lived experience and human fallout of an economic disruption that extended from work to neighborhoods, households, and life writ large. When the Covid-19 pandemic ended the eleven-year economic expansion that followed the Great Recession, workers had recovered many of their paid hours, but lost control of their time. Cheap, statistically sophisticated scheduling software and the surplus of job seekers for available work had made radically, systemically flexible scheduling a central workplace conflict (Greenhouse 2012).

When the Great Recession announced itself to the world during the 2008 financial crisis, employers had already succeeded in making work less secure and less generously compensated. The thirty-five-year employer war on "standard"—permanent, full-time, well-compensated—jobs had borne significant fruit. Wages for the bottom quarter of workers were falling rather than stagnating (Doussard, Peck, and Theodore 2009). Union busting and the aggressive introduction of contingent (that is, temporary, on-call, contract, or otherwise precarious) jobs ate away at the share of the workforce who could expect stable work, stable pay, and benefits (Mishel et al. 2012). And part-time work, once a tactic reserved for businesses with seasonal swings in labor demand, continued to displace opportunities for full-time work (Hatton 2011; Appelbaum, Bernhardt, and Murnane 2003). The recession unbalanced the ratio of unemployed workers to job openings, which rose from 1.5:1 in mid-2008 to nearly 7:1 (Bureau of Labor Statistics 2020).

Employers used their leverage to institute extreme scheduling flexibility for retail and service workers. Demands for "just-in-time" scheduling, the staffing equivalent of "just-in-time" inventory or manufacturing production, added a new set of problems for part-time workers (Gleason and Lambert 2014). Armed with sophisticated scheduling software and pressured by corporate mandates to cut paid hours, managers started to demand "open availability" as a condition of accepting job applications. In order to even win consideration for a position, workers had to pledge their availability to work any shift on any day, a condition to which employers invariably added the expectations that schedules were posted with one or two days' notice, that schedules could change at any time, and that workers could be sent home (or told not to clock in) when customers were scarce (Doussard 2013; Luce and Fujita 2012). As they faced cutbacks and penury in other parts of their lives, workers lost the flexibility to plan transit, childcare, and bill paying. In the process, they lost access to the basic capacities and services that could in principle facilitate escape from low-wage work and income insecurity.

Policy entrepreneurship provides the opportunity for workers to partially relieve these problems through municipal legislation. However, the nature of the problems themselves weakens many of the techniques behind minimum wage and targeted hiring laws. Workers and the public know intuitively what high pay and stable work looks like. The problems of paid time off and flexible scheduling by contrast exist more clearly in the law than in the popular imagination. As a result, campaigns to address these problems cannot draw on broad popular movements to demand change. At the same time, the policy solutions they propose require far more technical and legal negotiation than minimum wage and targeted hire legislation. Accordingly, the reform process elevates the role of both national and local policy entrepreneurs, who attempt to accomplish with the law what broad social movements set out to win before the New Deal. The result is incomplete: earned sick time and fair workweek laws take meaningful but limited action against the problems they address. To fully address these problems, however, current policy efforts will need the support of a broad and vocal movement to address workplace issues outside of wages.

Historically, visions linking justice at work to other kinds of justice—affordable housing, education, and most incisively, freedom from environmental harms—sprung not from studies of work but rather from studies of communities of color, conducted by scholars of color (Morello-Frosch, Pastor, and Sadd 2001; Darden 1990). This divide stands as a major problem for resurgent urban social movements allied with organized labor: how do movements built around the power of labor unions focused on hourly pay and narrow measures of job quality expand into movements that address the fuller range of related inequalities?

This chapter investigates the effectiveness of policy entrepreneurship for achieving justice *beyond* work by exploring policy campaigns that focus on the links between work and home. Earned sick time and fair workweek campaigns advocate policies that give workers more control over their time and more freedom to negotiate their household obligations. They face challenges in the problem stream, where activists struggle to concisely represent family care obligations and stable work schedules as problems that compel action as directly as does hourly pay. At the same time, the complexity of scheduling practices works against policy entrepreneurs developing simple solutions.

We have no choice but to approach these issues in a more speculative and open-ended way than we did the minimum wage and targeted hires. The networks that compel action on work-and-home policies and public finance are networks in the making. Because the problems they address lack popular recognition, grassroots organizing and problem definition play a smaller role in their campaigns. This elevates the role of policy entrepreneurs, who apply their skills to the daunting problem of devising legal solutions to complicated problems with little policy precedent.

ORGANIZING A PROBLEM WITHOUT A NAME

The Fight for $15 could draw upon commonsense understandings about good wages and the familiar machinery of minimum wage laws. Advocacy for targeted hiring programs benefited from tapping widespread understanding that communities of color had been locked out of the limited quantity of good jobs. By contrast, working conditions do not connect as directly to existing repertoires of activism and political imagery. The work of social reproduction itself—cleaning, caring, cooking, overseeing children's social and intellectual development—has historically been difficult to organize because it is "invisible" work (Daniels 1987). The limited repertoire of organizing strategies for making this work visible focuses not on household duties, but on *paid* work in caring professions, and on undervalued professional work that can usefully be conceptualized as invisible (Cross, Borgatti, and Parker 2002; Jurow et al. 2016; Whiting and Symon 2020).

Nightmarish scheduling arrangements, which are nightmarish because they make invisible work impossible to reconcile with wage labor, occur outside the boundaries of defined workplace regulations and impact communities and households whose problems lack standing as agreed-upon public problems (Hatton 2017). As a high-ranking union official counted off on his fingers to the authors, "We organize for the $15 minimum wage because (1) everybody understands it and (2) everybody knows that even if it's $15, it's not high enough." Other problems on the job, he explained, lack the same clarity. People who hold good jobs have limited experience of just-in-time scheduling, and no shared vocabulary, body of law, or social conventions for translating the narrative details of bad jobs, such as working without schedules, suffering injury, or working while sick, into a clear picture of a problem to be solved. Appealing to the abstract standard of "good" jobs does not clearly motivate or organize action.

To appreciate the slippage between the Fight for $15 campaign's demands and the web of problems confronting low-wage workers, just talk to a worker. When the authors asked striking fast food workers why they risked their jobs, most of them spoke not of low pay, but of scheduling. At the height of the Great Recession, securing more than twenty paid hours of work per week constituted a significant victory for most Fight for $15 participants. Even in windfall weeks that delivered thirty or thirty-five paid hours on the job, the problem of scheduling nullified many of work's benefits. Workers scheduled and began paying for childcare, only for managers to send them home early or cancel their shifts altogether. Chain retailers began to schedule "clopens"—split shifts in which a worker closes the store at the end of the day, then returns before dawn to open—with increasing frequency, all while budget cuts forced cutbacks in off-hours transit.

These problems mock the idea that work alone can support basic human needs, yet they do not appear in conventional labor statistics or discourse.

Thus, low wage workers' demands for justice on the job—justice *at* work—inevitably require the pursuit of justice *beyond* work. The separation of the two, the very idea that activism in the realm of material production can be separated from activism focused on social reproduction, is an artifact of the same twentieth-century settlements that urban social movements are struggling to overcome. Federal agencies—the Department of Labor, Department of Housing and Urban Development, Department of Health and Human Services—and the data they collect separate work from housing, education, health, and well-being. Yet before the Wagner Act inaugurated the current, workplace-centered model of union organizing, unions organized communities (and advocated for social housing) as much as they did workplaces (DeFilippis, Fisher, and Shragge 2010). The New Deal focused unions and scholars on workplace elections and on federal-level policy bargaining, to the detriment of the practice and theory of broader organizing (Montgomery 1989; Katznelson 1982).

The enterprise of separating work and home and collectivities also rested on the postwar era's racial and gender hierarchies (Hanson and Pratt 1995; Peck 1996; McDowell 2011, 1991; McCall 2001; Parker 2017). Hourly pay—the $15 workers now seek—provides a reliable measure of job quality only under certain conditions presumed to be normal (literally, "standard" in labor market terminology): one job per worker, and one waged laborer per household (McDowell 1991). Celebrations of, and nostalgia for, Fordism came at the cost of neglecting the social hierarchies that circumscribed access to stable work. Scholarship based on the lives and the experience of women and communities of color, and scholarship written by women and people of color, neither celebrated full-time, stable work nor conceptualized higher pay alone as a means to fuller and more dignified lives.

THE INCREMENTAL ADVANCE OF A POLITICS OF SOCIAL REPRODUCTION

The policy entrepreneurship networks engaged in issues of social reproduction developed in their current form in the late 1990s, in response to the Personal Responsibility and Work Opportunities Reconciliation

Act of 1996—the law with which Bill Clinton famously promised to "end welfare as we know it." Prior to Clinton's push to functionally eliminate basic welfare payments, Washington-based advocacy organizations took up antipoverty work as part of broader agendas focused on racial justice, civil rights, and political representation for marginalized social groups (Soss et al. 2011). Advocacy on poverty policy was only part of the portfolio of the most vocal and effective opponents of welfare reform (as the press labeled the abolition of Aid to Families with Dependent Children). Welfare reform spurred existing antipoverty organizations to pivot toward low-wage work, and led to the creation of several new advocacy organizations.

Marion Wright Edelman, the law's most vocal and damning critic, founded and ran the Children's Defense Fund, an organization devoted to childcare, disability advocacy, and education in addition to welfare access (Callahan 2015). The Center for Budget and Policy Priorities, which has advocated for alternatives to welfare reform, began as a broad budget analysis organization, pivoting toward poverty work as income inequality grew more apparent in the 1990s (Center for Budget and Policy Priorities 2020). Welfare reform also induced many organizations to shift focus to antipoverty work: prioritizing employment over income led to mounting public concern over the problem of working poverty (Shipler 2005). The Center for Law and Social Policy, which produces model sick time and scheduling legislation, began in 1971 with a broad commitment to social policy, but in its current form focuses on work and working mothers (Center for Law and Social Policy 2020). 9to5, a national organization active in state-level scheduling campaigns, began in 1971 as a women's professional advocacy organization but now focuses on low-wage work (9to5 2020). A more recent entrant, A Better Balance, was founded in 2006, as part of a successful effort to pass an earned sick time ballot initiative in San Francisco.

These organizations sponsored campaigns for paid sick days beginning in the mid-2000s, with organizers winning their first policy victory with a 2006 San Francisco ballot initiative (see Figure 12). Since the Great Recession, they have expanded into policy development and systematic, nationwide advocacy. The work is from the outset more difficult than advocacy for pay. In sharp contrast to the bright graphics illustrating the minimum wage's inadequacy,

PROBLEM	EXAMPLE FROM AUTHORS' FIELDWORK	COSTS TO WORKER	POLICY REMEDY
"Clopen": Late-night shift followed by the first morning shift	Miranda closes Earth's Bounty after midnight, waits more than an hour for a bus home, and must return before 6am to reopen.	*Opportunity costs:* Little chance to sleep Cannot provide care during dependents' waking hours *Lost time:* Infrequent off-hours bus and train service adds hours to commute	Minimum time between shifts Overtime pay rate for "clopening" $100 pay premium for "clopening"
Split shifts: Short shifts split by unpaid hours off	Keisha works 11–2 and 4–6 in the same retail job. She cannot work other jobs or return home in the space between shifts.	*Opportunity costs:* Gap between shifts cannot be used for work, study or care	Shift pay: minimum pay of at least four hours per shift
Early release: Manager sends worker home early	Desiree is sent home three hours before the end of her shift because retail traffic is slow.	*Direct costs:* Fewer paid hours Worker schedules and pays for unneeded childcare *Opportunity costs:* Cancelled shifts cannot be used to work second or third jobs Income variability and unpredictability impede household budgeting	Compensation hours: employer must pay for half of cancelled time
Call offs: Shift cancelled hours beforehand	Maria turns down a Thursday am shift at Retail Giant when her Young Fashions manager insists she work Thursday morning. On Thursday, the Young Fashions manager cancels the shift on one hour's notice.		
Off schedule: Employer limits or eliminates scheduled hours	Kemal asks his Sandwich Barn manager for Friday afternoon off, in order to care for his toddler son. The manager schedules him for zero shifts the following week "to make sure you have lots of time to look after your kid."	*Direct costs:* Large reduction in paid hours *Chilling effect:* Workers do not request raises, improved working conditions, extra hours, or favorable schedules	Opportunity to work: employer must offer new shifts to existing workers before hiring new workers Transparency: schedules must list weekly shifts and hours for all workers on payroll
Open availability: Employment conditioned on willingness to work all days and shifts	Annie's job at Forever Young only schedules 15–20 hours per week. Open availability prevents her from holding a second job to make up for the lost hours.	*Opportunity costs:* Worker cannot schedule second jobs, classes, doctors' appointments and basic household tasks	Advanced scheduling notice: Managers must post schedules at least two weeks in advance

FIGURE 12. Common scheduling challenges and consequences for workers. Source: Authors' interviews with low-wage workers in Chicago, St. Louis, and Indianapolis (Columns 1–3). Authors' analysis of existing fair workweek ordinances (Column 4).

advocacy materials for earned sick time and fair workweek legislation consist primarily of text. The statistics they invoke—that less than half of workers have the right to request a schedule, for example—come from informal surveys or back-of-the-envelope calculations, and they almost always skirt the central problem itself. The Bureau of Labor Statistics collects data on total work hours and total pay, but only for one job per worker, and it does not ask about split shifts, clopens, call-offs, or send-homes. Information about these very real and challenging problems comes in *narrative* form, where the details are devastating and the wordy whole is decidedly less than the potential sum of statistical parts (Figure 12).

Consider, for example, the representative challenges faced by Reggie, a striking fast food worker who explained his motivations to the authors over a hot chocolate on a cold February day in 2013. From 1997 through 2000, Reggie worked 80-hour weeks, split over two regularly scheduled 8-hour shifts at minimum-wage fast food restaurants. When a recession hit in early 2001, managers cut Reggie's shifts to 30 hours apiece, and cancelled employer-sponsored health insurance. Reggie continued to work those hours until 2008, when both franchises reduced all workers to a maximum of 20 paid hours per week and began to assign irregularly scheduled shifts. By 2013, Reggie worked a *total* of 25 hours per week, spread across a series of irregularly scheduled three- and four-hour shifts at two different establishments. He explained his motivations for striking this way: "I want respect from my managers, and I want to get my hours."

The difficulty workers face in both winning and using sick days constitutes a second problem, in terms of both life and organizing. Many low-wage retailers do not permit their employees to take sick days. At Earth's Bounty, an upscale supermarket on the North Side of Chicago, managers simply move sick workers from cash registers to jobs with limited customer contact, such as collecting shopping carts from the parking lot. At the Chicago Loop retailer Jenkins, sick workers "push plastic"—i.e., hand out credit card applications to customers as they enter the store. Miranda, a sales associate at Jenkins, works when she herself is under the weather, but often has to quit (or be fired) when her son falls ill and she cannot arrange childcare. Working for an employer who has a formal sick time policy, however, only helps marginally, due to the persistent threat of employer retaliation (Weil

2008). In the immediate aftermath of the Great Recession, short shifts and limited scheduling slots became their own discipline system: "If you do something your managers don't appreciate, like call off sick, they cut your hours on the next schedule," explains Yvonne, a Loop fast-food worker.

A third common problem originates in the difficulty of balancing multiple jobs with unstable schedules. Workers need high weekly hours to obtain economic self-sufficiency but can rarely sustain the logistical balancing act of fitting together multiple unstable work schedules. Consider the problems Jackie, another Loop sales associate, faced when she attempted to balance two jobs. In 2013, Jackie solved her hours problem by acquiring two separate 35-hour minimum-wage jobs with stable schedules, one in the early morning and one in late afternoon. This "perfect" arrangement lasted until Jackie asked the manager at her morning job to continue scheduling morning shifts, in order to clear the way for the afternoon job. "The minute I had that conversation, I was scheduled for *all* afternoon shifts. It was the most regular hours I ever got," she explains. After attempting to juggle the incompatible schedules for a month, she relented, quit the second job, and informed her manager she was back to a single paycheck. "I haven't been scheduled for a single afternoon since. Imagine that."

Statistical validation of these problems cannot come from federal data sources, which measure total hours worked without considering sick days, multiple jobs, or the length, frequency, and number of employment shifts. Scholars have responded by developing employer- and employee-based surveys that chart the extent and impact of just-in-time scheduling practices within participating retailers (Lambert, Fugiel, and Henly 2014; Gleason and Lambert 2014). The results show that scheduling software and firm-level restrictions on paid hours incentivize managers to shorten shifts (Lambert, Fugiel, and Henly 2014) and that women, people of color, and workers with lower levels of educational attainment are far more likely to suffer lost income and wasted expenses as the result of flexible schedules (Lambert, Haley-Lock, and Henly 2012). Unstable schedules also lead to diminished sleep, increased stress, and, generally, unhappiness (Schneider and Harknett 2019). The current challenge is less to understand or document these problems than to make them recognizable as problems upon which the political system must act.

WHAT'S THE PROBLEM? THE CHALLENGE OF FRAMING SOCIAL REPRODUCTION FOR POLITICAL ACTION

The complexity of workers' challenges with time works against efforts to render sick time and scheduling as broadly recognized problems. Prior to the Fight for $15, few community-labor coalitions mounted campaigns for earned sick time (Table 3) and only a single, New York City–based campaign focused on scheduling (Luce and Fujita 2012). Low-wage retail workers often complained about being sent home early, working while sick, and being forced to maintain "open" availability, but those problems took a clear secondary position to the basics of pay and job safety (Doussard 2013). Scheduling and sick time preoccupied Fight for $15 participants enough in the mid-2010s that local campaigns repeatedly tried to organize around the issues. Their attempts to frame the issue suffered from the complexity of the problems themselves and from the unclear position hours and family care occupy within the wage- and hours-based industrial relations framework authorized by the New Deal.

First, organizers opted to frame the issue as a moral one. Members of the predominantly female low-wage workforce, they argued, faced the impossible decision between earning money to support their loved ones and taking unpaid time to care for them:

> Everyone gets sick, but not everyone has time to get better. Every day, millions of working people in the United States face an impossible choice when they are sick: stay home and risk their economic stability or go to work and risk their health and the public's health. (National Partnership for Women and Families 2020, 1)

Alternately, proponents of earned sick time legislation focused on the threat that working sick poses to public health, a claim that resonated minimally before the Covid-19 pandemic:

> Businesses that don't provide paid sick time face the huge cost of lost business if they become known for infecting their customers. Nearly 90 percent of restaurant workers lack paid sick time, and "two-thirds report cooking, preparing, and serving food while sick." In a CDC study, 49 percent of food workers who had worked at least one shift while suffering from vomiting or diarrhea

Table 3. City and county earned sick time legislation

	LOCALITY (WORKERS COVERED 1,000)	WORK HOURS PER LEAVE HOUR EARNED	ENFORCEMENT	STATE (WORKERS COVERED, 1,000)
2006	San Francisco (59)	30	Office of Labor Standards	
2011	Seattle (150)	30	Office for Civil Rights	Connecticut (200)
2013	New York (1,200)	30	Department of Consumer Affairs	
2014	*San Diego (414)	30	Not specified	California (6,900)
	*Oakland (56)	30	Not specified	Massachusetts (900)
2015	Tacoma (40)	40	City finance director	Oregon (473)
	Philadelphia (200)	40	Not specified	
	Montgomery Cty, Md. (90)	30	Office of Human Rights	
	Emeryville, Calif. (5)	30	Not specified	
	Berkeley, Calif. (18)	35	Not determined	
	Pittsburgh (50)	35	Controller or other designee	
2016	Santa Monica, Calif. (12)	23-40	Not specified	Vermont (60)
	Minneapolis (62)	30	Department of Civil Rights	*Arizona (934)
	St. Paul (68)	30	Department of Human Rights and Equal Economic Opportunity	Washington (1,000)
	Los Angeles (650)	30	Office of Wage Standards	
	Chicago (460)	40	Department of Business Affairs and Consumer Protection	
	Cook Cty., Ill. (440)	40	Commission on Human Rights	
2017				Rhode Island (100)
2018	Austin (223)	30	Equal Employment Opportunity/Fair Housing Office	Maryland (750)
	San Antonio (345)	30	Metropolitan Health District	New Jersey (1,200)
	Duluth, Minn. (19)	50	City Clerk's Office	Michigan (no estimate) *#
	Westchester Cty., N.Y. (123)	30	Department of Weights and Measures, Consumer Protection	Nevada (no estimate) Maine (no estimate)
2019	Dallas (302)	30	Determined by City Manager	
2020				New York (2,600)

*Measure passed as ballot initiative; #State legislature intervened to weaken results of ballot initiative
Source: Authors' calculations from (National Partnership for Women and Families 2020) and Ballotpedia.

in the last year said that knowing they would not be paid if they stayed home influenced their decision to work while sick. If these ill workers get their customers sick, the business faces costs—decreased business, falling stock prices—from the loss of their good reputation. (Ziliak 2016, 1)

After 2015, advocates for earned sick time took yet another approach, this time tying sick days to the broader problem of family leave, and arguing for the technical fix of updating leave policies to match employment arrangements that continued to skew toward temporary, short-term, and short-hours:

> The way we work is changing and our laws must change with it. As workers increasingly find themselves in nonstandard, precarious, and insecure jobs, portable benefits—those that workers can take with them as they move from job to job or combine multiple sources of income—are increasingly essential. In the emerging future of work, portable benefits will be crucial to workers' economic security, to their job quality, and, ultimately, to their life quality. (A Better Balance 2018).

Campaigns for "fair workweek" laws—the moniker improves significantly on the prior handle of "predictive scheduling"—eschew these links in favor of a straight narrative approach to problem definition. The campaign messages reflect the role that women's professional and advocacy organizations play in fair workweek campaigns. Chicago's fair workweek coalition, for example, included local and national women's advocacy organizations (the Chicago Foundation for Women, the National Women's Law Center) as well as advocacy organizations for the feminized profession of social work and children's poverty programs:

> Low-wage workers and their families are struggling. Over the last decade, growing industries like retail, hospitality, and health care are creating an economy full of low-wage, no-benefit, part-time jobs with unreliable work hours. Corporate use of just-in-time scheduling is fueling massive under-employment and economic insecurity for working families.
> At the same time, workers endure debilitating stress due to

uncertainty about when they'll work and how much they'll earn each week. Unable to predict their hours or pay from day to day, hourly workers struggle to balance their job with college classes, enroll their children in quality child care, secure a second job, qualify for promotions, maintain healthy routines, or be there for their families. Women and workers of color, particularly in Black communities, are especially hard hit by the trend to structure hourly work in unstable part-time jobs. (Center for Popular Democracy 2019)

Collectively, these shifts in message, tone, and narrative strategy reflect a profound life problem that policy entrepreneurs struggle to convert into a recognizable policy problem (Figure 13). Better tactical skill and message-shaping acumen could perhaps resolve the problem, but that skill would need to overcome the broader disconnect between work and home in policy and discourse. Effective messages build on tropes that make abstract ideas concrete and that tie a particular problem to the dominant themes of American life—in the case of work, the imperative of economic growth (Fischer 2003). Imaginaries that center economic production while erasing or ignoring social reproduction shape the understanding of work, society, and politics in the United States, to an uncommon degree.

Critical approaches to this false conceptual division deploy a number of strategies for centering households, family, and the enormous range of work activities that public discourse does not acknowledge as work (Winders and Smith 2019). The task of making a compelling economic case for workers to have control of their own time and household obligations requires undoing this separation. That challenge places an unmanageable burden on tactical tropes and campaign messages. As Fischer and proponents of discourse analysis note, campaigns that advocate for positions this far outside the mainstream succeed not when they hit upon the right message, but rather when their supporting coalitions obtain enough power to amplify the message regardless of its secondary status (Fischer 2003).

Policy entrepreneurs engaged in the issues of earned sick time and fair workweek laws began in the late 2010s to add explicit racial justice dimensions to their work. 9to5, the national organization whose local affiliates introduce earned sick time and fair workweek legislation, states simply that "economic justice is racial justice is social justice."

PROBLEM	MORAL ARGUMENT	ECONOMIC ARGUMENT
Scheduling	*Unwaged work:* Fixed schedules support child-, family, and elder care. *Dignity:* Predictable schedules "reward work."	*Equity means growth:* An economy that "works for everyone" grows more.
Health care	*Equity:* Covering health insurance ensures basic rights and dignity for everyone.	*Efficiency wages:* Access to healthcare ensures productive workers remain on the job. *Public health:* Sick and unhealthy workers spread viruses and consume expensive emergency care. *Efficient economic growth:* States that pass Medicaid expansion minimize the shocks employers face from negotiating health insurance.
Sick time	*Rights:* It's a basic labor standard. *Justice:* Employers shouldn't punish workers for falling ill.	*Public health:* Sick workers will spread infection. *Efficiency wages:* Businesses lose skilled and productive workers when getting sick means quitting a job.
Transportation	*Equity:* Supporting public transit keeps the carless from being locked out of distant work opportunities.	*Externalities:* Firms and economies grow and diversify more effectively when people can circulate freely, fast, and cheaply.
Housing	*Citizenship:* Participation in politics and society rests on stable shelter.	*Externalities:* Expensive housing restricts the inter- and intraregional mobility on which efficient subnational labor markets depend.
Childcare	*Equity:* Universal prekindergarten ensures basic human development for all children.	*Efficiency:* Public childcare increases the workforce's size and the fit between workers and employers. *Long-term development:* Early childhood education will lead to a more capable workforce in twenty years.
Elder care	*Dignity:* Well-funded elder care allows individuals to age under ethical conditions. *Racial justice:* Well-funded elder care improves conditions for workers and residents of color.	*Efficiency:* Affordable elder care improves productivity by limiting workers' family burdens outside the job.

FIGURE 13. Problems and messages: How activists frame social reproduction challenges to low-wage work. Source: Authors' analysis of interview data and advocacy materials from A Better Balance, 9to5, the Center for Law and Social Policy, and the Center for Popular Democracy.

Scholars such as the Shift Project who use apps to collect scheduling data likewise prioritize race. However, none of the policy entrepreneurs active in this work identifies racial justice themes as the key to winning support for their agenda. Instead, they attribute success to their movement's current power to compel action from elected officials.

THE POLICY STREAM: NATIONAL ORGANIZATIONS, LOCAL LAWS

Since 2012, twenty cities and states have passed laws that mandate some form of paid time off, always in the form of paid sick days, and occasionally with additional provisions for paid vacation and family leave (Table 4). Like the minimum wage, laws mandating paid time off have the advantage of clear precedent in federal law. Since the New Deal, the Employee Retirement Income Security Act (ERISA) has induced employers to provide some paid leave for workers. We say *induced,* rather than *required,* because the mechanisms work indirectly and unevenly. ERISA provides no civil or punitive remedies for employers who do not make time off available to their workers. Instead, it offers tax incentives to those who meet time-off thresholds (typically amounting to just one week per year) that are the lowest in the industrialized world.

In addition to providing limited total amounts of time off, federal law contains numerous cut-outs that exempt (for example) workers at small businesses, farm employees, temps, contract workers, and many service-sector employees from accruing paid days off.[1] Thus, the majority of the paid time off laws passed since 2012 concern themselves primarily with closing loopholes and ensuring that most workers can expect to receive the meager benefits offered by law. Even so, recently passed legislation contains a highly varied and sometimes bewildering series of qualifications. Philadelphia's law exempts the health care industry, a prominent low-wage employer. Connecticut requires no time off for businesses with fifty or fewer employees. Other recent laws exempt local government, or federal employees, or both, and sometimes neither. The only clear legislative direction is to speed the rate at which workers accrue time off—to the still-low rate of one hour per thirty worked, which translates to about eight days off per year for a full-time worker. As we will show in some detail below, that constitutes an enormous hypothetical for an actually existing low-wage workforce whose members struggle to get as many as thirty hours per week.

Fair workweek policies exist in much smaller number, a fact that accurately reflects their novelty and low rate of success to date. Just six U.S. cities and three states have fair workweek laws on the books, and even that limited count creates a misleading picture: three of the laws do not cover food service and retail, the two industries most likely to insist that employees make themselves available to work any shift, any time, on any amount of advance notice. In fact, the existence of a fixed name, "fair workweek" laws, suggests a degree of internal coherence that the legislation itself lacks (Table 4). Proposed and enacted fair workweek laws introduce not a single regulatory change, but rather heterogeneous bundles of eight separate reforms (Cooke 2019):

Advance Notice of schedules
Advance Notice and Compensation for changes to schedule
Weekly Hours Estimate for all workers
On-Call Pay: Extra paid hours or higher wage rates for on-call shifts
Shift Pay: Minimum paid hours per shift
Part-Time Equity: Equal treatment for part- and full-time workers
Right to Request: A fair or predictable schedule
Right to Rest: A minimum number of hours between shifts, especially "clopens"
Opportunity to Work: Employers must offer additional hours to part-time employees before hiring new workers

These characteristics give fair workweek policy what policy mobilities scholars characterize as a high degree of "intrinsic mutation": where minimum wage law varies only in terms of the hourly rate and a handful of exceptional circumstances, we should *expect* fair workweek law to change as its proponents attempt to learn from past organizing campaigns and correct for problems in policy implementation (Peck and Theodore 2015).

National policy entrepreneurship networks shape final city-level legislation in some basic ways. First, although no national paid sick time or fair workweek legislation exists, national advocacy organiza-

Table 4. Development and diffusion of fair workweek laws

YEAR	MUNICIPALITY	TIME BETWEEN SHIFTS (HOURS)	NOTICE PERIOD (DAYS)	COMPENSATION FOR SHIFT CHANGE	COVERAGE THRESHOLD (MINIMUM # OF WORKERS) FOOD SERVICE	RETAIL	LODGING
2014	San Francisco*		14	4 hours pay	n/a	20	n/a
2016	Seattle	10	14	4 hours pay	500	500	n/a
	Emeryville, Calif. *	11	14		56	56	n/a
	San Jose*				35	35	35
	Washington, D.C.		21	4 hours pay	20 sites	5 sites	n/a
	New Hampshire			none	1	1	1
2017	Oregon	10	14	$500	500		
	New York City	11		$100	20	20	
2018	Philadelphia#	9	10	$250	250		
2019	Chicago	10	14	$200	200		

Grey shading: Fair workweek laws followed minimum wage legislation. *Ordinance passed via ballot initiative.
#Ordinance passed at same time as minimum wage legislation.
Source: Authors' analysis of fair workweek legislation passed in each jurisdiction

tions such as the Center for Law and Social Policy and the Center for Popular Democracy provide city-based activists with draft national bills that provide a template for local-level legislation. Second, staff attorneys at those national organizations provide answers to basic procedural questions about local laws: Do cities even have constitutional authority to regulate this? (Yes). Who enforces the law? (A local labor office and community organizations.) How do small businesses negotiate the mandates? (They manage.)

Over time, earned sick time and fair workweek laws make fewer concessions to employers. Tables 3 and 4 show a clear pattern of simplification and tightening standards as legislation progresses from a stage of initial compromise to stronger laws that omit fewer workers, cover more industries, and impose stricter penalties on noncompliant employers. Despite these successes, organizers and activists express reservations about the project of regulating the conditions of work through the law rather than workplace organizing.

Just-in-time scheduling has many varied causes: it's a strategic response to the surfeit of job seekers in low-wage labor markets (Doussard 2012); a desperate innovation created by retail managers who must meet unrealistic cost-cutting targets set by corporate headquarters (Lambert and Henly 2009); a matter of social norms and organization, including expectations about women's limited labor force attachment (Tilly and Tilly 1998); and a source of both competitively necessary flexibility and competitively unnecessary labor discipline in industries with unpredictable workflows (Doussard 2013). Even when unions win the ability to essentially write the law to deal with these problems, the results are speculative. They are currently winning the policy entrepreneurship process but making limited progress toward the bigger goal of work that provides dignity in workers' personal lives.

RIDING THE COATTAILS: SOCIAL REPRODUCTION AS THE NEXT STEP FOR MAYORS

At the height of the Fight for $15 campaign, fast food strikes appeared above the fold in major news dailies, featured prominently on national news casts, and joined Occupy Wall Street as symbols of America's deep economic inequalities. The problems of sick days and just-in-time scheduling never reached this status. Nevertheless, twenty cities now have paid sick time laws, and seven have passed fair workweek legislation. Policy entrepreneurs see their success in simple terms: they made inequality so substantial a political problem for elected officials that those officials had no choice but to act. Earned sick time and fair workweek laws passed as mechanisms mayors and city council members could use to dramatize their ongoing commitment to confronting their political weaknesses on the issue of economic inequality.

The slow and uneventful road these measures took to becoming law in Chicago provides an unusually clear window into the processes that compelled action. After securing a $13 minimum wage, Chicago's policy entrepreneurs maintained a public campaign to raise the minimum wage to $15, both to reach the peak wage soon and to eliminate the lower minimum wage for workers who receive tips. When labor organizers met with Emanuel's officials to discuss possible earned sick time legislation, their mandate was clear:

> When we first sat down with the mayor's policy people, it was all "De Blasio, De Blasio." "Does [New York mayor] de Blasio's law

say this? Does it do that? Is this what de Blasio's law does?" It's clear that he's taking such a beating in his popularity that he's really concerned to look liberal. (Interview, director, labor advocacy organization)

It's not like he's ever said "no" to our proposal. . . . I think that a lot of that's been influenced by De Blasio. . . . They seemed supportive of sick days from the start. (Interview, legislative director, advocacy organization)

When organizers grew dissatisfied with the speed of action from the Emanuel administration, they commissioned another nonbinding ballot initiative on earned sick time legislation, in the March 2015 primary election. It won 81 percent of the vote. Emanuel signed the law in early 2017, capping a short negotiation process with community and labor organizers. Even though Chicago's Earned Sick Time law took three years to pass after the minimum wage, sustained pressure on Emanuel's public image made organizers comfortable with the drawn-out process:

From the beginning, it was clear he had to pass this. The negotiation was about cut-outs and exemptions for businesses. The outcome was preordained. (Interview, director, legal advocacy organization)

This all fits austerity in City Hall. You can see a three-legged stool here: it's big with the working class, it costs nothing, and businesses could give a fuck. (Interview, director, labor advocacy organization)

The path to Chicago's fair workweek law involved continued pressure on elected officials—but not pressure about the fair workweek law itself. Soon after Emanuel's reelection in 2015, footage of Chicago police officers shooting unarmed teenager Laquan MacDonald in the back sixteen times undercut the mayor's political support. In 2018, the once-invulnerable mayor announced he would not stand for reelection. The race to succeed him dramatized the rapid change in sentiments among Chicago voters. The more conservative of the two candidates in the 2019 mayor election, Toni Preckwinkle, had used her powers on the Cook County Board to extend Chicago's minimum wage and earned sick time laws to more than 2 million residents outside the city limits. Her challenger, the victorious Lori Lightfoot, had prosecuted the officers who shot MacDonald and ran as an outsider. In a first, both candidates were black women, and both pledged support for a range of labor causes, including raising Chicago's minimum wage to $15. Even as Lightfoot took action on labor's agenda, however, organizers maintained pressure on her, going so far as to issue report cards giving the new mayor Ds and Fs on her first one hundred days (Quig 2019).

Community organizers attributed the ensuing legislative victory to their revised approach to power. Rather than attempting to win over individual city council members and the mayor, they used their memberships and connections to maintain broad pressure on everyone in power (Fulton and Doussard 2021):

> What I've kind of been learning from paid sick days is that community groups kind of have to take the issue direct to voters, direct to neighborhoods, to move the mayor. The alderman and the mayor aren't going to move unless it's safe to move something. And I think that [taking issues to voters] makes you a better coalition. (Interview, community organizer)

In the eyes of another activist, Chicago's fair workweek law had little to do with the issue of scheduling itself:

> Rahm's policy guy actually said "Why just paid sick days? What are other things we can be doing that matter to working people?" We declined to name it, though. We don't want them to negotiate paid sick days out for something else that's a lower priority.

These comments reflect the consensus position among organizers that earned sick time and fair workweek laws advance due to political pressure and, specifically, the same political pressure that yielded minimum wage laws. As with the minimum wage, securing commitments to pass the legislation moved negotiations to working groups charged with negotiating a policy solution with which all the involved parties could live.

The twin approach of pressuring elected officials from the outside and developing policies through negotiation within working groups has the added advantage of setting up additional campaigns. It also helps activists across cities to replicate the enviable opportunity San Francisco organizers have to revisit, revise, and rebuild earlier legislation (see above and chapter 5). Economic and racial justice coalitions put this power to use while working on earned sick time and fair workweek laws. Recent minimum wage victories had raised the challenge of cities struggling to enforce minimum wage laws for which they did not have workplace inspectors or protocols for identifying violations. Seattle established an Office of Labor Standards in 2014, as a result of pressure from organizers of the Fight for $15 campaign. New York, Chicago, Philadelphia, and others have followed by establishing their own offices—drawing on resources from national policy entrepreneurs, including a published labor standards "toolbox" (Round 2018). Chicago organizers describe the process both as a direct response to shortcomings in the implementation of the labor standards they won, and as an easy concession to win from municipal government. After working the technocratic process of tweaking earned sick time and fair workweek legislation, they successfully appealed to the mayor's representatives involved in that legislation on the good-government principal of smooth legal enforcement and administration.

PUTTING WORK IN ITS PLACE: THE CURRENT LIMITS AND LONG-TERM PROMISE OF URBAN POLICY ENTREPRENEURSHIP

Activism over working conditions currently yields policy victories despite organizers' failure to make the public recognize and act in response to inhumane scheduling practices. The fact that advocacy coalitions nonetheless secure support for paid sick time and fair workweek laws testifies to the current political power they hold. The barriers to building a politics of social reproduction with broad reach appear to lie with the problem itself. Other workplace regulations, including minimum wage laws, operate within the historically well-regulated and economically valorized world of wage labor, a world that provides ready-made measures for work's value and that has allowed activists to tap economistic arguments about the value of higher pay. The work of social reproduction, by contrast, remains invisible. There is no Bureau of Household Care to measure caring work, which is performed by household members without cash compensation or by care workers whose waged jobs confer little social status and less pay.

The diverse and contested imaginaries built around the work of social production limit the discursive tools policy entrepreneurs can bring to bear on the problem. That challenge is evident in the way activists continually try on and discard messages for their policies, which they have variously represented as solutions to contingent work, to the Great Recession, as a public health threat, as a drag on economic productivity, and as an affront to basic dignity. These messages proved adequate at times but did not create the breadth of policy opportunities that the Fight for $15 did.

The structure of the advocacy coalition for earned sick time and fair workweek policies also limits advocacy. The organizations overseeing policy development both nationally and locally have their roots in first-wave feminist movements focused on equity for professional women. The policy and professional focus of those organizations perhaps inevitably comes at the cost of organizing. Contrasting this structure to racial justice advocacy coalitions is instructive. For example, Chicago's racial justice advocates feature a number of direct organizing organizations, including Grassroots Collaborative, Action Now!, Southsiders Organized for Unity and Liberation, and Enlace Chicago. That same network includes a single organization devoted to women's issues, and that organization, Women Employed, does not conduct direct organizing. Limited capacity to engage gender inequalities—which are of course co-constituted with economic and racial inequalities—is a limitation of the current organization of advocacy.

Despite these limits, and the evident inability of organizers to define the problems of sick time and just-in-time scheduling in a way that resonates with the public, legislative victories on both issues continue. These successes owe to less durable forms of power: the current hold community and labor organizers have over candidates for office in large cities, and a robust legal policy network to provide model legislation, testimony, and answers to technical legal questions. The fact that the laws pass is significant, yet their impact is limited. Cities that enacted these laws quickly found that enforcement was a challenge (and often had to found new departments just to implement the rules). Particularly for fair workweek laws, these victories appear symbolic as much as practical. A more meaningful political and legal settlement for on-the-job problems that complicate social reproduction will ultimately require the movement to represent home, care, and control over time off the job as causes on equal footing with wages. Growing popular support for basic income programs provides some optimism, but the barriers to an effective politics of social reproduction in cities remain high.

These limits, however, do not mean that activism for justice beyond work has no clear path forward. In addition to developing policy solutions to the problems of family care and just-in-time scheduling, activists increasingly seek equity through the means of public goods: universal programs for social goods, and greater public investment in social programs that favor communities of color. Tax structures and shifts in public spending exist much further outside the typical worker's lived, tangible experience than does the drudgery of juggling schedules or attempting to reconcile irreconcilable demands to work for pay and work domestically at once. Despite those challenges, economic and racial justice coalitions continue to win policy change by strategically framing problems in their favor. These activities warrant investigation as a complement to advocacy for policies that reconcile work in home, not in the least because the key to victory appears to lie in the decision to foreground racial inequalities that generations of organizers had learned to bury.

7

"Wall Street Is a Racist Conspiracy"

RACIAL JUSTICE AND THE FIGHT AGAINST AUSTERITY

Workplaces are not islands. In order to eke out a living, much less realize one's full human potential, people need shelter, food, education, health care, family care, and transportation. Most of the world's industrialized states provide these basic resources to citizens as (supposedly) universal public goods. Actually existing democracies nearly always fail to meet these standards, but the question elsewhere is about the mismatch between aims and realities. The United States, by contrast, does not even claim to offer robust public goods. Furthermore, the ostensibly universal services that do exist, such as education, are riven by the same deepening inequalities against which citizens are furiously organizing today. Thus, winning a union, raising the minimum wage, and passing policies to guarantee some amount of sick time increase the possibility of winning a just society, but fall far short of providing the resources necessary to do so.

Justice movements in the United States often invoke the goal of "rebuilding the middle class," invoking a useful but limiting nostalgia for the political and economic arrangements of the post–World War II years. Postwar Fordism did provide material improvements and political power for workers. Even though the United States never invested in a welfare state to the extent of its counterparts, the basic provisions of the 1950s and 1960s—free or nearly free college education, pensions, public housing, welfare payments for low-income and unemployed workers, union representation for nearly two in five workers—supported citizens materially in ways that are unimaginable to younger generations. Yet Fordism still fell far short of providing a model or even an animating vision for a more just society.

U.S. Fordism was only adequate in comparison to what came before and after. Even at the height of the postwar boom, the United

States had persistently higher rates of poverty than other countries, weaker unions, and large segments of the population who saw few economic gains. The political foundation of Fordism was also extremely fragile. After 1948, the Taft-Hartley Act allowed individual states to "opt out" of the New Deal by attacking unions' finances (Peck 2016). Large employers, most notably the Big Three automakers, prevented universal health coverage by insisting on the socially and economically ruinous condition of tying health insurance to work. Political support for the stunted American welfare state rested on a shotgun marriage between Northern liberals and Southern conservatives who remained Democrats for vestigial reasons. Thus, politically durable support for U.S. Fordism functionally ended when the Republican Party's Southern Strategy separated the South from the Democratic Party (Perlstein 2008).

The most substantial limitation of Fordism as a vision for economic inequality results from the institutionalized racism and sexism on which the entire enterprise rested. Not only was the American welfare state weak in international comparison, but it also reserved the scarce supply of stable jobs, good housing, and quality education primarily for white citizens and men (McCall 2001). Invoking the economy of the 1950s or 1960s as a model for economic and racial justice (ERJ) coalitions calls for a return to a period whose formal economic rights could not compensate women and people of color for their diminished status and human rights. The Fight for $15, targeted hire programs, and movements for policies that align work with family care needs (chapters 4, 5, and 6) make significant but limited steps toward the goal of broader justice. The visions of justice embedded in each of these campaigns, however, require broader rights and resources than U.S. Fordism attempted. For organizers and activists, this increasingly means advocacy on public finance and fiscal austerity.

Austerity grew into a rallying cry for a range of political causes in the 2010s, but it has much deeper roots. Budget cuts in cities were part and parcel of the major transformations—deindustrialization, disinvestment, privatization—that in the 1970s initiated urban inequalities in their current form. Federal fiscal support to cities has fallen nearly continuously for fifty years: cities today receive less than one-quarter of their funding from the federal government (Center for Budget and Policy Priorities 2018). The resulting pressure on city budgets is both omnipresent and selective: investments in public education, social services, and public health have fallen virtually everywhere. Yet budgets for police and real estate development remain robust.

These realities make fiscal austerity an increasingly important target for ERJ coalitions, who cannot achieve their goals without the universal public goods people need to bridge the gap between unstable work and basic material needs. Such activism must confront two distinct challenges that make public finance an especially difficult organizing target. First, public finance is often bewilderingly complicated. Most people know too well what a bad boss or a bad job looks like, but financial details such as credit swaps, deferred pension payments, and tax increment financing (TIF) increments are abstract, intricate, and technical. This complexity poses a substantial barrier to building grassroots movements for fiscal fairness. Second, city finances cannot be standardized and compared in the same way that wages and basic working conditions can. The profusion of special districts and funds places most city budgets in webs of overlapping revenue sources and expenses. Each city designates, supports, and draws on funds from these districts in distinct ways, making apples-to-apples comparisons functionally impossible. This reality impedes policy entrepreneurship networks designed to move standardized policies and policy pieces across jurisdictions.

Nevertheless, policy entrepreneurship networks do provide an answer to these challenges, in the form of the ERJ coalition itself. While the byzantine details of city finances differ from one neighborhood, program, and district to the next, the underlying reality that city spending favors property owners, white residents, and their neighborhoods, does not. The post-2008 foreclosure crisis and the subsequent collapse of asset values for households of color highlighted these inequities in especially stark form. Activists responded by taking technical complexity out of their organizing message on austerity: simply and directly, they framed austerity as a problem of white supremacy itself. This discourse allowed them to take control of the problem stream that defined the political agenda on finance. It also supported movement building, by initiating and deepening relationships between ERJ organizations. These strong relationships placed coalitions in a position to act when windows of opportunity to address fiscal inequity opened.

Our plan for examining the work of ERJ coalitions against austerity reflects the heterogeneous issues and institutional arrangements that shape public spending. First, we focus on social and public goods, including elder care, childcare, prekindergarten, and basic education. These issues tie directly to low-wage work because fiscal austerity creates low-wage jobs by starving basic services of funding. They also tie to low-wage work indirectly: poorly funded and poor-quality basic services limit low-wage workers' ability to cover the gap between their wages and working conditions and life's basic needs. Second, we examine campaigns to reform TIF and regressive taxes. These campaigns target structural racism in the distribution of public resources and the structure of tax burdens—fiscal racism. *Fiscal racism* means that low-income households and communities of color bear the burden of funding public programs that redistribute resources upward toward services and investments in the built environment that favor white residents. Cruelly, it means that they also bear the burden of funding racist police forces.

The problems organizers take up in austerity and finance are heterogeneous, detailed, and complicated. The answer, however, is surprisingly simple. Prioritizing race and emphasizing racial justice messages works to both convert austerity and fiscal racism into actionable political problems and to assemble broad coalitions with the power to win changes. Accordingly, our approach here differs from prior chapters. We focus first on the broad problem stream related to austerity and race, then on the ways that individual campaigns negotiate politics and policy. The policy entrepreneurship at issue in these campaigns is an informal one in which participants address the way antiausterity campaigns frame issues rather than their legislative maneuvers. Some state-level policy campaigns, such as efforts to repeal or reform California's Proposition 13 and a plan to implement a progressive income tax in Illinois, generate potentially reproducible policy. Yet problem definition preoccupies activists so thoroughly that they monitor the messaging of those campaigns more than their legal maneuvers.

THE GREAT RECESSION: ACUTE AUSTERITY FOLLOWS A HALF CENTURY OF CHRONIC AUSTERITY

The Great Recession compounded fiscal austerity that Federalism had cultivated for decades. The brief uptick in social spending following the Johnson administration's War on Poverty quickly gave way to what was by the Great Recession a thirty-five-year norm of deliberate and systemic disinvestment from basic physical and social infrastructure (Kinder 2016). The resulting devastation for working people and low-income communities thus compelled the seemingly impossible course of finding place-specific and immediate solutions to a structural problem.

The fiscal constraints written into the U.S. Constitution and state constitutions complicate the challenge. U.S. cities and states rely primarily on their own tax collections for funding (Tiebout 1956) and—mortally threatening during recessions—they cannot run deficits. Continuous federal tax cuts add pressure to the budgets of programs ranging from physical infrastructure to education, shortfalls for which Congress compensated over time by creating "unfunded mandates": legal obligations for states to undertake work the federal government used to do, and to pay for it out of their own pockets. States responded by passing their own costs onto localities, where the buck finally stopped because there was no further level of government to which to devolve it (Xu and Warner 2016). On top of those problems, a majority of U.S. states passed tax and expenditure limits (TELs), measures that restrict local tax collection capacity, after 1980 (Wen et al. 2018).

The Great Recession began as a housing market problem and ended as an employment and consumption problem. In the process, it reduced collections of sales, income, and property taxes, the three principal sources of municipal income (Pagano 2013). The subsequent cutbacks to public spending were sudden, deep, and long lasting. In 2009 and 2010, nearly 90 percent of cities reported increased difficulty in meeting their basic fiscal needs; when the Covid-19 pandemic arrived to batter the economy in early 2020, U.S. cities had only just rebounded to their prerecession level of revenues, a full thirteen years after the prior peak (National League of Cities 2020). Municipal responses to recession often aggravated the underlying problem. Chicago, for example, patched a short-term revenue hole in 2009 by leasing the city's parking meters to Morgan Stanley for seventy-five years. The city burned through the $1.1 billion lease fee in thirty-odd months, and now faces more than a half century of reduced parking revenue (Ashton, Doussard, and Weber 2016). More subtly, a growing number of cities in this period exhausted their bonding capacity in order to fund basic physical infrastructure investments no longer financed by the federal government. Other fiscal problems too numerous to count followed this same basic structure. The challenge organizers faced was thus enormous and, like the prior challenges of deindustrialization and low-wage job growth, rooted in forces that lay beyond local control.

Despite these challenges, popular opinion continues to move toward demands for investment in people, with majorities of the public routinely voicing support for free college (Hartig 2020). Support for a federal basic income has also grown, to nearly half the population (Gilberstadt 2020). Antiausterity movements, from Occupy Wall Street to the successful demonization of Rahm Emanuel as "Mayor 1%," to current calls to defund the police in favor of investing in low-income communities, count growing portions of the public on their side. The language of antiracism plays a surprising and crucial role in this transformation.

PROBLEMS IN THE PROBLEM STREAM: "WE PRESENTED TOO MANY POWERPOINTS"

The complexities of finance pose enormous difficulties to any plan to organize systematic responses to austerity. Even the basic task of tallying a city's revenues and expenses requires analysts to understand foundational public accounting measures and the accounting methods of different funds, such as general and capital funds. Devolution, austerity, and the growth of fiscally entrepreneurial states complicate this picture (Harvey 1989a; Ashton, Doussard, and Weber 2016). Common organizing targets in today's U.S. cities include TIF arrangements (Baker et al. 2016), city agreements to privatize infrastructure and services (Ashton, Doussard, and Weber 2012; Kim and Warner 2016), publicly financed special authorities and agencies exempted from fiscal transparency requirements (Shi 2018), routine subsidies to developers and large employers, and a dizzying proliferation of public-private partnerships that spend unspecified volumes of resources with no public reporting criteria (Weber 2015). Each of these essentially bespoke agreements constitutes its own fiscal world, consisting of deal- and broker-specific accounting methods, measures, and reporting requirements. Organizers and organizing coalitions can with great difficulty decipher the finances of a given authority, TIF district, or detail, but the project of building a comprehensive picture of local finances from serial pieces of labor-intensive accounting remains beyond grasp.

Through the mid-2010s, organizers and activists responded to this challenge by attempting to become financial educators. In Chicago, early versions of this work included an activist-organized bust tour of TIF districts, in which participating journalists and elected officials were presented with alternative uses for TIF funds. The authors remember participating in several financial education trainings, including an ambitious event in which they presented a PowerPoint explaining economic base theory in Spanish to a room full of immigrant workers. Failed attempts to educate rank-and-file members on the technical complexities of financial information became a leitmotif of the period, as a Chicago organizer who began antiausterity education during the Recession explains:

> I think we were overly dependent on PowerPoints. We had to figure out how to make this into hands-on, experiential learning. The pieces of the [interest rate] swaps [Chicago negotiated on infrastructure asset sales], and all . . . It was really hard to figure out how much detail people needed.

A South Side organizer uses strikingly similar language. "We presented too many PowerPoints," he begins, but adds that failed PowerPoint presentations inadvertently led to a successful organizing message:

> We showed a bunch of graphs on subprime [mortgages]. And then, suddenly, it clicked. People said "Oh, I get it: it's a big conspiracy by the banks." . . . [That] ended up combatting individualistic victim stuff. . . . People said "I thought it was because I made shitty decisions, but now you're telling me that there was an engineered plan to sell houses in a way that led to all of this." It was really powerful, [it] got emotional.

Here the organizers detail a process of transformation sped by what Marshall Ganz terms "public narrative"—stories and tropes that compel action by acting on the insight that "values are experienced emotionally," not logically (Ganz 2011, 274). Using narratives of racial inequality and oppression both provided a simplifying language that stood in for the exhausting technical errata of mortgage financing and provided an emotionally compelling explanation of the problem to overcome (Ganz 2011, 275). Much as Occupy Wall Street simplified the issue of inequality by naming the 1 percent as inequality's architects, organizers gradually abandoned technical education on the mechanics of the finance system and financial instruments in favor of a narrative that named perpetrators. Crucially, they told stories that centered race.

The policy director of a Chicago advocacy organization explains its transformation through failed advocacy on property tax assessments. The problem is stark: lower-cost homes in Cook County are taxed by the assessor at a much higher rate than million-dollar homes (Kaegi and Ross 2019). The organization commissioned a study of the inequitable tax burden and brought an expert witness to the city council, where things quickly fell apart:

> We had our expert. And the other guys had their expert. It was the battle of the experts, and it went nowhere.... So we decided to take a different approach. (Policy director, advocacy organization)

Today, these same organizations use the language of race and antiracism strategically, as both a way to prioritize the racial dimensions of subjects they had formerly considered through the language of class and, more revealingly, as a way to strategically simplify organizing and activism around issues related to finance.

Successful advocacy campaigns for these policies have the common characteristics of finding a mechanism, such as a strike, to compel politicians to take action and create the capacity for *internal* policy development. While techniques for compelling political action against austerity circulate through policy entrepreneurship networks, the eventual policies ratified by necessity arose from long-term efforts of organizers and advocacy organizations to fit reform schemes to the complex particulars of a given jurisdiction's fiscal arrangements and political constituencies.

USING RACE TO DRAMATIZE SOCIAL REPRODUCTION: THE POLITICS OF ELDER CARE

The changing approach unions and advocacy groups take to the related issues of child- and elder care shows the impact of a race-centered analysis. Public programs supporting seniors, such as reduced-cost housing and home health care, have long suffered significant underfunding and as a result, low pay and poor working conditions. The stump speech Service Employees International Union members give to new home health workers begins by recounting the $1-and-change hourly wage home care workers earned before first unionizing in the 1980s. Despite some notable advances in funding child- and elder care federally and at the level of state government, cuts to both programs led to diminished service provision (at a time of heightened need) and, as ever, downward pressure on wages, hours and working conditions.

Women hold a disproportionate share of the jobs in care work, and women of color in particular. Placing these realities at the center of analysis and critique helped activists to dramatize the problem of austerity more effectively, to identify new connections to related organizations, and to understand the structural problems they faced more fully. The leader of a Chicago seniors' advocacy group explains the organization's transformation through race-focused work in these terms. The organization had long lobbied to increase budgets for senior housing and home care, to little effect. Then a cohort of young organizers convinced the organization's leadership to examine its attitudes about, and approaches to, race:

> Having the conversation about race points us to how we want the world to look like. We didn't understand the analysis well [at first].... I attribute it to young organizers and young organizers of color who challenged us on this. Organizing has tended to be white and male, what do people of color who do this work envision the world looking like and what are the real root causes that shape our problems?

Placing racial inequalities at the center of the organization's mission quickly led it to identify new organizing messages, targets, and allies:

> [Race] changes campaigns, for example [a recent] nursing home reform campaign. We could have said a lot of things, but we noted that South Side (black) homes were significantly understaffed compared to North Side (white). People on the South Side were getting significantly worse care. If we hadn't sat with seniors of color who had family members pass away, then we wouldn't have known that and we wouldn't have been able to call out owners as

racists. The only thing owners didn't want to be called was racist. *[So] everything we're saying about you is because you're racist.* You are racist because you are knowingly creating policies that lead to negative outcomes for people [of color]. Earlier, we would have said nursing homes are bad, care is bad, staffing is bad, we maybe could have gotten to the place of "and in all the African-American nursing homes staffing is even worse," but probably not. [emphasis added].

This shift in organizational focus and messaging helped to add new members to the organization's legislative coalition. Immediately following these recession-era changes, the organization won a number of notable legal and program victories, including a 2010 Illinois law that raised staffing levels in nursing homes, higher asset thresholds for eligibility for the state's Community Care Program, and extension of "homemaker" elder care services to evenings and weekends. Beyond these short-term changes, the organization plays a more central and visible role in current economic justice coalitions, where it has contributed its staff and political connections to campaigns for affordable housing, higher minimum wages, and investment in health care provider resources in the wake of Covid-19.

These victories followed cases in which organizers could endorse a clearly defined law or policy—i.e., cases in which the policy stream was already well developed. Chicago and Illinois's ongoing efforts to expand universal prekindergarten education offer an important counterexample to illustrate the point. Childcare advocacy organizations and unions have increasingly turned to the language of racial justice to build support for expanded and lower-cost prekindergarten programs, even winning trial grants to seed a Chicago-focused universal pre-K program. The Chicago-based trial program has limited prospects for expansion despite its early success, for the simple reason that its proponents cannot find alternatives to stubborn policy barriers, including the cost of expanding the program, the need to find thousands more day care providers to meet demand if the program became universal, and the looming reality that low-wage, in-home day care providers—the great challenge to the organized day care workers whose political support is crucial to expanding coverage—are the simplest and most efficient way to expand coverage. Nationally, the language of racial justice has expanded support for universal prekindergarten, without fashioning policy solutions to the technical barriers to the program.

THE START OF THE RED WAVE: CHICAGO TEACHERS CHALLENGE AUSTERITY AND WIN

The Chicago Teachers Union, the progenitor of the "red for ed" teacher strikes that swept seven states in 2018 and 2019, used racial justice organizing to expand its coalition of supporters. Foregrounding race in organizing messages and outreach allowed the union to build a citywide coalition of heterogeneous neighborhood and racial justice organizations spread across the city. This approach in effect used the city's entrenched segregation as an organizing tool—it converted the pervasive disparities in where and to whom funding flowed into fuel for neighborhood meetings, organizing house calls, and other direct outreach to low-income communities.

Public school budgets account for 40 percent of local tax expenditures across the United States, a characteristic that made organizing for improved funding and schools a long-term priority for community and labor organizers (National League of Cities 2017). Because school funding is local and often neighborhood specific, it intersects fiscal inequalities (Highsmith 2019). The introduction of charter schools that received public funding after public school closures deepened these problems (Farmer 2014), as did Chicago's aggressive use of TIF, which froze property tax revenues for disinvested areas and dedicated new tax revenues to subsidizing development—development that in turn drew higher-income in-migrants, who in turn made aggressive claims on public services funded through the fixed base of public taxes (Weber 2014). These long-term fiscal stresses became acute problems for low-income neighborhoods of color in Chicago after 2010, when Mayor Emanuel's "Renaissance" plan proposed closing dozens of schools in low-income neighborhoods on the South and West sides.

Emanuel's announcement of the planned school closures coincided with significant changes to the internal structure of the Chicago Teacher's Union, the bargaining unit that represented more than 20,000 employees of the Chicago Public Schools. For decades prior to the Great Recession, the Chicago Teachers Union bargained narrowly over pay and working conditions; its leadership rarely interacted with rank-and-file teachers and typically accommodated rather than challenged the city's finances (see Chapters 3–4). In the recession's aftermath, a cohort of activist teachers organized opposition within the union. The Caucus of Rank-and-File Educators (CORE) prioritized confrontation with the City and arguments for education that centered economic equality and racial justice. Their organizing decentered bargaining over pay and seniority in favor of activism that targeted the education system's intersections with Chicago's other inequalities. In particular, CORE members linked population declines and pressure to close schools to the Chicago Housing Authority's 1999 Plan for Transformation, which eliminated public housing units in favor of Section 8 vouchers for the private housing market. Eliminating public housing, CORE argued, both created the population loss that led to proposed school closures and seeded Chicago's recent homicide problem. A union leader explains:

> You had all these students on the South and West sides of the city who were the core of those schools. . . . Once you took away safe and secure housing, you introduce the many-headed hydra by breaking down the established gang structure in a school.

The union responded to austerity and the plan to close schools with a message that directly reversed the long-held counsel that unions and community organizations avoid the lightning rod of race. The school closure plan, the teachers argued, amounted to *educational apartheid*. The accompanying report, *The Black and White of Education in Chicago Schools*, combined racism, segregation, and austerity into a single analysis:

> 88 percent of students affected by CPS School Actions since 2001 are African American. Schools more than 99 percent students of color ("Apartheid schools") have been the primary target of CPS school actions—representing more than 80 percent of all affected schools. These students face a wide range of challenges outside of school, including high levels of violence and trauma, but are still expected to serve as test subjects for unproven school reform schemes. (Caref et al. 2012, 3)

The intertwined problems of segregation and educational disinvestment provided significant opportunities to convey this point of view to the public:

> Our organizing method was about going out to all the flashpoint opportunities—budget hearings, closure hearings, charter authorization hearings, TIF.... These would be spaces where the union [leadership] didn't bother to have a presence. So it was fertile ground and we started developing this huge list of parents [who supported CORE].... We even started in the steering meeting, inviting in presidents of the Local School Councils.... Before, the closure list was a contract. If you were on it, you got closed. After we started, you could see names were coming off the closure list. (Senior staff member, Chicago Teachers Union)

In 2011, Emanuel proposed extending teachers' work days by two hours, without additional pay or resources. The teachers countered by demanding conventional collective bargaining concessions on wages, hours, and working conditions. But they accompanied these with demands that lay outside of conventional employer-employee negotiations, including smaller class sizes, increased funding for arts and music programming, and social services for lower-income students. Emanuel and city representatives had expected the public to side with the city, but the themes of austerity and segregation built a surprisingly broad coalition in support of the teachers (Lipman 2013; Farmer and Noonan 2019). The City settled in little more than a week, granting the majority of the union's demands, and convincing other community and labor organizers about the value of using antiracism to build a political response to austerity. The closings, a long-tenured community organizer explains, clarified that

> what Rahm was about, [was] top-notch austerity and privatization politics. The uprising around CTU was a big movement to oppose Rahm and the politics he represents. That led to risk-taking: we did start exploring things that we were pretty sure Rahm wouldn't have agreed to beforehand.

This insight highlights an about-face in organizers' approach to risk. The classic postwar training for community organizers treated racial justice as a net negative for activist campaigns because it injected volatility into what was otherwise a well worked-out set of techniques for winning incremental reforms. After decades of widening inequality, the losses of the Great Recession and intense fiscal austerity, the unpredictability that racial justice discourse injects into activism began to appear as an asset: it promised the ability to change the rules of a losing game.

FROM TAX INCREMENT FINANCING TO DISPLACEMENT: RACE EXPANDS ADVOCACY ON FINANCE

Tax increment financing represents both a chronic fiscal problem and an acute crisis for low-income populations in Chicago. Illinois instituted TIF in 1977, when it enabled municipalities to earmark all future property tax growth within an area for special funds, simply by declaring that area "blighted" (Weber 2014). By 2000, TIF districts covered more than 30 percent of the city, and did so in ways that mocked the idea they responded to blight: TIFs enclosed areas of manufacturing disinvestment on the West and Far South Sides, but they also contained acres in the Loop, the expensive North Side Lake front, and a range of gentrifying and gentrified areas surrounding the city's core. The pervasiveness of TIF districts, the volume of resources they diverted, and the stark discrepancies between downtown and neighborhood TIFs made TIF an aspirational organizing target for Chicago's community and neighborhood organizers for decades. In the mid-2010s, these efforts finally gained a foothold when activists reframed the many problems of TIFs as problems of racial justice.

TIF presented residents with layers of challenges. Over the long term, TIF districts guaranteed austerity by freezing general purpose property-tax revenues at the level of the TIF district's founding year, and earmarking all future growth in assessed property values—the "increment"—for use on activities to counter supposed blight. The TIF formula does not account for inflation: as property values, taxes, and the cost of city-provided services rise over time like the cost of milk, the inflation-adjusted value of tax collections earmarked for general spending falls. This yields chronic pressure on basic public services, including schools and libraries. Because Chicago typically designates TIFs in areas of obvious interest to professionals and real estate developers, population and investment increase in many TIF districts, leaving the city with fewer dollars to fund services for more residents (Weber 2014).

Postrecession austerity added to these fiscal constraints, and the accompanying housing boom shifted attention to the uses of the TIF funds over which aldermen presided. Illinois law allows cities to use TIF dollars for a wide range of neighborhood and people-friendly uses, including job-training programs and investments in public health centers. In practice, however, TIF funds support developers, often crudely: more than half of TIF funds flow to developers through direct support or funding for infrastructure improvements, and just one-quarter are spent on economic development, a class of expenditures that includes much de facto support to business (City of Chicago n.d.). TIF's growing influence on both sides of the ledger—it underwrote gentrification while starving budgets that could in principle diminish gentrification's negative impacts—made the problem more urgent.

Thinking through race changed the way organizers framed the problem. The impetus to change came from the failed 2006 "Big Box" living-wage bill. Organizers had won a city council vote on the bill with an orthodox campaign focused on poverty and economic equality (Doussard 2015)—a victory then-mayor Richard M. Daley overturned by labeling the bill a racist attempt to price retail out of black neighborhoods. To organizers, the message was clear: talk about race yourself, or someone else will. Centering race transformed many organizations, including Grassroots Collaborative, a Partnership for Working Families (now PowerSwitch Action) affiliate that worked to unite community and labor campaigns. A Grassroots Collaborative leader explains how the organization's commitment to racial equity provided traction that had long eluded it in the struggle against TIF. Organizers piqued the public's interest by sidelining technical PowerPoints in favor of a de facto "gallery walk":

> We have this set of fifteen or twenty images with some words in it, showing in history the intersection of white supremacy and capitalism. It was useful in ... doing some of this fundamental work in terms of who broke the economy and who's responsible for fixing it.

One of the early messages was that Wall Street itself began as a literal slave trading post. By foregrounding rather than eliding racism's central role in capitalism, Grassroots Collaborative's messaging effectively simplified TIF and other previously obscure financial measures:

> People get it, and they get enough of a hook to know that when the city, or the schools or the state says there's no money, that's really not true. If you asked about the [interest-rate] swaps, very few people got the details, for sure, but people understood that they were decisions that people were making.

Foregrounding race transformed TIF from a technical issue into a kind of lingua franca for the problems of segregation, gentrification, and development writ large in Chicago. Community organizations throughout the city made similar transformations. Our Neighborhood, a community organization on the City's Northwest Side, started as a territorial organization dedicated to antipoverty and housing work in what became a gentrifying neighborhood. As gentrification displaced the neighborhood's Latinx population, Our Neighborhood shifted its focus from neighborhood territory to the process of displacement that threatened its members. TIF became a way to organize this work, a means of (literally) following the money and tying changes in the neighborhood to changes outside its boundaries. The organization's director explains:

> We'd like to use TIF to change the narrative on housing. There's so much in the slush fund, which is in the nine digits [hundreds of millions of dollars] citywide. Shouldn't TIF spend to zero? Every year, schools lose funding as a result.

Reconceptualizing TIF as a problem of racist development eventually led to changes in organizing, policy demands, and the administration of the TIF program itself. In 2018, organizers turned their attention to opposing $1.3 billion in proposed public subsidies for the North Side Lincoln Yards development, a multiacre project on the site of a closed foundry. In September 2019, the Chicago Lawyers' Committee for Civil Rights filed a lawsuit charging that the Lincoln Yards development and the TIF program writ large violated the Illinois

Civil Rights Act by steering public funds to TIFs in high-land-value, white neighborhoods at the expense of low-income neighborhoods of color (Raice 2019). The City immediately won its bid to dismiss the lawsuit, but the headlines and the claims of systemic racism led to other victories. In 2020, Mayor Lightfoot announced a series of TIF reforms, including the formation of community boards with input on TIF expenditures (Hinz 2020). None of the proposed reforms met the demands of anti-TIF activists, who maintained pressure on Lightfoot and the city council. Yet at the same time, the community council and legal reform enacted changes far beyond anything activists had won on TIF in the prior decades.

Foregrounding race had moved neighborhood organizations away from individual neighborhoods and toward a comprehensive analysis and critique of development. This critique builds on decades of research, outreach, organization building, and message development—activities that the language of antiracism converted into demands elected officials could not ignore.

SCALING UP: ANTIRACISM EXPANDS ACTIVISM TO STATE GOVERNMENT

Regressive tax structures add to the problems low-income communities and communities of color face. Most cities rely on property and sales taxes rather than income taxes, and eighteen U.S. states have flat income tax systems or sales-tax-based revenue systems, both of which charge more proportionally to low-income households. As ERJ coalitions expand beyond issues tied directly to the workplace, they increasingly take on state-level tax reform work. Rescaling to the state unfolds fluidly. As campaigns progressed, social movement participants and policy entrepreneurs moved in and out of coalitions and changed their roles, often in response to events originating in political pressure and legislative deadlines (Shore, Wright, and Però 2011).

Three state-level campaigns to address tax fairness featured in the November 2020 general elections, where Californians voted on a measure to restore some school funding cut by Proposition 13; Illinoisans voted on amending the state constitution to allow a progressive income tax; and Coloradans were scheduled to vote on a proposal to repeal the Taxpayer Bill of Rights (the Centennial State's Proposition 13) until a judge threw out the ballot initiative on a technicality. None of these proposals became law, but all demonstrate the evolution of the way activists frame problems.

Surrogates for California Proposition 15, the proposed repeal of the state's forty-three-year-old tax limit law, made their case in stark racial terms:

> Especially as Black Lives Matter protests continue across the country, now is a good time to consider the ways Prop 13 has contributed to inequality between the communities that have healthy neighborhoods, clean water, well-financed infrastructure and good schools, and the communities that don't. After all, it is precisely that inequality, which maps along racial lines, that is the crux of structural racism.
>
> California, for all its progressive values and best intentions, has among the worst racial disparities in the nation, including the highest levels of poverty and homelessness. For example, a count of homeless people in Oakland and Alameda County found a 47% increase in homelessness from 2017 to 2019, with nearly half of that population Black despite the fact that Alameda is only 11% Black. (Powell 2020)

Going further, other campaign surrogates argue that Proposition 13 and the antitax rebellions of the 1970s need to be understood as racist laws first and antitax measures second (Toppin 2019).

Instructions to organizers tasked with firming up votes for Illinois's constitutional amendment took a similar approach, with a July 2020 message to organizers advising them to lead by tying regressive taxes to the racial inequalities visible in the Covid-19 pandemic and police violence in communities of color:

> The tax code is both a symptom of and instrument of systemic racism. Racial inequity is furthered by Illinois' unfair tax system where low income and working people now pay twice as much as wealthy people as a share of their income. This inadequate tax system forces harmful cuts to state and local governments while pushing up property taxes, which also causes the tax burden to fall more heavily on Black and Latinx homeowners. . . . Fighting austerity requires dealing with state level policy, which can either

directly limit local expenditures, indirectly limit them by offloading needs, or starve institutions of the basic funding they need. (Vote Yes for a Fair Tax 2020)

As with fiscal policy issues related to elder care and education, building coalitions focused on racial justice work also provides the means of developing more effective organizing strategies and tactics. The postrecession efforts of a major fiscal policy advocacy group in Colorado illustrate these contributions well. The Colorado Fiscal Policy Institute has followed a common trajectory for ERJ organizations over the past quarter-century. It was founded as a semivolunteer organization in the 1990s, after the passage of the tax-freezing Taxpayers Bill of Rights (colloquially, TABOR) via a ballot initiative began to squeeze public revenues for education and basic services. The organization conducted a range of fiscal analyses and advocacy work in the 1990s and 2000s, drawing on its membership in the State Priorities Partnership, a national network of progressive fiscal policy organizations, for advice and ideas.

The Great Recession changed the institute's goals, tactics, and strategies. Growing austerity, combined with high levels of in-migration to Colorado and TABOR's limits on the revenue needed to provide basic services for nearly one-half million new Coloradans in the 2010s, added to the state's perennial fiscal challenges. The institute became a stand-alone organization in 2014, with five employees. By 2019, it had ten. The institute's new staff members include an outreach director charged with building alliances with community organizations and communities of color and a communications director tasked with creating resonant talking points about the complexities of fiscal policy. The difficulty of communicating on fiscal policy made the decision to foreground communications over fiscal analysis inevitable, as a senior member explains:

> You can do all the research you want to on policy, but most people find it boring, find it irrelevant to their lives.... You have to be really good at sort of tricking people into paying attention.... Once you trick people into focusing a little bit, they're kind of fascinated, and focused on what's important.... We've had forty years of antigovernment rhetoric, of antitax rhetoric. That's a thing we've spent a lot more time on.

The institute prioritized outreach to communities of color and environmental organizations, who play as significant a role in Colorado politics as organized labor does in the Midwest and Pacific states (Doussard 2020). The outreach to organizations representing people of color had the unexpected consequence of revealing failures in the institute's messaging. A senior official explains:

> We've done this work long enough to know that the conventional wisdom that [people of color] vote like Democrats. . . . Well, they just *don't*. We were working really hard to make sure that our materials were grounded in the experiences of people of color, and we were asking people in our partnerships to review our lit, design our lit, and we felt like we were doing the right thing. We were really proud of ourselves. And then I hear that there's this neighborhood organizing group that's come together to oppose our ballot measure [to raise school funding via a tax surcharge] in minority neighborhoods. What the hell? And then me, being the dumbass I am, call these people up, and what I was told—I'm embarrassed by it now—is that the city of Denver had just adopted a provision that said that if your schools don't meet performance standards, the district can take over running your local school and in fact they can close your local school. That had just happened in this historically black neighborhood. The City had just closed their school. And this parent said to me "Great, now that you've closed our neighborhood school, you want to take more of my money to fund someone else's neighborhood school. *I don't think so!*"

Dozens of encounters like this led the institute to adjust its organizing and messaging to demonstrate, rather than assume, the benefits to a more progressive tax code. The organization's extended network of relationships with community organizations made it effective with legislators after the Democrats won control of state government, even after the economic and public health crises induced by the Covid-19 pandemic. Prior to the pandemic, the institute had won the governor's backing to double the size of Colorado's earned income tax credit (EITC) to 20 percent of the federal eligibility threshold—an important victory, given the governor's stated commitment to cut taxes.

The pandemic's arrival in early March immediately cancelled the budget projections on which the proposed EITC rested. The institute's newly strong partnership with community organizations representing people of color provided a solution. When Colorado's legislature met in April to set the terms under which the state would use funds allocated to it under the CARES Act, the institute's partners pressured their legislators to close a tax loophole in CARES Act distribution, using the reserved funding to expand the state EITC to 15 percent of federal eligibility and adding eligibility for workers without valid social security numbers. The surprising accomplishment of winning additional resources for the poor in a tax-constrained state during a recession happened because the institute's outreach to racial justice organizations created both a bill more responsive to the needs of minority populations and a geographically and politically broader coalition.

FROM RACIAL JUSTICE FRAMES TO ANTIAUSTERITY POLICY

Austerity and racist inequalities in the funding of public goods and services pose problems that shape the current conflict over public health, police budgets, and post–Great Recession austerity. The need for public goods is a constant: even in the simpler and more localized economies around which urban movements organized prior to the New Deal, activists linked visions of dignity and well-being on the job to housing, education, and basic public health. The nationally and globally interwoven economy we inhabit nearly a century later expands the role these public services play in visions of justice, as access to health care; childcare; quality primary, secondary, and postsecondary education; and affordable housing grows more uneven. Organizing public finance and austerity in the same manner that justice movements organize workplaces and labor policy thus represents an essential step toward realizing visions of justice, both *at* work, where health, food, family care, and shelter provide basic conditions of possibility for holding and flourishing in a job, and *beyond* work, in domains of life, action, and human flourishing that collective bargaining itself will never be sufficient to realize.

The commitment to organize for justice beyond work thus poses a substantial challenge to ERJ coalitions whose roots lie in organized labor and the policy world the New Deal created. Strategies and tactics for winning change at work do not easily translate to public spending:

the abstractions of budgets exist beyond the lived experience of most workers and citizens, and the idiosyncratic, individualized nature of each public institution and funding stream blunts the power of policy entrepreneurship networks that flourish when the problem at issue varies only marginally across places.

Organizers' response to these problems—and the effectiveness of that response—seems surprising, at first. For most of the postwar era, community organizers learned to deemphasize the issue of race, which Saul Alinsky and other innovators in the practice of organizing saw as a figurative third rail in politics and policy. The decision to reverse course resulted less from the obsolescence of Alinsky's ideas than of his world: with the modest elements of the U.S. welfare state under assault and austerity severely restricting the range of public goods and services communities can hope to gain through incremental bargaining, the advantages to *emphasizing* the racial divisions that shape public policy far outweigh the tactical complications that come from making explicit the racist dimensions of racist policies (Lesniewski and Doussard 2017; chapter 3, this volume).

Antiracist discourse and campaign messages address the fundamental challenges to organizing around austerity directly. First, the language of antiracism offers a simplifying narrative that shapes the perceived problems of austerity and fiscal racism in ways that technical detail about financial instruments, regressive tax structures, and the mechanics of property assessment cannot. Labeling austerity, TIF, or any particular development deal, budget cut, or tax arrangement as racist both abstracts from financial particulars in a way that enables coalition building and supplies discreet organizing targets for currently powerful antiracist sentiment. It provides a potent "story of us" (Ganz 2011). The current call to defund the police illustrates these dynamics. On the one hand, invoking the goal of defunding the police, rather than addressing a particular budgetary issue or opportunity, broadens discontent with police violence in the service of producing a multiorganizational, multiethnic, multineighborhood agenda. On the other, arguing to defund the police gives broad antiracist sentiment a target, a set of priorities and decisions through which individuals and organizations can take action in the service of their goals.

Second, antiracist discourse accurately depicts long-standing problems in the provision of social goods and the de facto racism of austerity. As a growing body of conceptual and empirical work establishes in convincing detail, the story of persistent racial inequality in the United States cannot be told accurately without taking into account the bundle of financial advantages and intangible assets that whiteness, and living in white neighborhoods designated for superior services and public investments, confers (Chetty et al. 2014; Chetty, Hendren, and Katz 2016; Coates 2014; Sherman 2020; Boulton 2015; Wright et al. 2020). The message that austerity is racism motivates citizens because it is accurate.

Third, the discourse of racial justice calls into being new working relationships between community organizations (Fischer 2003). Paying attention to the material implications of messaging helps to identify the role antiracist discourse plays in diversifying, densifying, and thickening ERJ coalitions that were historically based in the intersectional, but narrower, relationships of service-sector organizing (Luce 2004; Doussard 2015). These changes are visible in each of the organizing campaigns we analyze in this chapter. Committing to antiracism led a senior-rights organization to ally with unions representing low-income elder care workers of color. It led the Chicago Teachers Union and its allies to build dozens of new relationships with community and neighborhood organizations with an interest in schools. It led the Colorado fiscal institute to both reach out to organizations representing communities of color *and* develop policies and messages that responded to those communities' needs.

These features of antiracist discourse help antiausterity activists to win control of the problem stream—that is, to shape what the public and elected officials understand as a policy problem worthy of action. The complicated and idiosyncratic character of individual financial arrangements, however, still works against reformers developing and deploying policies to answer the problems to which they draw attention. We can identify no systematic method or set of tools these organizations use to compel action on the problems they identify. Consider the diversity of mechanisms at play in generating responses to problems of collective consumption. The "red wave" of national teachers' walkouts uses the tool of the mass strike to move its issue to the center of the politics stream—a maneuver that works because they are employed by the state. The seniors' activist organization in Chicago used its existing relationships in the state capitol to win policy victories fitted to

ISSUE ROLE OF RACIAL JUSTICE ACTIVITIES	INITIAL ADVOCATES	ADVOCATES ADDED BY ERJ COALITION	PROBLEM STREAM MESSAGE AND DISCOURSE DRIVING PUBLIC ATTENTION	POLITICS STREAM MEANS OF COMPELLING ACTION	POLICY STREAM LEGAL REMEDIES
Elder care *Racial justice adds political allies*	Senior citizens' advocacy organizations	Service sector unions Racial justice organizations Neighborhood organizations	*Racism*: Poor elder services, low caregiver pay, and austerity result from racist neglect of programs for people of color	*Insider bargaining*: New allies allow activists to win larger concessions from state assembly	Developed *internally*: Advocacy organizations push for funding goals they themselves set
Education funding *Racial justice adds neighborhood and political allies*	Teachers unions	Neighborhood organizations Racial justice organizations	*Racist disinvestment*: School closures, privatization, underfunding, and segregation result from a budget that neglects communities of color	*Mass protest*: Strikes force attention to education funding	Developed *internally* through collective bargaining and externally through antiausterity
Tax increment financing *Racial justice adds issue allies*	Neighborhood development organizations	Neighborhood organizations Unions Issue-based advocacy groups Racial justice organizations	*Fiscal racism*: TIF transfers money from public services for communities of color to discretionary funds for real estate development	*Political organizing*: Long-term coalition-building elects sympathetic mayor and city council	Developed *internally* through decades of TIF-based organizing and advocacy
Regressive taxes *Racial justice adds political allies and changes campaign messages*	Fiscal policy organizations	Racial justice organizations Neighborhood organizations Environmental justice organizations	*Fiscal racism*: Regressive taxes fall on people of color; regressive tax structures limit resources for public services benefiting communities of color	*Ballot initiatives and exogenous shocks*: Covid-19 and CARES Act create window of opportunity for policy change	Developed *internally* through policy proposals fitted to state tax laws and political constituencies

FIGURE 14. Racial justice messaging and the three streams of antiausterity policy

its antiracist goals. Antiracist messages effectively shape public perception (Figure 14), but action still requires an *external* mechanism for bringing elected officials to the table.

By contrast, action on the problem of fiscal racism appears to be driven by the inside game of policy advocacy—but in an individualized, one-off manner that locates current solutions outside the machinery of multisited, nationally scaled policy entrepreneurship. The current horizon of this work lies in organizations finding a window of opportunity, as the Colorado Fiscal Institute did through the CARES Act, or applying the same pressure used to win reforms like fair workweek legislation to financial issues. On both types of policies, we see significant near-term opportunities for successful advocacy. With antiracist campaigns, however, the big picture appears to be more important. Using antiracism as a way to dramatize fiscal racism and the general inadequacy of public goods provision in the United States provides an imaginary that moves beyond nostalgia for the New Deal and Fordism: it imagines not a world that disappeared, but a better world that never was.

Conclusion
THE PROMISING WORK OF JUSTICE

The recent success of movements for social and economic justice in cities upsets a number of traditions in urban studies. It challenges the warning that mobile investors will punish cities for attempting redistribution. The method of victory also matters, as current justice movements succeed by uniting agendas—work and home, race and class—whose separation was long a distinguishing feature of urban social movements. Electoral and policy changes that advance justice as communities of color and working people see it are happening across a broad range of cities, a diverse set of policy areas, a multiplicity of political scales, and in areas, particularly racial justice, that economic justice activists long dared not to touch. The agenda continues to expand, and social movement participants at this moment find that adding new partners and issues to the agenda expands, rather than dilutes, their power. These developments compel us to look forward to the questions, problems, and possibilities contemporary justice movements face.

The pessimistic era of U.S. urban political economy centered growth machines, ruling coalitions, and mobile/reactionary homeowners and businesses. In the narrow sense, warnings about the veto power these reactionary interests hold are pragmatic and responsible. They focus students, activists, and scholars alike on the real and substantial barriers to left politics and policy in U.S. cities. We find little ground to contest those criticisms as they were made at the time. Yet the pragmatic decision to remain skeptical of winning justice through municipal government also came at a significant cost. The declared alternative of winning social and economic justice through *national* policy was scarcely more practical. That required a national electoral coalition with the power to overcome the sixty-vote threshold in the U.S. Senate, a means of circumventing electoral college and legislative maps that substantially overrepresent rural areas relative to cities, and building a geographically broad and diverse coalition that can clear these high bars while negotiating challenges that by definition inflame the racism that same political system empowers. This alternative to acting locally does not seem much of an alternative at all: it trades away the tangible power and capabilities of local networks, organizing, and action for the mechanically complicated and substantively difficult goal of assembling an enormous national political network. It also promises to make politics distant, formal, and procedural—detached from everyday lived experience.

The current reinvigoration of redistributive and equity-focused urban policy has many roots, including the economic globalization whose inequalities justice movements fight. The principal agents in this minirevolution are social movement participants who made the decision to embrace the power of cities, identity, and ideology over the insider's game of electoral politics. These movements succeed in moving policy because they use the resources of the city to build movements and set the agenda. The city is instrumentally useful in this goal, because it provides physical space, symbolic targets, and institutional relationships with which movements can set the agenda. More subtly, because cities are sites of collective consumption and social identity making—Marshall Ganz's "story of us"—these movements are broader and more diverse than their predecessors. Most provocatively, combining work, childcare, austerity, and other causes (which we could not explore in detail) into a single agenda dangles the tantalizing possibility that the current instantiation of justice movements is overcoming the separation of work and home thought to be central to urban politics in the United States (Katznelson 1982). They manage this in part by prioritizing racial justice in their analysis and messages, a decision that implements and builds on the understanding that capitalism and its inequalities work fundamentally, rather than incidentally, through race (Robinson 2005). They remain at their core economic justice movements, but they act on questions of justice in ways that more readily connect to proliferating antiracist movements (Bledsoe and Wright 2019). One of the simplest and most important contributions of our investigation of urban policy entrepreneurship is that it redirects attention from the weaknesses of economic and racial justice (ERJ) movements to their strengths. Those strengths really do appear numerous. Consider the objective of winning short-term, immediate policy victories. Addressing structural inequalities locally has several clear advantages for activists. Local action is cheaper and easier to organize. Acting locally also focuses scarce organizational and political resources on political institutions (city councils, mayors' offices) with lower barriers to access, and where elected officials represent comparatively diverse and politically supportive constituencies.

The city itself also provides extensive resources: central business districts and civic plazas where activists can shut down traffic and win attention, public meetings they can easily enter and organize, neighborhood and civic organizations to structure action and outreach. A classic line of argument in urban politics juxtaposes these resources of grassroots organizing to the movement-killing disappointments of failing to win a policy or election, or—worse yet—discovering that winning elections and passing laws produce their own disappointments. Our study of contemporary economic and racial justice coalitions shows this dichotomy to be false. The power ERJ coalitions currently possess on the minimum wage, earned sick time, antiausterity policy and a range of related reforms developed not despite long-term grassroots organizing, but because of it. Considered narrowly, living-wage and targeted-hire campaigns were failures: they won small and often unenforceable reforms, and they did so at great material and opportunity cost to the coalitions who worked to secure them. Yet those failures spurred durable changes in activism. The member organizations of ERJ coalitions developed techniques, discourses, and habits for working effectively together not despite the de facto failure of living-wage laws to live up to their promise, but because of it. ERJ movements, in short, do not develop as alternatives to short-term political and policy victories for working people and communities of color: they develop *through* political and policy campaigns.

HOW DURABLE ARE THESE CHANGES?

The status quo in urban studies suggests that the capacity for activists to win ERJ reforms is epiphenomenal, the product of luck and contingency rather than systematically applied skill. Our approach to the dilemmas of urban activism suggests that chance is often overcome by systematic power—power that ERJ coalitions developed deliberately. This finding raises the questions of how far activists' power stretches and, more fundamentally, how durable that power is. These questions carry extra importance after the social, economic, and political dislocations of 2020. Whatever the outcome to the interesting times in which we live, it is difficult to picture a return to the disciplined, incremental bargaining that characterized urban politics through the Great Recession. Disruptive changes are not coming—they are already here. A first question, or fear, is that they will wipe out the decades of work that built ERJ coalitions and urban policy entrepreneurship.

We begin with the threats to activists' power, as a way to clarify that our optimism about the activism we document in this book does not willfully look away from challenges. ERJ coalitions' current power has many sources, and diffuses through institutions—unions, community organizations, national advocacy networks—that systematize lessons and techniques for advocacy. Those institutions face their own threats. The recent *Janus* Supreme Court decision by design slashes revenue for public-sector unions, the unions most active in ERJ coalitions. Elsewhere, donor austerity and donors' politics often steer community organizations and national advocacy networks away from ERJ causes. These restraints do not play the role of clouds on the figurative horizon: they already limit advocacy coalitions' resources and agendas. Yet our research suggests that these constraints will change but not short-circuit advocacy. For example, several of the "red wave" teacher strikes took place in so-called "Right to Work" states that impose *Janus* funding conditions on all unions. As a whole, twenty-first-century labor organizations have won significantly larger policy victories than their predecessors did in the prior forty years, even though those predecessors counted significantly more members. Similarly, donors' reluctance to fund campaigns designed to "take away rich people's money," in the words of one of our informants, appears to be offset by their enthusiasm for funding racial justice work that leads to the same outcome. Ignoring the threats to ERJ coalitions marks a clear mistake, but so too does granting any of the challenges they face the status of a death blow.

ERJ coalitions' current power stems from multiple sources that are more or less durable. The basic precondition for activists to exercise leverage, the current urban "renaissance" of investment, innovation, and repopulation, represents a decades-long transformation of economy and society. Transformations at this scale and transformations involving this much investment, should be "sticky" for some time. But change always comes. Diminishing returns on current investments create crises (Harvey 1982), new technologies interrupt settled hierarchies and power structures unexpectedly (Storper and Walker 1989), and—this last point is decidedly empirical—global greenhouse gas emissions add risk and uncertainty to the global production networks and financial instruments that underlie the current urban boom. We will not speculate how or when, but the boom will end, and justice movements will be well-advised to adapt as quickly as they can. Here, we are somewhat optimistic that the work ERJ coalitions have done in expanding their coalitions and adding new issues, including climate change, to the economic justice agenda will prepare them for that future.

The ways ERJ organizations have refashioned their collaborations to take advantage of this leverage seem similarly durable: After twenty-plus years of working in coalitions, senior organizers and activists explain, with compelling detail, that they conceptualize and execute their work through partnerships. The policy entrepreneurship networks in which coalition members participate themselves appear to function as agents of economic and organizational efficiency whose capacity for learning and development makes each new policy campaign marginally cheaper to run and more effective. The authors themselves can attest to this: We spent and observed enormous effort in the failed 2006 Chicago campaign for a $10 minimum wage in big-box retail stores. The successful 2014 campaign for a $13 minimum wage required less time and fewer resources and the 2019 follow-up to raise Chicago's minimum wage to $15 fewer resources still. By the time the Illinois General Assembly entertained a bill to raise the state minimum wage to $15, legislative committees entertained limited testimony and never bothered to recall key witnesses, including the authors. The entire process took but a few weeks. The same pattern applies to living-wage laws, fair workweek legislation, free community college programs and teacher strikes against austerity: Policy entrepreneurship networks quickly convert the labor-intensive lesson learning of groundbreaking advocacy campaigns into reproducible campaigns, much as IKEA turns original designs into simply assembled off-the-shelf products.

POLICY ENTREPRENEURSHIP, NETWORK LEARNING, AND THE VALUE OF AGENDA SETTING

The policy entrepreneurship process itself fashions some useful lessons about how successful advocacy works. Most fundamentally, our four cases decenter city council and state assembly votes in favor of the discourses, protests and depictions of social problems that compel legislative bodies to act in the first place. The current wave of economic and (to an extent, racial) justice policy victories builds on the backbone of widespread public recognition that inequality threatens economies, housing, education and climate—that is, everything.

Only now, with hindsight, does this consensus feel like a foregone conclusion. The evidence about inequality was clear for decades, but ignored until the Great Recession, when Occupy Wall Street and increasingly aggressive economic justice organizers made inequality a problem too big to ignore. Defining problems in a way that captures the public imagination can paper over other, more intractable challenges to effective advocacy. Teachers' actions against austerity demonstrate the force of problem framing especially clearly: Briefly planned, highly effective teacher strikes often began without a clear proposal for policy solutions to the many problems poorly funded, segregated, and delegitimized public schools face. They won concessions from legislators not because of superior organizational skill or tactical acumen but rather because they had successfully rallied the public to their side.

Campaigns that struggle to define a persuasive social problem can also achieve their stated goals—but only when their power in the political stream can compensate. This reality explains the episodic advance of political organizing on behalf of fair workweek laws, which particularly powerful ERJ occasionally compel politicians to pass, even though they struggle to define the motivating problem. Dissecting policy and advocacy in terms of these multiple streams of action admittedly generates few hard and fast rules. The overlapping streams of problems, politics, and policy instead provide a way to rigorously organize questions about why, where, and how different policies take root or fail to. The broader challenges of framing problems and finding political pressure via elections, ballot initiatives, or strikes circumscribe a policy stream that develops quasi-independently.

ERJ coalitions owe their recent successes primarily to their skill at applying external pressure to set the political agenda. Our cases show that they complement this skill, to little fanfare, with inside negotiation with elected officials. The outside game of public pressure, in other words, sets up the inside game of old-fashioned bargaining and deal making (Imbroscio 2006). The first bargain struck within a national network of policy proposals appears to have agenda-setting power. For example, the negotiation between Seattle's Fight for $15 campaign and the mayor's minimum wage working group established employer size thresholds and other "coverage" measures that appeared, with some tweaking, in follow-up legislation, just as San Francisco's fair workweek and mandatory local hire laws developed the basic mechanisms that populated follow-up bills elsewhere. Negotiation, then, matters more as a pathway to entering the endgame of policy passage than as a vehicle for shaping outcomes. As a corollary, ERJ coalitions would benefit from expending extra resources in order to guarantee that the first negotiated bill for a given policy has the most favorable possible terms.

More mundanely, there exists a clear need to build in policy implementation and enforcement from the beginning. Many of the labor policy victories ERJ coalitions won faced the immediate challenge of enforcement, and specifically *lack of* enforcement. This problem forced organizers to expend their scarce political capital in order to revise the laws they won or to undertake new, follow-up campaigns to found city offices with the capacity to enforce (for example) the minimum wage, targeted hiring, and paid sick days laws. Here again, policy entrepreneurship networks provide an answer to the problem: recent minimum wage and fair workweek laws in Denver and Philadelphia (respectively) include provisions to found municipal labor standards offices as part of the initially ratified legislation.

THE PROBLEM OF JUSTICE, AND JUSTICE BEYOND WORK

The $15 minimum wage is not justice. Similarly, fair workweek legislation passes into law only episodically and provides limited support for workers struggling to integrate their paid and unpaid labor. Organizers have finally found some chinks in austerity's armor, but state support for shelter, food, medical care and other basic human needs remains woefully inadequate. Personal, organizational, and legal journeys toward the goal of equality go by the stated goal of justice, but justice is always qualified—economic justice, environmental justice, racial justice—and is by definition never complete (Greenberg 2014). We make these observations not to criticize justice movements' current demands, but rather to acknowledge their necessarily utopian character. As ERJ movements mature, the implied vision of justice they embrace by necessity changes. Tracking that vision of justice helps to diagnose their strengths, their limits, and the paths they will take.

Today's ERJ coalitions began by emphasizing the first word in their name. In the post–Great Society era of neighborhood-centered activism, they either strategically minimized or outright ignored the racial justice components of their goals. The economic justice they sought was itself narrowly conceived, less the result of fully realized visions for justice than a set of materialist demands fitted to the unique bargains and structure of the American welfare state. Activists invoked a narrowly material vision of justice: It centered wages, paid employment benefits, and access to expanding consumption. More narrowly still, those visions centered work, and specifically the kinds of jobs that rarely existed outside of the short-lived postwar compact in the United States. The names given to and aspirations heaped upon work reveal the limits of the encompassing vision. Activists demanded "standard" jobs offering ongoing employment at forty weekly hours; or "family-wage" jobs that paid enough for a single earner to support a spouse and dependents; or more desperately, "good" jobs offering pay and working conditions in excess of an undefined threshold.

Both the limited aspirations and the obvious shortcomings of these goals were creatures of their time. Incomes expanded along with the economy from the end of World War II through 1973 (Harrison and Bluestone 1990) and the expansions of the 1950s and 1960s delivered plentiful jobs in high-wage industries and occupations. These conditions papered over what the modern reader will identify as glaring problems in the underlying vision of justice, one which took for granted a delicate political-economic settlement that has now been in decline for a half-century. The postwar vision for justice in the workplace functioned as a vision of justice *through* the workplace. Among the numerous shortcomings and oversights to this vision were the way workplaces and unions themselves rationed access to "family wage" jobs to white workers and men; the subsequent decline in spending on basic public goods such as education and transit; the concurrent increase in housing, healthcare, and other costs that labor's wages are tasked with covering; the environmental costs of economic expansion based on producing ever-increasing volumes of physical goods; and the cost of repetitive work and inequitable democratic institutions to human flourishing, happiness, and development. Even fully just workplaces (which never actually existed) could contribute only partially to these goals.

We elaborate this old vision of justice at work because it still accounts for most of the contemporary vision of justice. The living-wage movement and the struggles that came out of it harnessed nostalgia for the postwar vision of justice, often pledging to "rebuild" the middle class. Our own study of current justice campaigns centers the Fight for $15—the contemporary justice that would be most recognizable to earlier generations. Unions, community organizations and the other institutions through which ERJ coalitions work, likewise developed through advocacy for older, narrower, and distinctly materialist visions of justice. They now attempt to use that same infrastructure to pursue broader visions of a fair society. Even so, they articulate no exhaustive or consistent definitions of justice.

Their actions, however, suggest the structure of a trinity, in which three broad domains of material justice in unison constitute a more substantive whole. In the sphere of economic production, they push to increase the share of waged work that pays enough to cover basic household needs, and to shrink inequalities in access to the limited quantity of such jobs. In the sphere of social reproduction, they push to expand resources and institutions that allow households to accomplish their own caring work and developmental goals alongside paid work. In the public sphere, they advocate for public goods that support individual well-being across the spheres of production and social reproduction. This vision evolves in pieces, through compromises, speculative leaps, and the constraints of inherited ideology, experience and organizational structure. It is of necessity inelegant and incomplete.

This rough de facto vision of justice reveals important information about current ERJ coalitions. First, the visions of economic justice these coalitions advance, clearly expand on the visions they inherited. In problem-framing, in political advocacy and in policy, coalitions increasingly combine the material and social dimensions of justice in the workplace: They treat communities of colors' access to high-quality jobs as a goal on equal footing with the long-standing goal of increasing the number of high-quality jobs. This advance seems small, but it marks a substantial advance from the long-held belief that the supply of desirable jobs could be divorced from questions of who gets those jobs.

Second, ERJ coalitions' current actions to address the problems of work, home and public goods together act on the understanding that none of these problems can be meaningfully addressed in isolation from the others. This understanding comes from history and experience. The political-economic bargain of Fordism faltered in substantial part because Fordist labor markets delivered adequate work only to a narrow slice of the population (Perlstein 2008; Henwood 2003; McDowell 1991). The partially realized vision of targeted hire programs represents an understanding that in addition to being normatively desirable, racially and gender-just allocations of work are practically necessary to maintaining the place-based bargaining power and the broader political economic bargains that make paid work better.

Third, and related, ERJ coalitions are attempting to expand their conceptions of and actions toward justice—beyond whatever their current bounds are. At the level of leadership, a growing number of the organizations we cover has placed women and people of color in directors' positions. The organizers and rank-and-file members we interviewed revealed, in surprising number and with disarming clarity, their frequent participation in meetings organized with the explicit goal of addressing the past racism of both the organization and *many of the people called to the meeting*. These efforts fall well short of the task of remedying past racism, and a great many organizations make no such efforts to begin with. Our interview subjects shared these critiques, and expressed them with disarming frankness and candor. The work is not perfect, but it is real.

These aspirations also point to several immediate challenges on which justice coalitions can usefully work. The first is the need to develop messages, tropes, discourses, and above all resonant *ideas* that frame problems of social reproduction and collective consumption with the same clarity that the image of the working poor frames the problem of economic inequality. The more optimistic (or naïve) permutations of discourse analysis imply that an heroically clear image or on-the-nose turn of phrase can move a problem from the shadows to sunlight. Maybe, but even if individuals can reliably summon such supreme acts of skill, those singular skills form a lousy basis for action plans. Studies of successful policy entrepreneurship suggest the less romantic, but more democratic, technique of trying as many formulations as possible (Kingdon 1984). Even then, the difference between successful and forgotten neologisms and turns of phrase results as much from the surrounding environment—the public's mood, the day's news—as from language itself. This argues for organizers and activists focusing their activities on shaping the public's mood itself. That is already one of the primary goals of grassroots organizing, and a process on which community and labor organizers have focused a growing portion of their efforts since the Great Recession (Doussard and Fulton 2020).

Negotiating the challenges of political scale also marks an immediate and important challenge for ERJ coalitions. The standard lines of argument about political scale within U.S. Federalism envision a contest within which politically opposed coalitions maneuver to capture state or national political forums whose laws supersede those of the lower-scale political institutions nested within them. ERJ activists often set out to "jump" scale to jurisdictions whose legislative actions can render local political authority and resistance irrelevant (Doussard 2015). But the contest also works the other way around, with politically reactionary organizations using control of state or federal government, or the judiciary branch, to preempt or remove legislative authority from states and cities (Lafer 2017). The politically conservative American Legislative Exchange Council (ALEC) deploys preemption aggressively and with tremendous success: Using ALEC's model legislation, states have passed dozens of preemption laws since 2010, covering everything from minimum wages to rent control to landlords' obligations to remove bedbugs from their properties.

This orthodox approach to the question of political scale often makes the situation seem hopeless for justice activists, simply because organized business interests possess far more resources with which to organize and fund the capture of different political scales (Lafer 2017). Our research with justice activists, however, points to the countervailing power of changes in the organizational relationships, democratic participation practices, and ideologies that shape the contest for scale. Most strikingly, we find real evidence that winning control of the problem, politics, and policy streams in cities, leads to control in state politics. The diffusion of minimum wage laws shows this pattern. Nine U.S. states (including the District of Columbia) have now passed a $15 minimum wage. All of them either previously passed the $15 minimum wage in large cities (as in California and Illinois) or have state legislatures dominated by city-based coalitions. In other words, control of the urban scale drove changes at higher political scales. Equally striking, the contest to pass those state-level minimum wage laws absorbed significantly fewer resources—less time, testimony and door-knocking—than city-level campaigns. Commonplace narratives of reactionary interests capturing higher political scales imply that such capture can be permanent. Yet city-based coalitions in state houses have begun to repeal recent preemption laws (as in the case of Colorado's former ban on municipal minimum wages). The post-2019 Democratic majority in Virginia even took steps to repeal that state's Right-to-Work law—a measure that Virginia voters nearly inscribed in the state constitution about a decade ago.

Both the near- and the long-term goals of justice coalitions will require action at those higher political scales. The impact of austerity budgets manifests most clearly in cities but originates with Federal and state budget cuts. For that reason, antiausterity campaigns by ERJ activists focus from the beginning on state tax codes, funding for schools, and the allocation of scarce resources. Here again, intensive organizing in recent decades appears to have borne fruit: Continued outreach and organizing around budgets have placed community and policy organizations who aspired to work together in positions to collaborate in ways that resonate with their members. Rather than focusing the analysis of scale on particular policy proposals, research would benefit from investigating the city-scaled relationships that lead urban coalitions to exert more power over time in state houses.

This leaves the question of how ERJ coalitions can make progress in developing and making readily available policy solutions to the problems on which they focus the public's attention. Our research indicates a clear answer: Try things. Across the policy domains we study, time and repetition stand out as two necessary conditions for the development of portable policies. Successful policy requires draft legislation and messages, events, testimony, and research necessary to compel elected officials to consider that legislation. Across the many issues we consider, legislators voted for change *after* activists spent years or decades refining messages, models, and supporting research. This argues for activists finding and taking more chances: trying new policies, reintroducing old ones, supporting new studies, trying on new messages, and just generally advancing justice campaigns by inventing, rather than waiting for, opportunities.

URBAN POLITICS AFTER GLOBALIZATION AND THE LIBERAL CONSENSUS

We propose the study of urban policy entrepreneurs to correct for the persistent focus of urban politics research on individual cities and on elected officials themselves. We see simple ways to drive forward each of these projects in the short term. Most simply, the framework of urban policy entrepreneurship provides a straightforward and practical way to examine the politics of cities *in relation* to one another, to global economic flows, and to other scales of government. Above all, the framework is practical. The three axes of policy entrepreneurship—problems, politics, and policies—provide a simple structure for comparing (1) the ways all three change when a given policy comes to a new jurisdiction, (2) the ways all three change when coalitions move from one policy to the next, and (3) the diagnostic strengths and weaknesses of different policy goals and campaigns. Each of these tasks provides a way to both develop and answer questions that move scholarship beyond the normative exhortation to consider cities relationally, and toward the systematic development of problems, agendas and questions to address with that multisited research. In the process of scrutinizing policy, this work will also add to our scarce knowledge about the communities and movements who push for policy change.

The study of urban policy entrepreneurs also makes progress on what might be termed the Goldilocks problem of studying urban politics. On the one hand, we live in an economically globalized reality in which finance, global production networks, and the power of transnational elites really do drive city futures. Telling the story of cities or social movements without foregrounding the challenges of global capitalism makes no sense. Yet emphasizing global economic structure with too heavy a hand flattens different places into a singular, undifferentiated "urban," and wrongly suggests that global structure will crush the agency and autonomy of everyday citizens and their movements.

Unfortunately, the alternative posture, of studying individual cities or social movements in isolation, creates an opposing problem. Juxtaposing coalitions of poorly resourced citizens to consolidated corporate economic power falsely suggests those citizens play a game they cannot win. And it is no way to build knowledge: Cities and their citizens differ in accidental and systematic ways that directly impact the development of their politics. Focusing on urban policy entrepreneurs provides a means of recognizing the *structured contingency* of individual places, problems, politics, and policy. The three streams of the Multiple Streams approach provide a way to organize and compare significant differences between places, without reducing their struggles to either the dominance of global capitalism or the heroic, isolated resistance of individual activists. Urban places differ along predictable lines, and in semipredictable ways. Our framework provides a means of learning from that valuable information instead of discarding it.

To these high-level conceptual considerations, we add the consideration that the framework of policy entrepreneurship makes detailed multisite research feasible *within the limited budgets and scarce time* that most scholars have available. Policy entrepreneurs are highly networked and view advocacy as an essential job description. This makes them willing to talk and predisposes them to narrate their actions in terms that echo the intellectual construction of multiple-streams analysis. Because their work consists of systematic experiments with policies, they also have interest in scholars' answers to questions about the three streams. Practically speaking, this means that scholars can develop empirically rich work by conducting a limited number of live and remote interviews, scrutinizing successful and failed policy proposals, and combing through campaign materials, messages, and legislative testimony. This model for research fits comfortably with both shrinking budgets for funding large-N, multisite studies and the difficulties overworked scholars employed at urban public universities face in finding the time and resources for detailed comparative work.

The way racial justice goals structure and change politics stands out as an important question for any such research to consider. As we conclude this in early 2021, newly visible police shootings of black men, protests, and backlash drive the daily news. Those events came to a head after urban studies scholars began to foreground critical race theory, intersectionality, and the idea that local states are inherently racist. Our research shows that the normative commitment to racial justice has materially useful consequences: It expands coalitions, compels organizers to resolve long-term problems in their own practice and discourse, and provides a framework for organizing and speaking compellingly about problems that remain on the edges of the public's radar.

CONCLUSION || 201

Remarkably, racial justice discourse has steered attention to long-standing problems that somehow escaped attention: disinvestment, undervalued caring work, rigged financial systems, police violence, and now the Covid-19 crisis. Justice movements worked for decades to make these issues or their antecedent causes into widely agreed-upon problems. The conceptual tools available in the postwar political era were simply not up to the job: They allowed activists to talk about fairness at the margins of unfair social and economic systems that the language and ideology of activism itself rarely contested. The speed and thoroughness with which those activists succeeded in framing Covid-19 as a racial justice (and environmental justice) problem attests to the change in orientation. Racial justice framing has its own challenges, including figurative and literal violent backlash from white reactionaries. It also has real conceptual power, and the rare ability to turn abstract inequalities into concrete and actionable problems. In organizing parlance, it cuts issues with great effectiveness.

The language of antiracism appears not only to unite ERJ activists in a call to action, but also to give these previously inchoate problems the quality of tangible, consensus problems about which individuals say *I know it when I see it*. There are many practical questions to limn and answer here: about additional conceptual problems to which antiracism could bring order, about supplementary changes to organizing practice and goals, about the durability of the current turn to antiracism, and about how organizing, problem definition, and activism will change if community and labor organizations continue to elevate to positions of power people of color. We can say many of the same things about climate justice activism, which also expands coalitions and provides a framework for organizing multi-issue activism. Our relative neglect of this issue follows from the limited attention it received from our research subjects: They are eager to incorporate climate justice into their work, but the economic justice ideals and practices on which their own activism has been built continue to push environmentalism to the margins. It is the next frontier to cross.

Finally, housing and the problem of nationwide, even planetary, gentrification punctuates the way ERJ activists develop, conceptualize, and talk about organizing campaigns. Prior to the New Deal, unions themselves devoted resources to developing housing, which they recognized as essential to visions of justice on the job. They did so, however, in a territorial way, solving the problem of housing by building housing. Addressing housing today requires addressing public policy, mapping and exposing the chains of finance that commodify shelter, and developing policy mechanisms, such as land banks and community land trusts, that remove shelter from the market. We have no solutions to this challenge but note its centrality to the work of justice ahead.

The biggest and most hopeful question about these changes in politics remains the possibility the contemporary justice movements will transcend the goals of liberal pluralism in addition to its institutional means. The activists participating in current justice coalitions pursue visions of justice rooted in the institutional materiel of the New Deal era: jobs, pay, housing. Even at their fullest, such visions invoke a reductionist, materialist vision of society, one that substitutes measurable material equity for the rights and power needed to obtain and sustain any such material distribution (Weaver 2018). We are partial to the practical and normative project of human development, whose measurement-ready focus on capabilities and emphasis on economy seem to make it ideally suited to the politics of the United States (Sen 1999). But excellent alternatives abound, including a growing body of thinking based in the work of Henri Lefebvre and the substantive project of the right to the city (Steil and Delgado 2019; Leeuwen 2020).

In all these permutations, the work of studying urban politics in the near future looks significantly different. For most of the postwar era, ERJ coalitions played hastily organized, often ad hoc defense. The institutions and rules of U.S. politics continue to disadvantage justice activists. Yet those activists increasingly shape rather than respond to problems. Mayors and city council members, who historically cemented their alliance with the growth machine by opposing activists, now pledge loyalty to the cause of racial and economic equality. The amount of work needed to make even incremental progress toward these visions of justice is daunting, if not overwhelming. Yet the work is happening virtually everywhere, and urban scholars have the conceptual and methodological tools to move citizens from the margins to the center of the stories we tell.

Acknowledgments

Acknowledgments are fun. Research and writing don't happen in a vacuum, and as we write this at the tail end of the pandemic, compiling a list of thank-yous is an excellent opportunity to recall better times. So many wonderful people and experiences helped us shape this book. We will fail to name all of you, so we ask preemptively for forgiveness from anyone we overlook. There are, after all, so many of you to single out for your support, direct, indirect, or otherwise.

Our frequent professional collaborators and co-conspirators played big roles in bringing these ideas to fruition through sharp comments and their own excellent work: Jennifer Clark, Pierre Clavel, James DeFilippis, Bill Lester, Nichola Lowe, Virginia Parks, Mildred Warner, and Laura Wolf-Powers all encouraged us, in different ways, to push these ideas forward and to write something optimistic. Jason Spicer and one anonymous reviewer gave extensive and unusually detailed comments that substantially improved the final project. Individual pieces of the argument benefited from a tour of the conference circuit, where some extremely sharp questions from the people already mentioned and some really lively discussants, including Jamaal Green, Bob Lake, Chris Tilly, and Kevin Ward, pushed us to do better.

The seeds of this book were planted in our graduate educations, when we had the real pleasure of being immersed in the intellectual worlds of people who care about work, economy, and politics—and who saw them as inseparable: Phil Ashton, Dennis Judd, Ann Markusen, David Perry, Joe Persky, Janet Smith, Nik Theodore, and Rachel Weber.

Hundreds of organizers, activists, and low-wage workers gave us big chunks of their time as we did this work. The screen of anonymity means we can thank few of you personally. Throughout, members of the Service Employees International Union, many of its locals, and Jobs with Justice and Partnership for Working Families affiliates were especially generous with their time. Thanks to you, we had the real luxury of building our work through long-term conversations that helped us to generate, refine, and improve our ideas. We hope the results aren't merely academic, and we really hope this book supports your work. In Chicago in particular, Adam Kader, Chirag Mehta, and Amisha Patel opened a lot of doors and challenged us when we needed challenging. Dozens of other people we cannot name did just as much.

Marc Doussard wishes to thank his excellent colleagues in Urban and Regional Planning at Illinois: Jesus Barajas, Lindsay Braun, Arnab Chakraborty, Mary Edwards, Andrew Greenlee, Stacy Harwood, Bumsoo Lee, Faranak Miraftab, Magdalena Novoa, Rob Olshansky, Rolf Pendall, Hugo Sarmiento, and Daniel Schneider. Further afield at UIUC: Trevor Birkenholtz, Jake Bowers, Julie Cidell, Dan Gilbert, Brian Jefferson, Andrew Weaver, and David Wilson. And lots of really sharp students: Max Eisenburger, Faizaan Qayyum, Steve Sherman, and Ozge Yenigun. Greg Schrock wishes to thank several current and former colleagues and students whose passion and collegiality have inspired him over the years: Ryan Allen, Ellen Bassett, Lisa Bates, Matthew Gebhardt, Karen Gibson, Edward Goetz, Aaron Golub, Jamaal Green, Charles Heying, Megan Horst, Jason Jurjevich, Jihye Kang, Dillon Mahmoudi, Stephen Marotta, Nathan McClintock, Thad Miller, Marisa Zapata, and countless others.

Our coauthors have also pushed us in ways that made this book a lot better. Marc Doussard thanks Brad Fulton, Ahmad Gamal, and Jacob Lesniewski, all of whom taught him a lot.

Committing to write a book, much less push it over the line during a pandemic, is a personal journey as much as a professional one. Marc Doussard benefited from Rita and Joe Doussard providing a respite, good company, and much-needed childcare while we all wore masks. Jessica Greenberg was and is always the best possible intellectual partner and source of mirth in this work, but she doesn't get the dedication this time. That goes to Gabriel and Julian, who were sort of aware this book was happening and definitely deserve the better world its subjects are trying to conjure.

Greg Schrock gives special thanks to his wife Leigh for being an excellent partner in their journey together, and dedicates this book to his parents, Wilma and Sam Schrock, for instilling in him—in their own understated ways—the importance of good work and fairness, which continue to motivate him every single day.

Notes

2. ECONOMIC AND RACIAL JUSTICE COALITIONS

1. In mandating a citywide living wage, rather than a wage for government contracts, living-wage legislation also addressed the burgeoning problem of privatization—local government outsourcing work to private contractors not bound by wage rules.

3. URBAN POLICY ENTREPRENEURS

1. These welcome updates remain mostly silent on the question of how changing politics yields changes to policy. Indeed, urban politics scholars tend to view cities' governance arrangements as deeply path dependent and singular—individual—in character (Rast 2015), especially when focusing on formal governmental institutions. In this institutionalist view, policy change is driven by "inner tensions of local political orders" (Rast 2015, 143), but with little further specification about the dynamics on the ground.

2. Sometimes referred to in the literature as the "multiple streams framework," or MSF (Herweg, Zahariadis, and Zohlnhöfer 2017).

3. This process does not intrinsically favor activists on the political left. The resources required to hop between legislative forums and scales privilege well-funded corporate donors with large volumes of resources.

4. Others have advanced speculative versions of this argument. De Leeuw and collaborators and Cairney and Jones reached this conclusion in their studies of subnational policy entrepreneurship (De Leeuw, Hoeijmakers, and Peters 2016; Cairney and Jones 2016). The limited body of work from scholars who have applied the multiple streams analysis to localities focuses on countries outside the U.S., where they argue, speculatively, that participants in politics may have more potential to shape the streams (Robinson and Eller 2010; De Leeuw, Hoeijmakers, and Peters 2016).

4. ORGANIZING FOR BETTER JOBS

1. The April 2014 strikes increased pressure on fast food employers by including employee walk-offs in Brazil, Japan, and the United Kingdom (Greenhouse 2014).

2. These worker constituencies expanded participation within limited bounds: none came to the Fight from $15 from outside of the labor movement, and most were involved in existing or aspirational SEIU bargaining units.

3. For example, Englewood, the low-income South Side neighborhood currently infamous for violent crime, is carved into seven separate wards, many of which stretch into majority-white neighborhoods with numerically dominant electorates.

4. The famously irate and profane mayor also donned an ugly sweater for campaign commercials.

5. GOOD JOBS FOR ALL

1. This language of "return on public investment" was typical framing, including in the very first local First Source ordinance in Portland, Oregon (Schrock 2015). This reflected a concern with how suburban communities were draining resources from central cities. Because racial divisions were typically stark between central cities and suburbs, the language of return on investment allowed urban mayors to justify local hiring programs without resorting to racial justifications.

2. Chicago Jobs Council (CJC), "Summary of Report to the First Source Task Force by the Construction Employers' Association (CEA)," June 17, 1987." CJC archives.

3. Chicago First Task Force, "Proposed Structure for Chicago First Program," 1986. Retrieved from Harold Washington Archival Collection, Chicago Public Library.

4. The U.S. Constitution's "Privileges and Immunities" clause restricts state and local governmental entities from discriminatory actions and policies against residents on an interstate basis, unless the government can demonstrate that out-of-state workers or businesses are an acute source of problems for that jurisdiction, motivating such restrictions. This does not preclude local governments from discriminating *within* their states, but in practice it means that local hire targets typically exempt hours worked by out-of-state workers from the denominator of total hours worked.

5. Organizer, Chicago policy advocacy organization, interview with author.

6. Organizer, Brightline Defense, interview with author.

7. Agency official, Baltimore Mayor's Office of Employment Development, interview with author.

8. Policy official, New Orleans, interview with author.

9. In 2018, the local and disadvantaged worker requirements increased to 50% and 30%, respectively.

10. Nashville, Tennessee, passed a Local Hire law in 2014, only to see the Tennessee Legislature immediately preempt it. At present, Tennessee and Ohio are the only two U.S. states that have passed preemptions on targeted hiring, but the threat remains in other states where cities have not attempted to pass local laws.

11. Staff, Puget Sound Sage, interview with author.

12. UCLA Labor Center played a key role in researching policy models, producing an extensive report for the City of Seattle that laid out policy alternatives that Seattle could adopt based on other cities' experience (Herrera et al. 2014).

13. Former staffer, City of Seattle, interview with author.

14. City of Seattle interview.

15. Puget Sound Sage interview.

16. Puget Sound Sage interview

6. JUSTICE BEYOND WORK

1. For those workers who *do* retain eligibility, rapid turnover in service-sector jobs results in a typical job tenure of around six months—meaning that few workers last long enough to use any time-off benefits they happen to gain.

Bibliography

A Better Balance. 2018. *Brief 2: Paid Family and Medical Leave & Nonstandard Employees.* Washington, D.C.: A Better Balance. https://pub.flowpaper.com/docs/https:/www.abetterbalance.org/wp-content/uploads/2019/02/ABB_Policy-Brief-2.pdf.

Aguiar, Luis L. M., and Shaun Ryan. 2009. "The Geographies of the Justice for Janitors." *Geoforum, Labouring Geography: Negotiating Scales, Strategies and Future Directions* 40 (6): 949–58.

Aldag, Austin M., Yunji Kim, and Mildred E. Warner. 2019. "Austerity Urbanism or Pragmatic Municipalism? Local Government Responses to Fiscal Stress in New York State." *Environment and Planning A: Economy and Space* 51 (6): 1287–305.

Alexander, Stephen J. 2007. "Equity Policies and Practices of the Harold Washington Administration: Lessons for Progressive Cities." In *Economic Development in American Cities: The Pursuit of an Equity Agenda*, edited by Michael I. J. Bennett and Robert P. Giloth, 213–35. Albany, N.Y.: SUNY Press.

Almeida, Paul. 2019. *Social Movements: The Structure of Collective Mobilization.* Berkeley: University of California Press.

Amin, Ash. 1994. *Post-Fordism: A Reader.* Studies in Urban and Social Change. Oxford: Blackwell.

Appelbaum, Eileen, Annette Bernhardt, and Richard J. Murnane. 2003. *Low-Wage America: How Employers Are Reshaping Opportunity in the Workplace.* New York: Russell Sage Foundation.

Archer, Nicole A., Ana Luz Gonzalez, Kimi Lee, Simmi Gandhi, and Delia Herrera. 2010. "The Garment Worker Center and the 'Forever 21' Campaign." *Working for Justice: The LA Model of Organizing and Advocacy*, edited by Ruth Milkman, Joshua Bloom, and Victor Narro, 154–64. Ithaca, N.Y.: ILR.

Ashton, Philip. 2009. "An Appetite for Yield: The Anatomy of the Subprime Mortgage Crisis." *Environment and Planning A* 41 (6): 1420–41.

Ashton, Philip, Marc Doussard, and Rachel Weber. 2012. "The Financial Engineering of Infrastructure Privatization: What Are Public Assets Worth to Private Investors?" *Journal of the American Planning Association* 78 (3): 300–312.

Ashton, Philip, Marc Doussard, and Rachel Weber. 2016. "Reconstituting the State: City Powers and Exposures in Chicago's Infrastructure Leases." *Urban Studies* 53 (7): 1384–400.

Baker, Tom, Ian R. Cook, Eugene McCann, Cristina Temenos, and Kevin Ward. 2016. "Policies on the Move: The Transatlantic Travels of Tax Increment Financing." *Annals of the American Association of Geographers* 106 (2): 459–69.

Baran, Hugh. 2018. "In Croson's Wake: Affirmative Action, Local Hiring, and the Ongoing Struggle to Diversify America's Building & Construction Trades." *Berkeley Journal of Employment and Labor Law* 39 (2): 300–375.

Beauregard, Robert A. 2018. *Cities in the Urban Age: A Dissent*. Chicago: University of Chicago Press.

Benford, Robert D., and David A. Snow. 2000. "Framing Processes and Social Movements: An Overview and Assessment." *Annual Review of Sociology* 26 (1): 611–39.

Benner, Chris, and Manuel Pastor. 2012. *Just Growth: Inclusion and Prosperity in America's Metropolitan Regions*. New York: Routledge.

Benner, Chris, and Manuel Pastor. 2015. "Brother, Can You Spare Some Time? Sustaining Prosperity and Social Inclusion in America's Metropolitan Regions." *Urban Studies* 52 (7): 1339–56.

Bennett, Larry. 1993. "Harold Washington and the Black Urban Regime." *Urban Affairs Quarterly* 28 (3): 423–40.

Berglund, Lisa. 2020. "Early Lessons from Detroit's Community Benefits Ordinance." *Journal of the American Planning Association* 87 (2): 254–65.

Bledsoe, Adam, Tyler McCreary, and Willie Wright. 2019. "Theorizing Diverse Economies in the Context of Racial Capitalism." *Geoforum* (July).

Bledsoe, Adam, and Willie Jamaal Wright. 2019. "The Anti-Blackness of Global Capital." *Environment and Planning D: Society and Space* 37 (1): 8–26.

Bluestone, Barry, and Bennett Harrison. 1982. *The Deindustrialization of America: Plant Closings, Community Abandonment, and the Dismantling of Basic Industry*. New York: Basic Books.

Boulton, Christopher. 2015. "Under the Cloak of Whiteness: A Circuit of Culture Analysis of Opportunity Hoarding and Colour-Blind Racism Inside US Advertising Internship Programs." *TripleC: Communication, Capitalism & Critique. Open Access Journal for a Global Sustainable Information Society* 13 (2): 390–403.

Brady, Shane R., and Jacob Lesniewski. 2018. "Rabble Rousing in a Red State: Lessons Learned from Organizing for Worker Rights in a Highly Conservative State." *Journal of Community Practice* 26 (2): 236–51.

Briggs, James. 2017. "Indy Council Approves $13 'Living Wage' for City,

County Workers." *Indianapolis Star,* August 27. https://www.indystar.com/story/news/local/marion-county/2017/08/14/indy-council-approves-13-living-wage-city-county-workers/565806001/.

Brogan, Peter. 2014. "Getting to the CORE of the Chicago Teachers' Union Transformation." *Studies in Social Justice* 8 (2): 145–64.

Brooks, David. 2020. "Opinion | Where Do Republicans Go From Here?" *New York Times,* August 7. https://www.nytimes.com/2020/08/07/opinion/sunday/republican-party-trump-2020.html.

Brown, Megan. 2018. "The $15 Wage Movement Moves South: Politics of Region in Labor Union Campaigns." *Antipode* 50 (4): 846–63.

Broxmeyer, Jeffrey D., and Erin Michaels. 2014. "Faith, Community, and Labor." In *New Labor in New York: Precarious Workers and the Future of the Labor Movement,* edited by Ruth Milkman and Edward Ott, 70–87. Ithaca, N.Y.: Cornell University Press.

Bureau of Labor Statistics. 2020. "Job Openings and Labor Turnover Survey Highlights January 2020." https://www.bls.gov/web/jolts/jlt_labstatgraphs.pdf.

Cairney, Paul. 2013. "Standing on the Shoulders of Giants: How Do We Combine the Insights of Multiple Theories in Public Policy Studies?" *Policy Studies Journal* 41 (1): 1–21.

Cairney, Paul, and Michael D. Jones. 2016. "Kingdon's Multiple Streams Approach: What Is the Empirical Impact of This Universal Theory?" *Policy Studies Journal* 44 (1): 37–58.

Cairney, Paul, and Nikolaos Zahariadis. 2016. "Multiple Streams Approach: A Flexible Metaphor Presents an Opportunity to Operationalize Agenda Setting Processes." In *Handbook of Public Policy Agenda Setting,* edited by Nikolaos Zahariadis, 87–105. Cheltenham, U.K.: Edward Elgar.

Callahan, Kathe. 2015. "Edelman, Marion Wright." In *Encyclopedia of Public Administration and Public Policy-5 Volume Set,* 1018–20. New York: Routledge.

Cantrell, Jennifer D., Suparna Jain, and James B. McDaniel. 2013. "Enforceability of Local Hire Preference Programs." Washington, D.C.: US Department of Transportation, National Cooperative Highway Research Program. http://onlinepubs.trb.org/onlinepubs/nchrp/nchrp_LRD_59.pdf.

Caref, Carol, Sarah Hainds, Kurt Hilgendorf, Pavlyn Jankov, and Kevin Russell. 2012. *The Black and White of Education in Chicago's Public Schools: Class, Charters and Chaos.* Chicago: Chicago Teacher's Union.

Castañeda, Ernesto. 2019. *Building Walls: Excluding Latin People in the United States.* Lanham, Md.: Lexington Books.

Castells, Manuel. 1983. *The City and the Grassroots: A Cross-Cultural Theory of Urban Social Movements.* Berkeley: University of California Press.

Castells, Manuel. 1996. *The Rise of the Network Society.* Cambridge, Mass.: Blackwell.

Center for Budget and Policy Priorities. 2018. "Policy Basics: Federal Aid to State and Local Governments." Center on Budget and Policy Priorities. https://www.cbpp.org/research/state-budget-and-tax/federal-aid-to-state-and-local-governments.

Center for Budget and Policy Priorities. 2020. "Mission and History." https://www.cbpp.org/about/mission-history.

Center for Law and Social Policy. 2020. "About." https://www.clasp.org/about.

Center for Popular Democracy. 2019. "Workers Tell Congress Why We Need a Fair Workweek." November 6. https://populardemocracy.org/blog/workers-tell-congress-why-we-need-fair-workweek.

Chetty, Raj, Nathaniel Hendren, and Lawrence Katz. 2016. "The Effects of Exposure to Better Neighborhoods on Children: New Evidence from the Moving to Opportunity Project." *American Economic Review* 106 (4): 855–902.

Chetty, Raj, Nathaniel Hendren, Patrick Kline, and Emmanuel Saez. 2014. "Where Is the Land of Opportunity? The Geography of Intergenerational Mobility in the United States." *Quarterly Journal of Economics* 129 (4): 1553–623.

Chinese for Affirmative Action and Brightline Defense Project. 2010. *The Failure of Good Faith: Local Hiring Policy Analysis and Recommendations for San Francisco.* San Francisco: Chinese for Affirmative Action.

City of Chicago. 1984. *"Chicago Works Together": 1984 Chicago Development Plan.* Chicago: City of Chicago.

City of Chicago. n.d. "Tax Increment Financing: Annual Financial Analysis." http://chicago.github.io/annual-financial-analysis/TIF/.

Clark, Jennifer. 2013. *Working Regions: Reconnecting Innovation and Production in the Knowledge Economy.* London: Routledge.

Clavel, Pierre. 1986. *The Progressive City: Planning and Participation, 1969–1984.* New Brunswick, N.J.: Rutgers University Press.

Clavel, Pierre. 2010. *Activists in City Hall: The Progressive Response to the Reagan Era in Boston and Chicago.* Ithaca, N.Y.: Cornell University Press.

Clawson, Dan. 2003. *The Next Upsurge: Labor and the New Social Movements.* Ithaca, N.Y.: Cornell University Press.

Coates, Ta-Nehisi. 2014. "The Case for Reparations." *The Atlantic* 313 (5): 54–71.

Cohen, Larry, Rev Calvin Morris, and Sarita Gupta. 2013. *Jobs with Justice: 25 Years, 25 Voices.* Oakland, CA: PM.

Congressional Budget Office. 2014. *The Effects of a Minimum-Wage Increase on Employment and Family Income.* Washington, D.C: Congressional Budget Office. https://www.cbo.gov/sites/default/files/113th-congress-2013-2014/reports/44995-MinimumWage_OneColumn.pdf.

Cooke, Adrienne. 2019. "Stolen Wages, Stolen Lives: A Critical Analysis of the Fair Workweek Policy." Master's thesis, University of Illinois at Urbana-Champaign.

Cox, Kevin R. 1993. "The Local and the Global in the New Urban Politics: A Critical View." *Environment and Planning D: Society and Space* 11 (4): 433–48.

Cross, Rob, Stephen P. Borgatti, and Andrew Parker. 2002. "Making Invisible Work Visible: Using Social Network Analysis to Support Strategic Collaboration." *California Management Review* 44 (2): 25–46.

Cummings, Scott L. 2001. "Community Economic Development as Progressive Politics: Toward a Grassroots Movement for Economic Justice." *Stanford Law Review* 54 (3): 399–493.

Daniels, Arlene Kaplan. 1987. "Invisible Work." *Social Problems* 34 (5): 403–15.

Darden, Joe. 1990. *Detroit: Race and Uneven Development*. Philadelphia: Temple University Press.

Darrah-Okike, Jennifer. 2019. "Disrupting the Growth Machine: Evidence from Hawai'i." *Urban Affairs Review* 55 (2): 428–61.

Davidoff, Paul. 1965. "Advocacy and Pluralism in Planning." *Journal of the American Institute of Planners* 31 (4): 331–38.

Dávila, Jerry. 2013. *Dictatorship in South America*. Chichester, U.K.: Wiley-Blackwell.

Dean, Amy. 2012. "Mobilizing the Unorganized: Is 'Working America' the Way Forward?" *New Labor Forum* 21: 61–68.

Dean, Amy B., and David B. Reynolds. 2011. *A New New Deal: How Regional Activism Will Reshape the American Labor Movement*. Ithaca, N.Y.: ILR.

DeFilippis, James. 2016. *Urban Policy in the Time of Obama*. Minneapolis: University of Minnesota Press.

DeFilippis, James, Robert Fisher, and Eric Shragge. 2010. *Contesting Community: The Limits and Potential of Local Organizing*. New Brunswick, N.J.: Rutgers University Press.

de Leeuw, Evelyne, Marjan Hoeijmakers, and Dorothee TJM Peters. 2016. "Juggling Multiple Networks in Multiple Streams." *European Policy Analysis* 2 (1): 196–217.

Donegan, Bob. 2015. Donegan (Bob) oral history interview conducted by Michael McCann. Transcript. University of Washington, Special Collections. Oral History Collection. SeaTac Seattle Minimum Wage History

Project records. https://digitalcollections.lib.washington.edu/digital/collection/ohc/id/1966/rec/12.

Doussard, Marc. 2012. *Chicago's Growing Low-Wage Workforce: A Profile of Falling Labor Market Fortunes.* Chicago: Women Employed.

Doussard, Marc. 2013. *Degraded Work: The Struggle at the Bottom of the Labor Market.* Minneapolis: University of Minnesota Press.

Doussard, Marc. 2015. "Equity Planning Outside City Hall: Rescaling Advocacy to Confront Complex Problems." *Journal of Planning Education and Research* 35 (3): 296–306.

Doussard, Marc. 2016. "Organizing the Ordinary City: How Labor Reform Strategies Travel to the US Heartland." *International Journal of Urban and Regional Research* 40 (5): 918–35.

Doussard, Marc. 2020. "The Frontier of Equity Politics: Denver and the Future of Community-Labor Coalitions after Organized Labor." *Cities* 96: 102450.

Doussard, Marc, and Brad R. Fulton. 2020. "Organizing Together: Benefits and Drawbacks of Community-Labor Coalitions for Community Organizations." *Social Service Review* 94 (1): 36–74.

Doussard, Marc, and Ahmad Gamal. 2016. "The Rise of Wage Theft Laws: Can Community-Labor Coalitions Win Victories in State Houses?" *Urban Affairs Review* 52 (5): 780–807.

Doussard, Marc, and Jacob Lesniewski. 2017. "Fortune Favors the Organized: How Chicago Activists Won Equity Reforms under Austerity." *Journal of Urban Affairs* 39 (5): 618–34.

Doussard, Marc, Jamie Peck, and Nik Theodore. 2009. "After Deindustrialization: Uneven Growth and Economic Inequality in 'Postindustrial' Chicago." *Economic Geography* 85 (2): 183–207.

Douthat, Thomas H., and Nancey Green Leigh. 2017. "First Source Hiring: An Essential Tool for Linking the Poor to Employment or a 'Dead Letter' Progressive Policy?" *Urban Affairs Review* 53 (6): 1025–63.

Dreier, Peter, and Bruce Ehrlich. 1991. "Downtown Development and Urban Reform: The Politics of Boston's Linkage Policy." *Urban Affairs Review* 26 (3): 354–75.

Dreier, Peter, and Christopher R. Martin. 2010. "How ACORN Was Framed: Political Controversy and Media Agenda Setting." *Perspectives on Politics* 8 (3): 761–92.

Dube, Arindrajit, T. William Lester, and Michael Reich. 2010. "Minimum Wage Effects across State Borders: Estimates Using Contiguous Counties." *Review of Economics and Statistics* 92 (4): 945–64.

Ehrenfeucht, Renia, and Marla Nelson. 2013. "Young Professionals as Ambivalent Change Agents in New Orleans after the 2005 Hurricanes." *Urban Studies* 50 (4): 825–41.

Farmer, Stephanie. 2014. "Cities as Risk Managers: The Impact of Chicago's Parking Meter P3 on Municipal Governance and Transportation Planning." *Environment and Planning A* 46 (9): 2160–74.

Farmer, Stephanie, and Sean Noonan. 2019. "Chicago Unions Building a Left-Labor-Community Coalition, United Working Families, to Restore Working-Class Democracy." *Labor Studies Journal* 44 (4): 388–95.

Farmer, Stephanie, and Chris D. Poulos. 2019. "The Financialising Local Growth Machine in Chicago." *Urban Studies* 56 (7): 1404–25.

Feit, Josh. 2014. "The Secret History of Seattle's Minimum Wage Law." *Seattle Met,* July 30. https://www.seattlemet.com/news-and-city-life/2014/07/history-of-seattles-minimum-wage-law-august-2014.

Feldman, Maryann, Theodora Hadjimichael, Lauren Lanahan, and Tom Kemeny. 2016. "The Logic of Economic Development: A Definition and Model for Investment." *Environment and Planning C: Government and Policy* 34 (1): 5–21.

Fields, Desiree. 2017. "Unwilling Subjects of Financialization." *International Journal of Urban and Regional Research* 41 (4): 588–603.

Fischer, Frank. 2003. *Reframing Public Policy: Discursive Politics and Deliberative Practices.* Oxford: Oxford University Press.

Fraser, Nancy. 2019. *The Old Is Dying and the New Cannot Be Born: From Progressive Neoliberalism to Trump and Beyond.* New York: Verso Books.

Freeman, Richard B., and James Medoff. 1984. *What Do Unions Do?* New York: Basic Books.

Frege, Carola, John Kelly, and John E. Kelly. 2004. *Varieties of Unionism: Strategies for Union Revitalization in a Globalizing Economy.* Oxford: Oxford University Press on Demand.

Frey, William H. 2020. "American Cities Saw Uneven Growth Last Decade, New Census Data Show." *Brookings,* May 26. https://www.brookings.edu/research/new-census-data-show-an-uneven-decade-of-growth-for-us-cities/.

Frieden, Bernard J., and Lynne B. Sagalyn. 1991. *Downtown, Inc.: How America Rebuilds Cities.* Cambridge, Mass.: MIT Press.

Friedmann, John, and Goetz Wolff. 1982. "World City Formation: An Agenda for Research and Action." *International Journal of Urban and Regional Research* 6 (3): 309–44.

Fulton, Brad R., and Marc Doussard. 2021. "Sustaining the Grassroots: How Community Organizations Mitigate the Downsides of Collaborating with Unions." *Journal of Urban Affairs,* 1–20.

Fulton, Brad R., Michelle Oyakawa, and Richard L. Wood. 2019. "Critical Standpoint: Leaders of Color Advancing Racial Equality in Predominantly White Organizations." *Nonprofit Management and Leadership* 30 (2): 255–76.

Gale, William, Surachai Khitatrakun, and Aaron Krupkin. 2017. "Winners and Losers after Paying for the Tax Cuts and Jobs Act." *Tax Policy Center*, December 8. https://www.taxpolicycenter.org/publications/winners-and-losers-after-paying-tax-cuts-and-jobs-act/full.

Ganz, Marshall. 2000. "Resources and Resourcefulness: Strategic Capacity in the Unionization of California Agriculture, 1959–1966." *American Journal of Sociology* 105 (4): 1003–62.

Ganz, Marshall. 2011. "Public Narrative, Collective Action, and Power." In *Accountability through Public Opinion: From Inertia to Public Action*, edited by Sina Odugbemi and Taeku Lee, 273–89. Washington, D.C.: World Bank.

Gibson, Timothy A. 2004. *Securing the Spectacular City: The Politics of Revitalization and Homelessness in Downtown Seattle*. Lanham, Md.: Lexington Books.

Gilberstadt, Hannah. 2020. "More Americans Oppose than Favor the Government Providing a Universal Basic Income for All Adult Citizens." *Pew Research Center*, August 19. https://www.pewresearch.org/fact-tank/2020/08/19/more-americans-oppose-than-favor-the-government-providing-a-universal-basic-income-for-all-adult-citizens/.

Gilman, Hollie. 2016. "Engaging Citizens: Participatory Budgeting and the Inclusive Governance Movement within the United States." *Ash Center Occasional Paper Series*. Cambridge, Mass.: Ash Center of Harvard Kennedy School. http://ash.harvard.edu/files/ash/files/participatory-budgeting-paper.pdf?m=1455295224.

Gilmore, Ruth Wilson. 2007. *Golden Gulag: Prisons, Surplus, Crisis, and Opposition in Globalizing California*. Berkeley: University of California Press.

Glaeser, Edward L. 2011. *Triumph of the City: How Our Greatest Invention Makes Us Richer, Smarter, Greener, Healthier, and Happier*. New York: Macmillan.

Glasmeier, A. K., and R. M. Leichenko. 1996. "From Free Market Rhetoric to Free Market Reality: The Future of the US South in an Era of Globalization." *International Journal of Urban and Regional Research* 20 (4): 601–15.

Gleason, Carrie, and Susan Lambert. 2014. "Uncertainty by the Hour." *Open Society Foundations*. http://static.opensocietyfoundations.org/misc/future-of-work/just-in-time-workforce-technologies-and-low-wage-workers.pdf.

Gleeson, Shannon. 2016. *Precarious Claims: The Promise and Failure of Workplace Protections in the United States*. Berkeley: University of California Press.

Goetz, Edward G. 1990. "Type II Policy and Mandated Benefits in Economic Development." *Urban Affairs Review* 26 (2): 170–90.

Got Green Project. 2010. "Got Green? Environment, Equity and Opportunity." https://gotgreenseattle.files.wordpress.com/2010/03/got-green-news-2-10-for-web.pdf.

Greenberg, Jessica. 2014. *After the Revolution: Youth, Democracy, and the Politics of Disappointment in Serbia*. Stanford, CA: Stanford University Press.

Greenberg, Miriam, and Penny Lewis. 2017. *The City Is the Factory: New Solidarities and Spatial Strategies in an Urban Age*. Ithaca, N.Y.: Cornell University Press.

Greenhouse, Steven. 2012. "A Part-Time Life, as Hours Shrink and Shift." *New York Times*, October 27. https://www.nytimes.com/2012/10/28/business/a-part-time-life-as-hours-shrink-and-shift-for-american-workers.html.

Greenhouse, Steven. 2013a. "Fast-Food Workers Plan Second Strike for More Pay." *New York Times*, April 4. https://www.nytimes.com/2013/04/04/nyregion/fast-food-workers-plan-second-strike-for-more-pay.html.

Greenhouse, Steven. 2013b. "A Day's Strike Seeks to Raise Fast-Food Pay." *New York Times*, July 31. https://www.nytimes.com/2013/08/01/business/strike-for-day-seeks-to-raise-fast-food-pay.html?pagewanted=all.

Greenhouse, Steven. 2014. "A Day's Strike Seeks to Raise Fast-Food Pay." *New York Times*, December 10. https://www.nytimes.com/2013/08/01/business/strike-for-day-seeks-to-raise-fast-food-pay.html.

Gross, Julian, Greg LeRoy, and Madeline Janis-Aparicio. 2005. *Community Benefits Agreements: Making Development Projects Accountable*. Washington, D.C.: Good Jobs First and California Partnership for Working Families. http://www.goodjobsfirst.org/sites/default/files/docs/pdf/cba2005final.pdf.

Hackworth, Jason. 2015. "Right-Sizing as Spatial Austerity in the American Rust Belt." *Environment and Planning A* 47: 766–82.

Hackworth, Jason. 2007. *The Neoliberal City : Governance, Ideology, and Development in American Urbanism*. Ithaca, N.Y.: Cornell University Press. http://www.loc.gov/catdir/toc/ecip0617/2006023306.html.

Hajer, Maarten A. 2009. *Authoritative Governance: Policy Making in the Age of Mediatization*. Oxford: Oxford University Press.

Halpern, Robert. 1995. "Community Economic Development." In *Rebuilding the Inner City: A History of Neighborhood Initiatives to Address Poverty in the United States*, 127–48. New York: Columbia University Press.

Hanson, Susan, and Geraldine Pratt. 1995. *Gender, Work, and Space*. London: Routledge.

Harrison, Bennett, and Barry Bluestone. 1990. *The Great U-Turn: Corporate Restructuring and the Polarizing of America*. New York: Basic Books.

Hartig, Hannah. 2020. "Democrats Overwhelmingly Favor Free College Tuition, While Republicans Are Divided by Age, Education." *Pew Research Center,* February 21. https://www.pewresearch.org/fact-tank/2020/02/21/democrats-overwhelmingly-favor-free-college-tuition-while-republicans-are-divided-by-age-education/.

Hartley, Daniel A., Nikhil Kaza, and T. William Lester. 2016. "Are America's Inner Cities Competitive? Evidence from the 2000s." *Economic Development Quarterly* 30 (2): 137–58.

Harvey, David. 1982. *The Limits to Capital.* Oxford: Basil Blackwell.

Harvey, David. 1989a. "From Managerialism to Entrepreneurialism: The Transformation in Urban Governance in Late Capitalism." *Geografiska Annaler. Series B, Human Geography* 71 (1): 3–17.

Harvey, David. 1989b. *The Urban Experience.* Baltimore, MD: Johns Hopkins University Press.

Hatton, Erin. 2011. *The Temp Economy: From Kelly Girls to Permatemps in Postwar America.* Temple University Press.

Hatton, Erin. 2017. "Mechanisms of Invisibility: Rethinking the Concept of Invisible Work." *Work, Employment and Society* 31 (2): 336–51.

Henwood, Doug. 2003. *After the New Economy.* New York: New Press.

Herod, Andrew. 1997. "Labor's Spatial Praxis and the Geography of Contract Bargaining in the US East Coast Longshore Industry, 1953–1989." *Political Geography* 16 (2): 145–69.

Herrera, Lucero E., Saba Waheed, Tia Koonse, and Clarine Ovando-Lacroux. 2014. *Exploring Targeted Hire: An Assessment of Best Practices in the Construction Industry.* Los Angeles: UCLA Labor Center.

Hertel-Fernandez, Alex. 2019. *State Capture: How Conservative Activists, Big Businesses, and Wealthy Donors Reshaped the American States—and the Nation.* Oxford: Oxford University Press.

Herweg, Nicole, Nikolaos Zahariadis, and Reimut Zohlnhöfer. 2017. "The Multiple Streams Framework: Foundations, Refinements, and Empirical Applications." In *Theories of the Policy Process,* edited by Christopher M. Weible and Paul A. Sabatier, 4th ed., 17–53. New York: Routledge.

Highsmith, Brian. 2019. "The Implications of Inequality for Fiscal Federalism (or Why the Federal Government Should Pay for Local Public Schools)." *Buff. L. Rev.* 67: 407.

Hinz, Greg. 2020. "Lightfoot Reveals Her TIF Overhaul Plan." *Crain's Chicago Business,* February 5. https://www.chicagobusiness.com/greg-hinz-politics/lightfoot-reveals-her-tif-overhaul-plan.

Ho, Stacy, and Jeremy Hays. 2011. *High Road Outcomes in Portland's Energy Efficiency Upgrade Pilot.* Oakland, CA: Green For All.

Hong, Jonathan. 2016. "The 421-a Tax Abatement Program: Affordable

Housing Policy and Its Effect on Characterizing Brooklyn Communities." Senior capstone project, Vassar College.

Houser, Erik, Craig W. Thomas, and Stephen Page. 2017. *$15 Now?! Combat and Collaboration in Seattle's Historic Minimum Wage Debate (B).* Seattle: University of Washington, Evans School of Public Policy & Governance.

Houston, Serin D. 2019. *Imagining Seattle: Social Values in Urban Governance.* Lincoln: University of Nebraska Press.

Hwang, Jackelyn. 2020. "Gentrification without Segregation? Race, Immigration, and Renewal in a Diversifying City." *City & Community* 19 (3): 538–72.

Hyra, Derek. 2012. "Conceptualizing the New Urban Renewal: Comparing the Past to the Present." *Urban Affairs Review* 48 (4): 498–527.

Imbroscio, David L. 2006. "Shaming the Inside Game: A Critique of the Liberal Expansionist Approach to Addressing Urban Problems." *Urban Affairs Review* 42 (2): 224–48.

Imbroscio, David. 2013. "From Redistribution to Ownership: Toward a Post Neoliberal Urbanism." *Urban Affairs Review* 49 (6): 787–820.

Jayaraman, Sarumathi, and Immanuel Ness. 2015. *The New Urban Immigrant Workforce: Innovative Models for Labor Organizing.* London: Routledge.

Jefferson, Brian. 2020. *Digitize and Punish: Racial Criminalization in the Digital Age.* Minneapolis: University of Minnesota Press.

Jonas, Andrew E. 1998. "Investigating the Local-Global Paradox: Corporate Strategy, Union Local Autonomy, and Community Action in Chicago." In *Organizing the Landscape: Geographical Perspectives on Labor Unionism,* edited by Andrew Herod, 325–50. Minneapolis: University of Minnesota Press.

Jonas, Andrew E, and David Wilson. 1999. *The Urban Growth Machine: Critical Perspectives, Two Decades Later.* Albany: State University of New York Press.

Jones, Michael D., Holly L. Peterson, Jonathan J. Pierce, Nicole Herweg, Amiel Bernal, Holly Lamberta Raney, and Nikolaos Zahariadis. 2016. "A River Runs through It: A Multiple Streams Meta-Review." *Policy Studies Journal* 44 (1): 13–36.

Judd, Dennis R., and Dick W. Simpson. 2011. *The City, Revisited: Urban Theory from Chicago, Los Angeles, and New York.* Minneapolis: University of Minnesota Press.

Jurow, A. Susan, Leah Teeters, Molly Shea, and Erica Van Steenis. 2016. "Extending the Consequentiality of 'Invisible Work' in the Food Justice Movement." *Cognition and Instruction* 34 (3): 210–21.

Kaegi, Fritz, and M. P. A. Ross. 2019. "Closing the Divide: How the Cook

County Assessor's Office Is Translating Electoral Victory into Meaningful Policy Reform." Panel presentation, 85th annual conference of the International Association of Assessing Officers, September.
Kain, John H., and Joseph J. Persky. 1969. "Alternatives to the Gilded Ghetto." *The Public Interest* 14: 74.
Kantor, Paul. 1995. *The Dependent City Revisited: The Political Economy of Urban Development and Social Policy.* Boulder, Colo.: Westview.
Karch, Andrew. 2007. *Democratic Laboratories: Policy Diffusion among the American States.* Ann Arbor: University of Michigan Press.
Karjanen, David J. 2016. *The Servant Class City: Urban Revitalization versus the Working Poor in San Diego.* Minneapolis: University of Minnesota Press.
Katznelson, Ira. 1982. *City Trenches: Urban Politics and the Patterning of Class in the United States.* Chicago: University of Chicago Press.
Kaufmann, Karen M. 2005. "Still Waiting for the Rainbow Coalition? Group Rationality and Urban Coalitions."
Keegan, Caroline. 2020. "'Black Workers Matter': Black Labor Geographies and Uneven Redevelopment in Post-Katrina New Orleans." *Urban Geography* 42 (3): 340–59.
Kim, Yunji, Austin M. Aldag, and Mildred E. Warner. 2020. "Blocking the Progressive City: How State Pre-Emptions Undermine Labour Rights in the USA." *Urban Studies* 58 (6): 1158–75.
Kim, Yunji, and Mildred E. Warner. 2016. "Pragmatic Municipalism: Local Government Service Delivery after the Great Recession." *Public Administration* 94 (3): 789–805.
Kinder, Kimberley. 2016. *DIY Detroit: Making Do in a City without Services.* Minneapolis: University of Minnesota Press.
Kingdon, John. 1984. *Agendas, Alternatives, and Public Policies.* New York: HarperCollins.
Krippner, Greta R. 2005. "The Financialization of the American Economy." *Socio-Economic Review* 3 (2): 173–208.
Krumholz, Norman. 1994. "Advocacy Planning: Can It Move the Center?" *Journal of the American Planning Association* 60 (2): 150–51.
Krumholz, Norman, Janice M. Cogger, and John H. Linner. 1975. "The Cleveland Policy Planning Report." *Journal of the American Institute of Planners* 41 (5): 298–304.
Krumholz, Norman, and John Forester. 1990. *Making Equity Planning Work: Leadership in the Public Sector.* Philadelphia: Temple University Press.
Lafer, Gordon. 2017. *The One Percent Solution: How Corporations Are Remaking America One State at a Time.* Ithaca, N.Y.: Cornell University Press.

Lambert, Susan J., Peter J. Fugiel, and Julia R. Henly. 2014. *Precarious Work Schedules among Early-Career Employees in the US: A National Snapshot.* Research Brief. Chicago: University of Chicago, Employment Instability, Family Well-Being, and Social Policy Network (EINet).

Lambert, Susan J., Anna Haley-Lock, and Julia R. Henly. 2012. "Schedule Flexibility in Hourly Jobs: Unanticipated Consequences and Promising Directions." *Community, Work & Family* 15 (3): 293–315.

Lambert, Susan J., and Julia R. Henly. 2009. "Scheduling in Hourly Jobs: Promising Practices for the Twenty-First Century Economy." Washington, D.C.: Mobility Agenda. https://ssascholars.uchicago.edu/work-scheduling-study/files/lambert_and_henly_scheduling_policy_brief.pdf.

Larson, Eric D. 2016. "Black Lives Matter and Bridge Building: Labor Education for a 'New Jim Crow' Era." *Labor Studies Journal* 41 (1): 36–66.

Lees, Loretta, Hyun Bang Shin, and Ernesto López-Morales. 2016. *Planetary Gentrification.* Cambridge: Polity.

Leeuwen, Bart van. 2020. "What Is the Point of Urban Justice? Access to Human Space." *Acta Politica*: 1–22.

Lefebvre, Henri. 1991. *The Production of Space.* Translated by Donald Nicholson-Smith. Cambridge: Blackwell.

Leitner, Helga, Eric Sheppard, and Kristin M. Sziarto. 2008. "The Spatialities of Contentious Politics." *Transactions of the Institute of British Geographers* 33 (2): 157–72.

Lesniewski, Jacob, and Marc Doussard. 2017. "Crossing Boundaries, Building Power: Chicago Organizers Embrace Race, Ideology, and Coalition." *Social Service Review* 91 (4): 585–620.

Lester, T. William. 2014. "The Role of History in Redistributional Policy Discourse: Evidence from Living Wage Campaigns in Chicago and San Francisco." *Journal of Urban Affairs* 36 (4): 783–806.

Lipman, Pauline. 2013. "The Rebirth of the Chicago Teachers Union and Possibilities for a Counter-Hegemonic Education Movement." *Monthly Review* 65 (2): 1.

Locker, Philip. 2015. Locker (Philip) oral history interview conducted by Garrett Strain. Transcript. University of Washington, Special Collections. Oral History Collection. SeaTac Seattle Minimum Wage History Project records. https://digitalcollections.lib.washington.edu/digital/collection/ohc/id/1847/rec/28.

Logan, John R., and Harvey Molotch. 1987. *Urban Fortunes: The Political Economy of Place.* Berkeley: University of California Press.

Lowe, Nichola. 2007. "Job Creation and the Knowledge Economy: Lessons from North Carolina's Life Science Manufacturing Initiative." *Economic Development Quarterly* 21 (4): 339–53.

Lowe, Nichola J., and Laura Wolf-Powers. 2018. "Who Works in a Working Region? Inclusive Innovation in the New Manufacturing Economy." *Regional Studies* 52 (6): 828–39.

Luce, Stephanie. 2004. *Fighting for a Living Wage*. Ithaca, N.Y.: Cornell University Press.

Luce, Stephanie. 2015. "$15 per Hour or Bust: An Appraisal of the Higher Wages Movement." *New Labor Forum* 24: 72–79.

Luce, Stephanie. 2017. "Living Wages: A US Perspective." *Employee Relations* 39 (6): 863–74.

Luce, Stephanie, and Naoki Fujita. 2012. *Discounted Jobs: How Retailers Sell Workers Short*. New York: CUNY Murphy Institute and Retail Action Project.

MacDonald, Ian Thomas, ed. 2017. *Unions and the City: Negotiating Urban Change*. Ithaca, N.Y.: Cornell University Press.

Madland, David. 2015. *Hollowed Out: Why the Economy Doesn't Work Without a Strong Middle Class*. Berkeley: University of California Press.

Mah, Julie. 2020. "Gentrification-Induced Displacement in Detroit, Michigan: An Analysis of Evictions." *Housing Policy Debate*, 1–23.

Marantz, Nicholas J. 2015. "What Do Community Benefits Agreements Deliver? Evidence from Los Angeles." *Journal of the American Planning Association* 81 (4): 251–67.

Markusen, Ann, Peter Hall, Scott Campbell, and Sabina Deitrick. 1991. *The Rise of the Gunbelt: The Military Remapping of Industrial America*. New York: Oxford University Press.

Markusen, Ann. 1980. *Regions and Regionalism : A Marxist View*. Berkeley, Calif.: Institute of Urban and Regional Development Dept. of City and Regional Planning, University of California.

Markusen, Ann, and Greg Schrock. 2009. "Consumption-Driven Urban Development." *Urban Geography* 30 (4): 344–67.

Martin, Isaac. 2001. "Dawn of the Living Wage: The Diffusion of a Redistributive Municipal Policy." *Urban Affairs Review* 36 (4): 470–96.

Martin, Isaac. 2006. "Do Living Wage Policies Diffuse?" *Urban Affairs Review* 41 (5): 710–19.

Massey, Douglas S., and Nancy A. Denton. 1993. *American Apartheid: Segregation and the Making of the Underclass*. Cambridge, Mass.: Harvard University Press.

Massey, Douglas S., Jorge Durand, and N. Malone. 2002. *Beyond Smoke and Mirrors: Immigration Policy and Global Economic Integration*. New York: Russell Sage Foundation.

McAdam, Doug, Sidney Tarrow, and Charles Tilly. 2003. "Dynamics of Contention." *Social Movement Studies* 2 (1): 99–102.

McAlevey, Jane. 2016. *No Shortcuts: Organizing for Power in the New Gilded Age*. Oxford: Oxford University Press.

McCall, Leslie. 2001. *Complex Inequality: Gender, Class, and Race in the New Economy*. New York: Routledge.

McCann, Eugene. 2013. "Policy Boosterism, Policy Mobilities, and the Extrospective City." *Urban Geography* 34 (1): 5–29.

McClendon, Robert. 2014. "Labor-Advocacy Group Renews Calls for Community Benefits on $546 Million Airport Project." *Times-Picayune*, August 13. https://www.nola.com/news/politics/article_904478ee-b0ea-5d1f-b550-46cfc6673efd.html.

McDowell, Linda. 1991. "Life without Father and Ford: The New Gender Order of Post-Fordism." *Transactions of the Institute of British Geographers* 16 (4): 400–419.

McDowell, Linda. 2011. *Capital Culture: Gender at Work in the City*. New York: John Wiley & Sons.

McKittrick, Katherine, and Clyde Adrian Woods. 2007. *Black Geographies and the Politics of Place*. Cambridge, Mass.: South End.

Metzl, Jonathan M. 2019. *Dying of Whiteness: How the Politics of Racial Resentment Is Killing America's Heartland*. New York: Basic Books.

Mian, Atif, and Amir Sufi. 2015. *House of Debt: How They (and You) Caused the Great Recession, and How We Can Prevent It from Happening Again*. Chicago: University of Chicago Press.

Milkman, Ruth. 2006. *LA Story: Immigrant Workers and the Future of the U.S. Labor Movement*. New York: Russell Sage Foundation.

Milkman, Ruth. 2019. "U.S. Labor and the Neoliberal Turn." *Reviews in American History* 47 (1): 125–31.

Milkman, Ruth, Joshua Bloom, and Victor Narro. 2010. *Working for Justice: The LA Model of Organizing and Advocacy*. Ithaca, N.Y.: ILR.

Milkman, Ruth, and Ed Ott. 2014. *New Labor in New York: Precarious Workers and the Future of the Labor Movement*. Ithaca, N.Y.: Cornell University Press.

Minard, Lina. 2013. "Should Seattle Mandate That Construction Companies Hire Locally?" *The Stranger*, March 21. https://www.thestranger.com/slog/archives/2013/03/21/should-seattle-mandate-that-construction-companies-hire-locally.

Mishel, Lawrence, Josh Bivens, Elise Gould, and Heidi Shierholz. 2012. *The State of Working America*. 12th ed. Ithaca, N.Y.: Cornell University Press.

Mitchell, Mary. 2019. "Universal Basic Income May Be a Way to Break Cycle of Violence." *Chicago Sun-Times*, February 8. https://chicago.suntimes.com/2019/2/8/18339758/universal-basic-income-may-be-a-way-to-break-cycle-of-violence.

Mollenkopf, John H. 1983. *The Contested City*. Princeton, N.J.: Princeton University Press.

Mollenkopf, John H., and Manuel Castells. 1991. *Dual City: Restructuring New York*. New York: Russell Sage Foundation.

Molotch, Harvey. 1976. "The City as a Growth Machine: Toward a Political Economy of Place." *American Journal of Sociology* 82 (2): 309–32.

Montgomery, D. 1989. *The Fall of the House of Labor: The Workplace, the State, and American Labor Activism, 1865–1925*. Cambridge: Cambridge University Press.

Mooney, Christopher Z. 2001. *The Public Clash of Private Values: The Politics of Morality Policy*. New York: Chatham House.

Morel, Domingo. 2018. "Race and State in the Urban Regime." *Urban Affairs Review* 54 (3): 490–523.

Morello-Frosch, Rachel, Manuel Pastor, and James Sadd. 2001. "Environmental Justice and Southern California's 'Riskscape' the Distribution of Air Toxics Exposures and Health Risks among Diverse Communities." *Urban Affairs Review* 36 (4): 551–78.

Moretti, Enrico. 2012. *The New Geography of Jobs*. Boston: Houghton Mifflin Harcourt.

Moyn, Samuel. 2012. *The Last Utopia: Human Rights in History*. Cambridge, Mass.: Harvard University Press.

National Employment Law Project. 2011. *The Good Jobs Deficit: A Closer Look at Recent Job Loss and Job Growth Trends Using Occupational Data*. http://www.nelp.org/page/-/Final%20occupations%20report%207-25-11.pdf?nocdn=1.

National League of Cities. 2017. "State and Local Expenditures." State and Local Backgrounders. Washington, D.C.: National League of Cities. https://www.urban.org/policy-centers/cross-center-initiatives/state-and-local-finance-initiative/state-and-local-backgrounders/state-and-local-expenditures.

National League of Cities. 2020. *City Fiscal Conditions 2020*. Washington, D.C.: National League of Cities. https://www.nlc.org/sites/default/files/users/user57221/City_Fiscal_Conditions_2020_FINAL.pdf.

National Partnership for Women and Families. 2020. *Paid Sick Days Improve Public Health*. Washington, D.C. http://www.nationalpartnership.org/research-library/work-family/psd/paid-sick-days-improve-our-public-health.pdf.

Ness, Immanuel, and Stuart Eimer, eds. 2015. *Central Labor Councils and the Revival of American Unionism: Organizing for Justice in Our Communities*. Armonk, N.Y.: M. E. Sharpe.

New Orleans Airport Expansion Community Evaluation Commission. 2014. "Community RFP Findings."

Nicholls, Walter J. 2008. "The Urban Question Revisited: The Importance of Cities for Social Movements." *International Journal of Urban and Regional Research* 32 (4): 841–59.

Nicholls, Walter, Byron Miller, and Justin Beaumont, eds. 2013. *Spaces of Contention: Spatialities and Social Movements*. Aldershot, U.K.: Ashgate.

9to5. 2020. "About 9to5." https://9to5.org/about-9to5/.

Pagano, Michael A. 2013. *Metropolitan Resilience in a Time of Economic Turmoil*. Urbana: University of Illinois Press.

Paik, A. Naomi. 2020. *Bans, Walls, Raids, Sanctuary: Understanding US Immigration for the Twenty-First Century*. Berkeley: University of California Press.

Parikh, Sejal. 2015. Parikh (Sejal) oral history interview conducted by Megan Brown. Transcript. University of Washington, Special Collections. Oral History Collection. SeaTac Seattle Minimum Wage History Project records. https://digitalcollections.lib.washington.edu/digital/collection/ohc/id/1898/rec/36.

Parker, Brenda K. 2017. *Masculinities and Markets: Raced and Gendered Urban Politics in Milwaukee*. Athens: University of Georgia Press.

Parks, Virginia, and Dorian Warren. 2009. "The Politics and Practice of Economic Justice: Community Benefits Agreements as Tactic of the New Accountable Development Movement." *Journal of Community Practice* 17 (1–2): 88–106.

Pastor, Manuel, Chris Benner, and Martha Matsuoka. 2009. *This Could Be the Start of Something Big: How Social Movements for Regional Equity Are Reshaping Metropolitan America*. Ithaca, N.Y.: Cornell University Press.

Peck, Jamie. 1996. *Work-Place: The Social Regulation of Labor Markets*. New York: Guilford.

Peck, Jamie. 2016. "The Right to Work, and the Right at Work." *Economic Geography* 92 (1): 4–30.

Peck, Jamie, and Nik Theodore. 2010. "Mobilizing Policy: Models, Methods, and Mutations." *Geoforum* 41 (2): 169–74.

Peck, Jamie, and Nik Theodore. 2015. *Fast Policy*. Minneapolis: University of Minnesota Press.

Peck, Jamie, and Heather Whiteside. 2016. "Financializing Detroit." *Economic Geography* 92 (3): 235–68.

Perlstein, Rick. 2008. *Nixonland: The Rise of a President and the Fracturing of America*. New York: Scribner.

Peterson, Paul E. 1981. *City Limits*. Chicago: University of Chicago Press.

Piketty, Thomas. 2014. *Capital in the 21st Century*. Cambridge, Mass.: Belknap.

Piven, Frances Fox. 1970. "Whom Does the Advocate Planner Serve." *Social Policy* 1 (1): 32–37.

Podesta, John, and Cecilia Martinez. 2020. "Covid-19 Relief and Economic

Recovery Must Dismantle Environmental Racism." *The Hill,* July 18. https://thehill.com/opinion/energy-environment/507529-covid-19-relief-and-economic-recovery-must-dismantle-environmental.

Powell, John A. 2020. "Repealing Proposition 13 Would Shrink Racial Equity Gaps." *Sacramento Bee,* July 23. https://www.sacbee.com/opinion/california-forum/article244415522.html.

Pulido, Laura. 2017. "Geographies of Race and Ethnicity II: Environmental Racism, Racial Capitalism and State-Sanctioned Violence." *Progress in Human Geography* 41 (4): 524–33.

Quig, A. D. 2019. "Lightfoot Gets Low Marks from Progressive Groups on First 100 Days." *Crain's Chicago Business,* August 26. https://www.chicagobusiness.com/government/lightfoot-gets-low-marks-progressive-groups-first-100-days.

Raice, Shayndi. 2019. "Activists Try to Stop a Huge Chicago Development Over $1.3 Billion in Tax Incentives." *Wall Street Journal,* July 11. https://www.wsj.com/articles/activists-try-to-stop-a-huge-chicago-development-over-1-3-billion-in-tax-incentives-11562849876.

Rast, Joel. 1999. *Remaking Chicago: The Political Origins of Urban Industrial Change.* Dekalb: Northern Illinois University Press.

Rast, Joel. 2015. "Urban Regime Theory and the Problem of Change." *Urban Affairs Review* 51 (1): 138–49.

Reese, Laura A., Gary Sands, and Mark Skidmore. 2014. "Memo from Motown: Is Austerity Here to Stay?" *Cambridge Journal of Regions, Economy and Society* 7 (1): 99–118.

Reich, Michael, Sylvia Allegretto, and Anna Godoey. 2017. "Seattle's Minimum Wage Experience 2015–16." *Center on Wage and Employment Dynamics Policy Brief,* June. https://www.researchgate.net/profile/Sylvia_Allegretto/publication/317840606_Seattle%27s_Minimum_Wage_Experience_2015-16/links/594d8a870f7e9be7b2d66120/Seattles-Minimum-Wage-Experience-2015-16.pdf.

Reich, Michael, Ken Jacobs, and Miranda Dietz. 2014. *When Mandates Work: Raising Labor Standards at the Local Level.* Berkeley: University of California Press.

Reynolds, David, and Jen Kern. 2001. "Labor and the Living-Wage Movement." *WorkingUSA* 5 (3): 17–45.

Rivera, Guillermo. 2015. Rivera (Guillermo "Memo") oral history interview conducted by Megan Brown. Transcript. University of Washington, Special Collections. Oral History Collection. SeaTac Seattle Minimum Wage History Project records. https://digitalcollections.lib.washington.edu/digital/collection/ohc/id/1904/rec/39.

Robinson, Cedric J. 2005. *Black Marxism: The Making of the Black Radical Tradition.* Chapel Hill: University of North Carolina Press.

Robinson, Scott E., and Warren S. Eller. 2010. "Participation in Policy Streams: Testing the Separation of Problems and Solutions in Subnational Policy Systems." *Policy Studies Journal* 38 (2): 199–216.

Rolf, David. 2015a. *The Fight for $15: The Right Wage for a Working America.* New York: New Press.

Rolf, David. 2015b. Rolf (David) oral history interview conducted by Garrett Strain. Transcript. University of Washington, Special Collections. Oral History Collection. SeaTac Seattle Minimum Wage History Project records. https://digitalcollections.lib.washington.edu/digital/collection/ohc/id/1996/rec/40.

Rolf, Pendall. 2005. "Up Against the Sprawl: Public Policy and the Making of Southern California." *Economic Geography* 81 (3): 331.

Rosen, Jovanna, and Lisa Schweitzer. 2018. "Benefits-Sharing Agreements and Nonideal Theory: The Warning Signs of Agreement Co-Optation." *Planning Theory* 17 (3): 396–417.

Rosenfeld, Jake. 2014. *What Unions No Longer Do.* Cambridge, Mass.: Harvard University Press.

Rothstein, Richard. 2017. *The Color of Law: A Forgotten History of How Our Government Segregated America.* New York: Liveright.

Round, Jenn. 2018. "The Labor Standards Enforcement Toolbox." Rutgers School of Management and Labor Relations. https://smlr.rutgers.edu/faculty-research-engagement/center-innovation-worker-organization-ciwo/strengthening-labor-standards.

Russon Gilman, Hollie, and Brian Wampler. 2019. "The Difference in Design: Participatory Budgeting in Brazil and the United States." *Journal of Public Deliberation* 15 (1): 7.

Saito, Leland. 2019. "Urban Development and the Growth with Equity Framework: The National Football League Stadium in Downtown Los Angeles." *Urban Affairs Review* 55 (5): 1370–401.

Saito, Leland, and Jonathan Truong. 2015. "The LA Live Community Benefits Agreement: Evaluating the Agreement Results and Shifting Political Power in the City." *Urban Affairs Review* 51 (2): 263–89.

Sams-Abiodun, Petrice, and Gregory Rattler Jr. 2013. *Recognizing the Underutilized Economic Potential of Black Men in New Orleans.* New Orleans: Lindy Boggs National Center for Community Literacy.

Sassen, Saskia. 2001. *The Global City: New York, London, Tokyo.* Princeton, N.J.: Princeton University Press.

Savitch, H. V., and Paul Kantor. 2002. *Cities in the International Marketplace: The Political Economy of Urban Development in North American and Western Europe.* Princeton, N.J.: Princeton University Press.

Schmitt, John. 2013. "Why Does the Minimum Wage Have No Discernible Effect on Employment?" *Center for Economic and Policy Research* 22: 1–28.

Schneider, Daniel, and Kristen Harknett. 2019. "Consequences of Routine Work-Schedule Instability for Worker Health and Well-Being." *American Sociological Review* 84 (1): 82–114.

Schragger, Richard. 2016. *City Power: Urban Governance in a Global Age.* New York: Oxford University Press.

Schrock, Greg. 2013. "Reworking Workforce Development: Chicago's Sectoral Workforce Centers." *Economic Development Quarterly* 27 (3): 163–78.

Schrock, Greg. 2015. "Remains of the Progressive City? First Source Hiring in Portland and Chicago." *Urban Affairs Review* 51 (5): 649–75.

Scott, Allen J. 2014. "Beyond the Creative City: Cognitive–Cultural Capitalism and the New Urbanism." *Regional Studies* 48 (4): 565–78.

Scott, Allen J. 2019. "City-Regions Reconsidered." *Environment and Planning A: Economy and Space* 51 (3): 554–80.

Sen, Amartya. 1990. "Development as Capability Expansion." In *Human Development and the International Development Strategy for the 1990s,* edited by Keith Griffin and John Knight, 41–58. London: Macmillan.

Sen, Amartya. 1999. *Development as Freedom.* Oxford: Oxford University Press.

Service Employees International Union. 2021. "Racial Justice." https://www.seiu.org/racial-justice.

Shabazz, Rashad. 2015. *Spatializing Blackness: Architectures of Confinement and Black Masculinity in Chicago.* Urbana: University of Illinois Press.

Sheppard, Eric, Vinay Gidwani, Michael Goldman, Helga Leitner, Ananya Roy, and Anant Maringanti. 2015. "Introduction: Urban Revolutions in the Age of Global Urbanism." *Urban Studies* 52 (11): 1947–61.

Sherman, Stephen Averill. 2020. "From Revanchism to Inclusion: Institutional Forms of Planning and Police in Hyde Park, Chicago." *Journal of Planning Education and Research* 40 (2):139–50.

Shi, Yu. 2018. "An Empirical Assessment of Local Autonomy and Special District Finance in the US." *Local Government Studies* 44 (4): 531–51.

Shipler, David K. 2005. *The Working Poor: Invisible in America.* New York: Vintage.

Shore, Cris, Susan Wright, and Davide Però. 2011. *Policy Worlds: Anthropology and the Analysis of Contemporary Power.* New York: Berghahn.

Sites, William. 2003. *Remaking New York: Primitive Globalization and the Politics of Urban Community.* Minneapolis: University of Minnesota Press.

Sites, William, Robert J. Chaskin, and Virginia Parks. 2007. "Reframing Community Practice for the 21st Century: Multiple Traditions, Multiple Challenges." *Journal of Urban Affairs* 29 (5): 519–41.

Smith, Neil. 2002. "New Globalism, New Urbanism: Gentrification as Global Urban Strategy." *Antipode* 34 (3): 427–50.

Sonn, Paul K., and Stephanie Luce. 2008. "New Directions for the Living Wage Movement." In *The Gloves-Off Economy: Workplace Standards at the Bottom of America's Labor Market*, edited by Annette Bernhardt, Heather Boushey, Laura Dresser, and Chris Tilly, 269–86. Ithaca, N.Y.: Cornell University Press.

Soss, Joe, Richard C. Fording, Sanford F. Schram, and Sanford Schram. 2011. *Disciplining the Poor: Neoliberal Paternalism and the Persistent Power of Race*. Chicago: University of Chicago Press.

Spicer, Jason S., and Evan Casper-Futterman. 2020. "Conceptualizing U.S. Community Economic Development: Evidence from New York City." *Journal of Planning Education and Research*.

Spirou, Costas, and Dennis R. Judd. 2016. *Building the City of Spectacle: Mayor Richard M. Daley and the Remaking of Chicago*. Ithaca, N.Y.: Cornell University Press.

Squires, Gregory D. 1989. *Unequal Partnerships: The Political Economy of Urban Redevelopment in Postwar America*. New Brunswick, N.J.: Rutgers University Press.

Squires, Gregory D. 1994. *Capital and Communities in Black and White: The Intersections of Race, Class, and Uneven Development*. Albany: State University of New York Press.

Stabrowski, Filip. 2015. "Inclusionary Zoning and Exclusionary Development: The Politics of 'Affordable Housing' in North Brooklyn." *International Journal of Urban and Regional Research* 39 (6): 1120–36.

Steil, Justin P., and Laura Humm Delgado. 2019. "Limits of Diversity: Jane Jacobs, the Just City, and Anti-Subordination." *Cities* 91: 39–48.

Stone, Clarence. 1989. *Regime Politics: Governing Atlanta, 1946–1988*. Lawrence: University Press of Kansas. http://www.getcited.org/pub/102798356.

Stone, Clarence N. 2015. "Reflections on Regime Politics: From Governing Coalition to Urban Political Order." *Urban Affairs Review* 51 (1): 101–37.

Stone, Clarence N. 2017. "Trends in the Study of Urban Politics: A Paradigmatic View." *Urban Affairs Review* 53 (1): 3–39.

Storper, Michael, and Richard Walker. 1989. *The Capitalist Imperative: Territory, Technology, and Industrial Growth*. New York: Basil Blackwell.

Sugrue, Thomas J. 1996. *The Origins of the Urban Crisis: Race and Inequality in Postwar Detroit*. Princeton, N.J.: Princeton University Press.

Swarts, Heidi, and Ion Bogdan Vasi. 2011. "Which US Cities Adopt Living Wage Ordinances? Predictors of Adoption of a New Labor Tactic, 1994–2006." *Urban Affairs Review* 47 (6): 743–74.

Sykes, Bryan L., and Michelle Maroto. 2016. "A Wealth of Inequalities: Mass Incarceration, Employment, and Racial Disparities in US Household Wealth, 1996 to 2011." *RSF: The Russell Sage Foundation Journal of the Social Sciences* 2 (6): 129–52.

Tattersall, Amanda. 2013. *Power in Coalition: Strategies for Strong Unions and Social Change*. Ithaca, N.Y.: Cornell University Press.

Thomas, Brianna. 2015. Thomas (Brianna) oral history interview conducted by Megan Brown. Transcript. University of Washington, Special Collections. Oral History Collection. SeaTac Seattle Minimum Wage History Project records. https://digitalcollections.lib.washington.edu/digital/collection/ohc/id/1919/rec/49.

Thomas, June Manning. 1990. "Planning and Industrial Decline Lessons from Postwar Detroit." *Journal of the American Planning Association* 56 (3): 297–310.

Thurow, Lester C. 1975. "Job Competition: The Labor Queue." In *Generating Inequality: Mechanisms of Distribution in the U.S. Economy*, 75–97. New York: Basic Books.

Tiebout, Charles M. 1956. "A Pure Theory of Local Expenditures." *Journal of Political Economy* 64 (5): 416.

Tilly, Chris, and Charles Tilly. 1998. *Work Under Capitalism*. Boulder, Colo.: Westview.

Toppin, E. J. 2019. "The Impact of Proposition 13 on Mental Health Services in California." *Other & Belonging Institute* (blog). January 3.

Turner, Lowell, and Daniel B. Cornfield. 2007. *Labor in the New Urban Battlegrounds: Local Solidarity in a Global Economy*. Ithaca, N.Y.: Cornell University Press.

UC Berkeley Labor Center. 2020. "Inventory of US City and County Minimum Wage Ordinances." http://laborcenter.berkeley.edu/minimum-wage-living-wage-resources/inventory-of-us-city-and-county-minimum-wage-ordinances/.

UCLA Labor Center. 2014. *Worker Profile in City of Seattle Construction Projects*. Los Angeles: UCLA Labor Center.

Uitermark, Justus, and Walter Nicholls. 2017. "Planning for Social Justice: Strategies, Dilemmas, Tradeoffs." *Planning Theory* 16 (1): 32–50.

Van Horn, Carl E., Robert A. Beauregard, and David S. Ford. 1986. "Local Economic Development and Job Targeting." In *Local Economies in Transition*, edited by Edward M. Bergman, 226–47. Durham, N.C.: Duke University Press.

Vote Yes for a Fair Tax. 2020. "Fair Tax and Racial Equity: Guide on Discussing How the Fair Tax Advances Racial Equity." https://www.lwvwilmette.org/uploads/1/0/5/5/105539455/vyft-fair-tax-and-race-equity.pdf.

Weaver, Timothy P. R. 2018. "A City of Citizens: Social Justice and Urban Social Citizenship." *New Political Science* 40 (1): 84–102.

Weaver, Timothy P. R. 2021. "Charting Change in the City: Urban Political Orders and Urban Political Development." *Urban Affairs Review*.

Weber, Rachel. 2002. "Extracting Value from the City: Neoliberalism and Urban Redevelopment." *Antipode* 34 (3): 519–40.

Weber, Rachel. 2014. "Tax Increment Financing in Theory and Practice." In *Financing Economic Development in the 21st Century*, edited by Sammis B. White and Zenia Z. Kotval, 297–315. London: Routledge.

Weber, Rachel. 2015. *From Boom to Bubble: How Finance Built the New Chicago*. Chicago: University of Chicago Press.

Weil, David. 2008. "Mighty Monolith or Fractured Federation? Business Opposition and the Enactment of Workplace Legislation." In *The Gloves-off Economy: Workplace Standards at the Bottom of America's Labor Market*, edited by Annette Bernhardt, heather Boushey, Laura Dresser, and Chris Tilly, 287–316. Champaign: University of Illinois at Urbana-Champaign.

Weir, Margaret. 1992. *Politics and Jobs: The Boundaries of Employment Policy in the United States*. Princeton, N.J.: Princeton University Press.

Weller, Christian. 2020. "Systemic Racism Makes Covid-19 Much More Deadly for African-Americans." *Forbes*, June 18. https://www.forbes.com/sites/christianweller/2020/06/18/systemic-racism-makes-covid-19-much-more-deadly-for-african-americans/.

Wen, Christine, Yuanshuo Xu, Yunji Kim, and Mildred E. Warner. 2018. "Starving Counties, Squeezing Cities: Tax and Expenditure Limits in the US." *Journal of Economic Policy Reform* 23 (2): 1–19.

Whelan, Robert K., and Denïse Strong. 2018. "Rebuilding Lives Post-Katrina: Choices and Challenges in New Orleans's Economic Development." In *Race, Place, and Environmental Justice after Hurricane Katrina: Struggles to Reclaim, Rebuild, and Revitalize New Orleans and the Gulf Coast*, edited by Robert D. Bullard and Beverly Wright, 183–203. New York: Routledge.

Whiting, Rebecca, and Gillian Symon. 2020. "Digi-Housekeeping: The Invisible Work of Flexibility." *Work, Employment and Society* 34 (6): 1079–96.

Wiewel, Wim, and Nicholas C. Rieser. 1989. "The Limits of Progressive Municipal Economic Development: Job Creation in Chicago, 1983–1987." *Community Development Journal* 24 (2): 111–19.

Williams, Jessica. 2015. "City Makes Concessions to Both Sides under HireNOLA Rules; Labor Activists Still Dissatisfied." *Times-Picayune*, December 15. https://www.nola.com/news/politics/article_32cfae14-6344-5144-8a94-e7770a2cb 71 a.html.

Wilson, Sage. 2015. Wilson (Sage) oral history interview conducted by Megan Brown. Transcript. University of Washington, Special Collections. Oral History Collection. SeaTac Seattle Minimum Wage History Project records. https://digitalcollections.lib.washington.edu/digital/collection/ohc/id/1874/rec/55.

Wilson, William Julius. 1996. *When Work Disappears: The World of the New Urban Poor.* New York: Knopf.

Winders, Jamie, and Barbara Ellen Smith. 2019. "Social Reproduction and Capitalist Production: A Genealogy of Dominant Imaginaries." *Progress in Human Geography* 43 (5): 871–89.

Wolf-Powers, Laura. 2010. "Community Benefits Agreements and Local Government." *Journal of the American Planning Association* 76 (2): 141–59.

Woods, Clyde Adrian. 1998. *Development Arrested: The Blues and Plantation Power in the Mississippi Delta.* London: Verso.

Wright, Erik Olin, and Rachel E. Dwyer. 2003. "The Patterns of Job Expansions in the USA: A Comparison of the 1960s and 1990s." *Socio-Economic Review* 1 (3): 289–325.

Wright, Howard. 2015. Wright (Howard) oral history interview conducted by Emilie Wood and Garrett Strain. Transcript. University of Washington, Special Collections. Oral History Collection. SeaTac Seattle Minimum Wage History Project records. https://digitalcollections.lib.washington.edu/digital/collection/ohc/id/1993/rec/56.

Wright, James, Ronald W. Whitaker, Muhammad Khalifa, and Felecia Briscoe. 2020. "The Color of Neoliberal Reform: A Critical Race Policy Analysis of School District Takeovers in Michigan." *Urban Education* 55 (3): 424–47.

Xu, Yuanshuo, and Mildred E. Warner. 2016. "Does Devolution Crowd Out Development? A Spatial Analysis of US Local Government Fiscal Effort." *Environment and Planning A* 48 (5): 871–90.

Zahariadis, Nikolaos. 2014. "Ambiguity and Multiple Streams." *Theories of the Policy Process* 3: 25–59.

Ziliak, Stephanie. 2016. "The Business Benefits of Paid Sick Time: Healthy Employees Lead to Healthy Ledgers." Center for Law and Social Policy. https://www.clasp.org/sites/default/files/public/resources-and-publications/publication-1/Business-Case-for-HFA-1.pdf.

Zotti, Ed. 2019. "End Black Flight, and Chicago Can Grow to 3 Million People Again." *Chicago Sun Times,* December 10. https://chicago.suntimes.com/columnists/2019/12/10/21010315/chicago-growth-population-african-american-black-flight-ed-zotti-lori-lightfoot.

Index

Page numbers in italics signify figures or tables.

ACORN (Association of Community Organizations for Reform Now), 48, 49, 50, 53, 72, 127
Action Now! (Chicago), 158
affirmative action, 115, 119
Affordable Care Act, 68
AFL-CIO, 47, 92
AFSCME (American Federation of State, County and Municipal Employees), 47, 190
agenda setting, 70
agenda windows, 70, 77–79, 80–81, 205n4
Agnos, Art, 46
Alinsky, Saul, 6, 37, 38, 49, 73, 181
American Federation of State, County and Municipal Employees (AFSCME), 47, 190
American Legislative Exchange Council (ALEC), 197
American Recovery and Reinvestment Act (ARRA) (2009), 123, 131
American Rescue Plan, 86
antiausterity activism. *See* public finance activism
Arkansas, minimum-wage campaigns, 108
austerity policies: education and, 171, 172, 173; elder- and childcare and, 169; Great Recession and, 53, 57, 58, 84, 164–66, 174, 179; limits on power of cities and, 64, 165; racial justice focus and, 84, 182–83; roots of, 162–63; tax increment financing (TIF) and, 175; urban rebound and, 17
authors' research approaches and methods, 3, 79–81, 84–86

Baker, Ella, 59
ballot initiatives: minimum-wage campaigns and, 81, 82, 92–93, 95, 96, 97–98, 101, 105, 106, 108; urban policy entrepreneurs and, 8, 9, 77, 80
Baltimore, 125
Ban the Box measures, 115
basic income programs, 159, 166
Benner, Chris, 34, 40
Better Balance, A, 142
Big Box bill (Chicago), 57, 175, 191
Black Friday strikes (2012), 94
Black Lives Matter, 54, 128
Boston, 44, 45, 119
Brightline Defense (BD) (San Francisco), 123–25
Brown, Michael, 54
Bureau of Labor Statistics, 144
Burlington, Vermont, 44
Bush, George W., administration, 68

California, 177, 178. *See also* Los Angeles; San Francisco
Camden, New Jersey, 119

233

capitalism. *See* racial capitalism analysis
CARES Act, 181
Casper-Futterman, Evan, 76
Castells, Manuel, 35, 38–40
Caucus of Rank-and-File Educators (CORE), 172
CBAs (community benefits agreements), 120–22, 135
Center for Budget and Policy Priorities, 142
Center for Law and Social Policy, 142, 153
Center for Popular Democracy, 153
Central Labor Councils (CLCs), 47, 56
Chavez, Cesar, 59
Chicago: austerity policies, 17, 58; authors' research methods and, 84–85; Chicago Teachers Union strike, 4, 56, 103, 104, 171–74; electoral politics, 77, 105–6; ERJ coalition development, 54, 56, 57–59; ERJ coalition networks, 37–38; gerrymandering, 103, 206n3; labor movement, 56; living-wage movement, 49, 57, 103, 175, 191; minimum-wage campaigns, 26, 38, 77, 102–6, 107, 110–11; neighborhoods movement, 44–45, 103; public finance activism, 21, 58–59, 166, 167–68, 169–70, 174–77; targeted hiring programs, 117–18, 119, 121–22; urban rebound and, 16–17, 26, 51; work-and-home policies, 26, 154–56, 157
Chicago Association of Neighborhood Development Organizations, 44, 45
Chicago First program, 118, 119
Chicago Foundation for Women, 148
Chicago Jobs Coalition (CJC), 117, 118
Chicago Jobs Council, 45
Chicago Lawyers' Committee for Civil Rights, 176–77
Chicago Teachers Union, 4, 56, 103, 104, 171–74
"Chicago Works Together" (Mier), 44, 45
Children's Defense Fund, 142
Chinese for Affirmative Action (CAA) (San Francisco), 123–25
Cincotta, Gale, 37
cities, limits on power of, 64–65, 165
Cleveland: neighborhoods movement, 43–44, 46; targeted hiring programs, 119
Clinton, Bill, 142
collective action frames, 66
Colorado: minimum-wage campaigns, 108, 198; public finance activism, 177–78, 179–81
Colorado Families for a Fair Wage, 108
Colorado Fiscal Policy Institute, 179–80
Commerce Clause, 119
community benefits agreements (CBAs), 120–22, 135
community benefits movement, 30–31, 39, 42, 50–52, 120–22
community development corporations, 41, 103
community organizing: living-wage movement and, 7, 39, 48; racism and, 6, 37, 41, 49, 181
Community Renewal Society (CRS) (Chicago), 121–22
community workforce agreements, 131
Community Workshop for Economic Development (Chicago), 45

Connecticut, minimum-wage campaigns, 109
Construction Jobs Equity Coalition (Seattle), 131
consumption base, 32–33
CORE (Caucus of Rank-and-File Educators), 172
Couch, David, 108
coupling events, 68, 70, 78, 125. *See also* agenda windows
Covid-19 pandemic, 2, 180–81, 201

Daley, Richard M., 49, 57, 118, 175
de Blasio, Bill, 154–55
deindustrialization: austerity policies and, 162; growth machine theory on, 19–20; inequalities and, 28; minimum-wage campaigns and, 87; neighborhoods movement and, 39, 44, 46, 60
Denver, 54, 85, 121
Department of Economic Development (Chicago), 45
desegregation, 115
Detroit: growth machine theory on, 21; minimum-wage campaigns, 94–95; urban rebound and, 15–16
discourse coalitions theory, 65–66, 79
disinvestment, 4, 17, 18, 50–51, 162–63
downtowns, 21

East Bay Alliance for a Sustainable Economy (EBASE), 55
Economic Action Research Network (EARN), 93, 112
economic and racial justice (ERJ) coalitions: antiracism work within, 196; challenges for, 7, 40–42, 61–62, 188–89; durability of, 189–91; historical isolation of, 38–39; network structures of, 35, 37–38; opportunities for, 3, 24; political scale and, 197–98; process similarities, 34; racial capitalism analysis and, 35–36; roots of, 6–7, 35, 183, 188; successes of, 38, 187, 191–93; UPE collaboration with, 71, 72, 77; visions of justice and, 193–94, 195, 196–97. *See also* ERJ coalition development
economic and social inequalities. *See* inequalities
economic changes. *See* urban rebound
economic development, 31–33
Economic Policy Institute, 93, 106, 112
Edelman, Marion Wright, 142
elder- and childcare, 168–71
electoral politics: disappointment with, 53, 189; minimum-wage campaigns and, 26, 76, 77, 81–82, 92–93, 95, 98–100, 105–6, 109, 112, 206n4; multiple streams approach and, 69–70; neighborhoods movement and, 44–45; urban policy entrepreneurs and, 76–77, 79–80, 189; urban scholarship focus on, 4; work-and-home policies and, 155–56. *See also* ballot initiatives; politics stream
Emanuel, Rahm: austerity and, 57–58; Chicago Teachers Union strike and, 104, 171, 173; minimum-wage campaigns and, 26, 102, 103, 105, 106, 206n4; politics stream and, 77; public finance and, 166; work-and-home policies and, 37, 154–55, 156
Emerald Cities Collaborative, 129

Employee Retirement Income Security Act (ERISA), 151
Enlace Chicago, 158
environmental sustainability, 130–31
ERJ coalition development, 39–62, 42; community benefits movement as precursor, 50–52; Great Recession and, 53–54, 57; living-wage movement as precursor, 6–7, 39, 42, 47–50, 57; neighborhoods movement as precursor, 39, 42, 43–47; racial capitalism analysis and, 59–60; racial justice focus and, 54–57, 58, 59, 60–61. *See also* economic and racial justice (ERJ) coalitions
ERJ coalitions. *See* economic and racial justice (ERJ) coalitions

fair workweek legislation, 83, 148, 152, 156, 158, 192. *See also* scheduling challenges
Fight for a Fair Economy, 96
Fight for $15. *See* minimum-wage campaigns
financialization, 19, 20–21, 28
First Source Hiring programs, 117–18, 122, 206n1
fiscal austerity. *See* austerity policies
fiscal racism, 164, 185. *See also* public finance activism
Fischer, Frank, 66
Florida, 107
Floyd, George, 59, 85
Flynn, Ray, 44, 45, 46
Fordism, 115, 141, 161–62, 194–95, 196
foreclosure crisis. *See* Great Recession
Freiboth, David, 101

Front Range Economic Strategy Center (Denver), 54

Ganz, Marshall, 167, 188
Garcia, Jesus "Chuy," 103, 105, 106
Gateway Project (Chicago), 121–22
gender advocacy. *See* women
gentrification, 16, 51–52, 74, 174, 175, 176, 201–2
gerrymandering, 103, 206n3
Gilmore, Ruth Wilson, 36
globalization, 3, 199–200
Goldilocks problem, 199
Got Green (Seattle), 131
Grassroots Collaborative (Chicago), 37, 38, 54, 57–59, 158, 175
Greater Birmingham Ministries (GBM), 55–56
Great Recession (2007–2009), 39, 41; austerity policies and, 53, 57, 58, 84, 164–66, 174, 179; community benefits movement and, 51–52; ERJ coalition development and, 53–54, 57; impact of, 52–53, 137; living-wage movement and, 49; mainstream attention to inequalities and, 192; minimum-wage campaigns and, 53–54, 93–94; public finance activism and, 163, 179; racial justice focus and, 174; targeted hiring programs and, 121, 123; work-and-home policies and, 137–38, 140–41, 142, 145
growth imperative, 21, 26–27, 30–31, 41–42, 51
growth machine theory, 4, 19–20, 21, 24, 25, 29

Hire NOLA, 127, 128–29
HireNYC program, 125

INDEX || 237

home-and-work policies. *See* work-and-home policies
housing, 201–2
human development approach to economic development, 32
Hurricane Katrina, 127, 134

Illinois: minimum-wage campaigns, 109; public finance activism, 177, 178–79. *See also* Chicago
Imbroscio, David L., 88
immigrants, 49–50, 55
Indianapolis, 84–85, 107
Industrial Areas Foundation, 37, 38
inequalities: mainstream attention to, 2, 15, 17, 192; minimum-wage campaigns and, 102, 107; persistence of, 1–2, 21–24, 23; public finance activism and, 168; targeted hiring programs and, 130, 134; urban rebound and, 3, 24–25, 27, 28, 29–30; work-and-home policies and, 154. *See also* racism
inside-outside campaigns: ERJ coalition successes and, 192–93; minimum-wage campaigns and, 101, 193; multiple streams approach and, 71, 72; targeted hiring programs and, 117, 136; work-and-home policies and, 156–57
Interfaith Worker Justice, 54, 55–56
ISAIAH Minnesota, 55

Janus v. AFSCME, 190
Jobs with Justice, 54
justice, visions of, 193–97, 202
Justice for Janitors, 78
just-in-time scheduling, 138, 154–55. *See also* scheduling challenges

Kantor, Paul, 34
King, Martin Luther, Jr., 94
King County Labor Federation, 96
Kingdon, John, 64, 67–68, 69, 73

Laborers Union (Seattle), 131, 132
labor movement: durability of ERJ coalitions and, 190; elder- and childcare and, 169; Fordism and, 162, 194–95; immigrants and, 55; *Janus v. AFSCME* and, 190; living-wage movement and, 6, 47–48; minimum-wage campaigns and, 92–93, 95–96, 100, 103, 104, 112, 206n2; racial justice focus and, 56; racism and, 6, 37, 41, 47–48, 50, 133; targeted hiring programs and, 82, 120, 123, 130, 131, 132, 136; visions of justice and, 194–95; work-and-home policies and, 139, 141
Landrieu, Mitch, 85, 127, 128, 134
land use, 45–46
Lightfoot, Lori, 17, 26, 107, 156, 177
living-wage movement: challenges to, 103; durability of ERJ coalitions and, 191; minimum-wage campaigns and, 92, 93, 96; network structures and, 54; as precursor to ERJ coalitions, 6–7, 39, 42, 47–50, 57; privatization and, 205n1; public finance activism and, 175; racial justice focus and, 61, 115; visions of justice and, 195. *See also* minimum-wage campaigns
Living Wage Resource Center, 72
Logan, John, 63
Los Angeles, 51, 54, 121
Los Angeles Alliance for a New Economy (LAANE), 51, 54, 121
Louisiana, 129. *See also* New Orleans

MacDonald, Laquan, 155
Make the Road New York, 54
Marxian political economy theory, 25, 36
Matsuoka, Martha, 34, 40
McDonald's, 93
McGinn, Mike, 100
McKittrick, Katherine, 36
media: minimum-wage campaigns and, 100; urban resources and, 74
messaging: discourse coalitions theory on, 66; growth imperative and, 41–42; public finance activism and, 163, 167–68, 169–71, 180; targeted hiring programs and, 117, 132, 206n1; visions of justice and, 196–97; work-and-home policies and, 142, 144, 158. *See also* problem stream; racial justice focus
Mier, Rob, 44, 45
minimum-wage campaigns, 33, 87–113; ballot initiatives and, 81, 82, 92–93, 95, 96, 97–98, 101, 105, 106, 108; Chicago, 26, 38, 77, 102–6, 107, *110–11*; chronology of, 93–95; development of (2000s), 92–93; diffusion of, 88–92, *89–90, 91,* 106–9, 197–98; electoral politics and, 26, 76, 77, 81–82, 92–93, 95, 98–100, 105–6, 109, 112, 206n4; follow-up campaigns, 88–89; Fordism and, 162; Great Recession and, 53–54, 93–94; inside-outside campaigns and, 101, 193; municipal government and, 100–102; national policy entrepreneurs and, 74, 107, 112–13; network structures and, 87, 93; racial justice focus and, 56, 94–95; SeaTac, 95–98, *110–11*; Seattle, 26, 98–102, *110–11*, 193;
strikes and, 74, 93, 94–95, 99–100, 103, 109, 112, 154, 205n1, 206n2; success of, 4, 9, 25–26, 38; urban policy entrepreneurs and, 87, 99, 101, 109, *110–11*, 112–13; urban resources and, 9, 75, 87, 98; work-and-home policies and, 88, 140, 141
Minneapolis, 108
MLK Labor (Seattle), 56
Molotch, Harvey, 63
multiple streams approach (MSA), 67–70, 200, 205n2; ERJ coalition successes and, 192; inside-outside campaigns and, 71, 72; national vs. urban policy entrepreneur roles in, 73; public finance activism and, 183–85. *See also* urban policy entrepreneurs
municipal government: minimum-wage campaigns and, 100–102; neighborhoods movement and, 46; targeted hiring programs and, 117–18, 119, 127–29, 131, 132, 133, 134; urban scholarship on, 65, 205n1; work-and-home policies and, 154–56. *See also* inside-outside campaigns
Murray, Ed, 100–101

Nashville, 207n10
National Employment Law Project, 93, 106, 112
National People's Action, 38
national policy entrepreneurs: constraints on, 8, 77–78; durability of ERJ coalitions and, 191; minimum-wage campaigns and, 74, 107, 112–13; politics stream and, 76; problem stream and, 74; public finance activism and, 163, 179; roles of, 72, 73; targeted

hiring programs and, 129; work-and-home policies and, 141–42, 152–53
National Women's Law Center, 148
neighborhoods movement: community development corporations and, 41, 103; as precursor to ERJ coalitions, 39, 42, 43–47; vision of justice and, 194
network structures, 8, 37–38; complexity of, 37; Great Recession and, 54; living-wage movement and, 7; minimum-wage campaigns and, 87, 93; policy stream and, 74–75, 80–81; targeted hiring programs and, 121; urban resources and, 3; urban scholarship and, 5, 200; venue shopping and, 8, 64, 75, 205n3. *See also* national policy entrepreneurs; urban policy entrepreneurs
New Deal, 2, 22, 46, 141, 146, 162, 181
New Jersey, 109
New Orleans: authors' research methods and, 85; targeted hiring programs, 126–29, 134, 136, 206n9
New Orleans Worker Center for Racial Justice (NOWCRJ), 127
Newsom, Gavin, 124
New York, 51, 54, 157
9to5, 142

Obama administration, 53, 54
O'Brien, Mike, 131
Occupy Wall Street, 73, 166, 168, 192
Ohio, 207n10. *See also* Cleveland
Our Neighborhood (Chicago), 176

Parikh, Sejal, 100
Parks, Virginia, 51

Partnership for Working Families (PowerSwitch Action), 38, 51, 55, 121, 175
Pastor, Manuel, 34, 40
Patel, Amisha, 57
Peck, Jamie, 66
Personal Responsibility and Work Opportunities Reconciliation Act (1996), 141–42
Philadelphia, 151, 157
Pilipino Workers Center (California), 56
Podesta, John, 2
police funding, 59, 85–86
police racism, 1, 16, 54, 65, 85–86, 155, 164, 200
policy entrepreneurs. *See* national policy entrepreneurs; urban policy entrepreneurs
policy leverage sources: community benefits movement and, 52; ERJ coalition development and, 40–41, 60; urban rebound and, 27, 28, 29, 31. *See also* urban resources
PolicyLink, 125, 129
policy mobilities theory, 66
policy stream: inside-outside campaigns and, 72; minimum-wage campaigns and, 99; national vs. urban policy entrepreneur roles in, 73; network structures and, 74–75, 80–81; overview, 68–69; urban resources and, 71, 74–75; work-and-home policies and, 151–54, 153, 207n1
policy windows. *See* agenda windows
political scale, 197–98
politics stream: inside-outside campaigns and, 72; minimum-wage campaigns and, 98–99, 105; national vs. urban policy

entrepreneur roles in, 73; overview, 69–70; public finance activism and, 183, *184*; research approach on, 79–80; targeted hiring programs and, 125–26; urban resources and, 71, 75–77. *See also* electoral politics
Portland, Oregon, 85, 118, 206n1
positive feedback effects, 100
post-Fordism, 18–19, 20–21, 27, *28*, 29
PowerSwitch Action (Partnership for Working Families), 38, 51, 55, 121, 175
Preckwinkle, Toni, 155–56
preemption laws, 197, 198
press. *See* media
privatization, 162, 205n1
Privileges and Immunities Clause, 119, 206n4
problem stream: inside-outside campaigns and, 72; minimum-wage campaigns and, 77, 93, 95, 98, 102; national vs. urban policy entrepreneur roles in, 73; overview, 68; public finance activism and, 84, 163, 166–68, 183; research approach on, 79; targeted hiring programs and, 132; urban resources and, 71, 73–74; work-and-home policies and, 146, 148–49, *150*, 151
Project Labor Agreements (PLA), 132, 133
Proposition 1 (SeaTac, Washington), 96, 97–98
Proposition 13 (California), 177, 178
protest culture, minimum-wage campaigns and, 98, 103
public finance activism, 33, 163–85; challenges to, 83–84, 163, 181–82; constraints on cities, 165; elder- and childcare and, 168–71; Fordism and, 161–62; multiple streams approach and, 183–85; problem stream and, 84, 163, 166–68, 183; public goods and, 33, 163, 181, 182–83; racial justice focus and, 85, 163, 167–68, 174, 175–76, 182–83; state-level campaigns, 177–81, 198; targeted hiring programs and, 122; tax increment financing (TIF), 21, 121, 163, 166, 167, 171, 174–77. *See also* austerity policies
public goods, 33, 163, 168–71, 181, 182–83
public narrative, 167
Puget Sound Sage, 40, 54, 131–32

racial capitalism analysis, 35–36, 59–60, 129–30
racial justice focus: austerity policies and, 84, 182–83; education and, 171, 173–74; elder- and childcare and, 168–71; ERJ coalition development and, 54–57, 58, 59, 60–61; living-wage movement and, 61, 115; minimum-wage campaigns and, 56, 94–95; multiple streams approach and, 183–85; neighborhoods movement and, 61; public finance activism and, 85, 163, 167–68, 174, 175–76, 182–83; racial capitalism analysis and, 35–36, 59–60, 129–30; tax fairness and, 178–80; tax increment financing (TIF) and, 174, 175–76; urban scholarship and, 200–201; work-and-home policies and, 151, 158. *See also* targeted hiring programs

racism: community organizing and, 6, 37, 41, 49, 181; disinvestment and, 50–51; ERJ coalition development and, 41; Fordism and, 194–95; Great Recession and, 52, 54; labor movement and, 6, 37, 41, 47–48, 50, 133; living-wage movement and, 49, 57, 175; neighborhoods movement, 43; policing and, 1, 16, 54, 65, 85–86, 155, 164, 200; public finance activism and, 164; targeted hiring programs and, 118, 130, 135. *See also* inequalities; racial capitalism analysis
Rainier Beach Action Coalition, 134
Raise the Floor, 112
rational-choice theory, 25
Rauner, Bruce, 58
real estate investment, 75–76
referenda. *See* ballot initiatives
regime theory, 21, 25
regional movements, 16, 32, 40
reinvestment: inequitable, 50–51; targeted hiring programs and, 120–21, 130, 134. *See also* urban rebound
research methods. *See* urban scholarship
Resident Jobs Policy (Boston), 119
"return on investment" messaging, 117, 206n1
rights-based discourses, 50
Right to Work laws, 62, 94, 190, 198
Robinson, Cedric, 35–36
Rules for Radicals (Alinsky), 6

San Francisco: neighborhoods movement, 46; targeted hiring programs, 122–25, 135; work-and-home policies, 142, 157

Savitch, H. V., 34
Sawant, Kshama, 98–99, 100
scheduling challenges, 83, 138, 140–41, *143*, 154–55
scholarship. *See* urban scholarship
SeaTac minimum-wage campaign, 95–98, *110–11*
Seattle: authors' research methods and, 85; electoral politics, 26, 98–100; ERJ coalition development, 54; living-wage movement, 56; minimum-wage campaign, 26, 98–102, *110–11*, 193; targeted hiring programs, 121, 129–34, 136, 207n12; work-and-home policies, 157
Seattle Priority Hire program, 133–34
Seattle process, 132
SEIU (Service Employees International Union), 47, 56, 93, 95–96, 100, 112, 169
Sen, Amartya, 32
Service Employees International Union (SEIU), 47, 56, 93, 95–96, 100, 112, 169
service sector growth, 27, *28*, 29, 31
Shift Project, 151
sick days, 144–45, 148, 155
situated knowledge, 36
social goods. *See* public goods
social reproduction. *See* work-and-home policies
Southern Strategy, 162
Southsiders Organized for Unity and Liberation (Chicago), 158
Spicer, Jason S., 76
Stand with Dignity (STAND) (New Orleans), 127–28, 129, 134
State Priorities Partnership, 179
St. Louis, 84–85, 94, 107

Stokes, Carl, 44–45
Stone, Clarence N., 65
St. Paul, minimum-wage campaign, 108
strikes: minimum-wage campaigns and, 74, 93, 94–95, 99–100, 103, 109, 112, 154, 205n1, 206n2; teachers, 4, 56, 103, 104, 171–74, 190, 192
structured contingency, 67, 200

Taft-Hartley Act, 162
targeted hiring programs, 33, 82, 115–36; approaches to, *116*; challenges to, 116–17, 118–20; Chicago, 117–18, 119, 121–22; community benefits movement and, 120–22; defined, 115–16; diffusion of, 124–25; Fordism and, 162, 196; inside-outside campaigns and, 117, 136; labor movement and, 82, 120, 123, 130, 131, 132, 136; network structures and, 121; New Orleans, 126–29, 134, 136, 206n9; policy waves, *124*; Portland, 206n1; "return on investment" messaging and, 117, 206n1; San Francisco, 122–25, 135; Seattle, 121, 129–34, 136, 207n12; urban policy entrepreneurs and, 125, *126*
tax and expenditure limits (TELs), 165
tax fairness, 177–78
tax increment financing (TIF), 21, 121, 163, 166, 167, 171, 174–77
Tennessee, 207n10
Theodore, Nik, 66
think tanks, 68–69
TIF (tax increment financing), 21, 121, 163, 166, 167, 171, 174–77
Trump administration, 21–22, 41

UC Berkeley Labor Center, 93, 101
UCLA Labor Center, 132, 207n12
unions. *See* labor movement
United for a New Economy (UNE) (Colorado), 55
Unleash Local campaign (Louisiana), 129
urban policy entrepreneurs (UPEs), 64; agenda windows and, 77–79, 205n4; comparison analysis and, 9–10; ERJ coalition collaboration with, 71, 72, 77; importance of, 199–200; minimum-wage campaigns and, 87, 99, 101, 109, *110–11*, 112–13; multiple streams approach on, 67–70; national policy entrepreneurs and, 72, 73, 74; targeted hiring programs and, 125, *126*; urban resources and, 8–9, 70–71, *71*, 73–77, 188–89; work-and-home policies and, 138. *See also* network structures
urban rebound, 1; durability of ERJ coalitions and, 190–91; inequalities and, 3, 24–25, 27, *28*, 29–30; policy leverage and, 27, *28*, 29, 31; process of, 18–21; selectivity of, 15–17; temporary nature of, 17–18
urban resources: minimum-wage campaigns and, 9, 75, 87, 98; network structures and, 3; urban policy entrepreneurs and, 8–9, 70–71, *71*, 73–77, 188–89; urban rebound and, 24, 30
urban scholarship, 199–200; authors' research approaches and methods, 3, 79–81, 84–86; capital and electoral focus of, 3–4; discourse coalitions theory and, 65–66, 79; Goldilocks problem, 199–200; growth machine theory

and, 4, 19–20, 21, 24, 25, 29; limits of focus of, 64–65; Marxian political economy theory and, 25, 36; multisite perspective, 9, 34, 63–64; on municipal government, 65, 205n1; neglect of urban social movements, 3–4, 35, 38; network structures and, 5, 200; policy mobilities theory and, 66; racial justice focus and, 200–201; rational-choice theory and, 25; regime theory and, 21, 25; structured contingency and, 67, 200. *See also* multiple streams approach

urban social movements: ERJ coalitions as, 39–40; scholarly neglect of, 3–4, 35, 38; scholarship on, 34, 64–65. *See also* economic and racial justice (ERJ) coalitions

Virginia, 198

War on Poverty, 115, 165
Warren, Dorian, 51
Washington, D.C., 119
Washington, Harold, 37, 44–45, 46, 117, 118
Weaver, Timothy P. R., 65
welfare reform, 141–42
welfare rights movement, 48
Westin, Jonathan, 94
White, Kevin, 119

White supremacy. *See* racial justice focus; racism
Wiewel, Wim, 45
women: elder- and childcare and, 169; work-and-home policies and, 141, 148, 149–50, 154, 158
Women Employed (Chicago), 158
Woo, Michael, 130–31, 134
Woods, Clyde Adrian, 36
work-and-home policies, 33, 82–83, 137–59; challenges to, 138–39, 157–58; Chicago, 26, 154–56, 157; data insufficiency and, 142, 144–45; Fordism and, 162; Great Recession and, 137–38, 140–41, 142, 145; importance of, 140–41; inside-outside campaigns and, 156–57; minimum-wage campaigns and, 88, 140, 141; national policy entrepreneurs and, 141–42, 152–53; policy stream and, 151–54, 153, 207n1; problem stream and, 146, 148–49, 150, 151; racial capitalism analysis on, 59–60; scheduling challenges and, 83, 138, 140–41, 143, 154–55; successes, 158–59, 192. *See also* minimum-wage campaigns
Worker Center for Racial Justice (WCRJ) (Chicago), 56
Wright, Howard, 101–2

Marc Doussard is associate professor of urban and regional planning at the University of Illinois at Urbana–Champaign. He is author of *Degraded Work: The Struggle at the Bottom of the Labor Market* (Minnesota, 2013).

Greg Schrock is associate professor of urban studies and planning at Portland State University.